680
SE

Sequoia, Anna

The complete
catalogue of mail-
order kits

DATE			
MAR. 2 1981			
JUN. 7 1983			
MR 30 '87			
MR 9 '89			
AG 26 '89			
APR 05 '95			
MAY 26 '97			
OCT 18 '01			
JUN 12 '10			

© THE BAKER & TAYLOR CO

The Complete Catalogue of Mail-Order Kits

The Complete Catalogue of Mail-Order Kits

ANNA SEQUOIA

RAWSON, WADE PUBLISHERS, INC.

New York

Library of Congress Cataloging in Publication Data

Sequoia, Anna.
    The complete catalogue of mail-order kits.

    Includes index.
    1. Handicraft—United States—Directories.
2. Handicraft—United States—Catalogs. I. Title.
II. Title: Kits.
TT12.S46   680.29′73   80-5984
ISBN 0-89256-158-0   AACR2
ISBN 0-89256-174-2 (pbk.)

Copyright © 1981 by Anna Sequoia
Published simultaneously in Canada by McClelland and Stewart, Ltd.
Composition by American–Stratford Graphic Services, Inc.
Brattleboro, Vermont
Printed and bound by R. R. Donnelley & Sons Co.,
Crawfordsville, Indiana

DESIGNED BY JACQUES CHAZAUD

First Edition

ACKNOWLEDGMENTS

This book would have been infinitely more difficult to research and write without the encouragement, cooperation, and/or kit testing of the following people: Barbara Bahoshy, Arthur Berkoski, Norman Brilliant, Patricia Cammarota, Diane Cleaver, Rebecca Dominguez-Blum, Michael Edison, Judd Gabey, Sarah Gallick, Sandy Goldbeck, Diane Greene, Jason Gruen, Charles Haber, Neil Hart, Jules Hecht, Dr. James L. Januzzi, Annette Kastalick, Renee Kashdan, Joanie Miller, Deanna Moinester, Robert Perry, Eleanor Rawson, Peggy Schneider, Steve Schneider, Joel Siegel, and Steve Werner. Special thanks also to those manufacturers and kit distributors who cooperated so enthusiastically.

CONTENTS

CONTENTS APPENDIX

Introduction

How to Use This Book

The Complete Catalogue of Mail-Order Kits can help you save 35 percent to 60 percent off the "normal" retail price of everything from hand-knitted sweaters to dollhouses to stereo speakers. *It could save you hundreds of dollars the first year you own it.*

Most of the kits in this book don't require specialized tools or skills. Since each kit arrives with complete and clear instructions, you don't have to be a genius to put it together. And if you do have a problem, all you have to do is look in the Appendix in the back of this book for the kit manufacturer's telephone number, and call them for help; kit manufacturers are, almost without exception, good helpful people who have an investment in your success and satisfaction. They know that if you enjoyed your kit, you'll tell your friends, who'll probably wind up buying one too.

The Appendix, beginning on page 189, is an important part of this book. It contains the address of the manufacturers or suppliers mentioned in each chapter; it tells you what other merchandise a supplier may carry and how much each charges for its catalogue.

Every chapter of the book has its own section in the Appendix; for example, chapter 8: Transportation. Say you've read about a helicopter kit you'd like. Look in the Contents/Appendix (page x) for the chapter 8: Transportation listing. You'll see there a subhead that reads "Sources of Kits for Airplanes, Helicopters and Gliders." That's what you want. Once you turn to the correct page, you'll find suppliers listed there in alphabetical order. Also, you'll note that there's another section right after it titled "Additional Sources of Kits for Airplanes, Helicopters, and Gliders." This section provides addresses and information about manufacturers whose kits I simply didn't have room to detail in the text of chapter 8. So each time you see a section like that—"Other Sources of Kits for Patchwork and Appliqué" or "Thirty-five Additional Sources of Model Railroad Kits"—realize that you're getting a bonus.

When I started research for this book, I knew there were a lot of kits, but I had no *idea* how many. It really is mind-boggling. I think that what surprised me most was how many kits there were for log cabins and other types of homes. But it really does make sense to build or make what you want from a kit. In most cases, you buy directly from the manufacturer, cutting out the cost of all the middlemen who ordinarily add their percentages to what you have to pay, and you save the cost of labor for assembly. On a big purchase, like a cabin or a harpsichord, these kits can save you thousands of dollars.

Best of all, most kits are fun to put together. If you're part of a family, especially if you're working on one of the largest projects, like a boat kit, or a home computer, or a four-poster bed, you'll find that it doesn't take long before everyone within a six-room radius gets happily involved. Besides, kits expand your skills. When I began this book, even after a lifelong involvement with needlework of various kinds, I hadn't done much needlepoint. But after working with a few kits, I've now developed to the point where I'm designing and making my own needlepoint Christmas tree ornaments. It's the same with dollhouses (or almost any other type of kit described in this book); thanks to some of the dollhouse kits detailed in the text of chapter 6, I've gotten to the point where I'm about to begin work on a large Country Victorian dollhouse that I plan to supply with electricity so that all the little chandelier and lamp kits inside will light up.

The Complete Catalogue of Mail-Order
Kits

1

Furniture–Also Incorporating Rugs, Clocks, Decorative Accessories, and Stained-Glass Lamps

For most of us, furnishing our homes is a project that takes years. First of all, there's the cost: prohibitive. Second, most of us want just the right accessories—a rug, which picks up the colors of the walls and the upholstery, in a size that unifies and balances the room; a little shelf clock whose sound reminds us of happy weekends in the country; a footstool that's just the right height for proper relaxation.

Just when things begin to pull together, after two years, or eight years, or even after twenty years, we move. And we begin again to weed out, to refurbish, to replace, and to augment the things we love with still more things we love.

This chapter is intended for people who have more taste than money. For example, if you would like an elegant four-poster canopy bed but don't feel like paying Bloomingdale's $400 or more, you can order Cohasset Colonials beautiful pumpkin pine tester bed with 77″ maple posts copied from originals in the Yankee Pedlar Inn, Holyoke, Massachusetts. This wonderfully simple double bed sells for a remarkably inexpensive $195 in kit form, and it comes with a wrench, glue, stain, and all necessary hardware. It's not difficult to put together. Or if you'd like a fine oak or walnut Regulator clock, you may want to order one in kit form from Craft Products Company, St. Charles, Illinois. These sell for about $120; I've seen similar clocks in Gimbel's for more than $200. Or perhaps you'd like Windsor chairs. Several furniture kit companies have these, and the ones I've seen (and included in the section that follows) are all beautiful and half the price you'd pay at Lord & Taylor, or Altman's, or Sloane's.

If you like Shaker furniture, you'll adore many of the Shaker reproduction kits from Yield House, Shaker Workshops, and several other kit companies. Shaker chair kits, for example, are almost without exception well executed copies of fine antiques. Cohasset Colonials, to name just one source, has a magnificent 34½" sturdy yet elegant high chair, only $59, the original of which is in the collection of the Concord Antiquarian Society; the design is so beautiful that you'd probably be willing to pay a little more than twice the price for it, preassembled, at retail. Shaker Workshops, of Concord, Massachusetts, specializes in chair kits—all of which come to you with their backs preassembled, squared up, glued, and pinned. You'll particularly like their Elder's Chair, a classic rock-maple Shaker armchair that measures 51½" high, with a generous 18" x 22" seat. The seat height is 18". This stately, comfortable chair has magnificent proportions, with finials on the rear posts and "mushroom" turnings on the armrests copied in precise detail from the original. At $104.40, including shipping and handling, this has to be one of the best buys you can find for your home; assembled, it's easily worth twice the price.

Whatever your taste, whether for rustic or more refined furniture, there are kits to fit your decor—and your pocketbook. The Bartley Collection, for example, is known for its top-quality reproductions of American Queen Anne, and Chippendale originals in the Henry Ford Museum. And soon they'll be introducing what should be one of the finest furniture kits available, a stately cherry corner cupboard that will cost under $1,000. If you've looked for corner cabinets or hutches lately, you know that's extraordinarily cheap; I've seen badly constructed and designed pine junk selling for $600 more. Bartley's own price for this corner cupboard, preassembled and finished (with an estimated two-year wait) is $2,350.

But best of all, you don't have to be a mechanical or woodworking genius to assemble most of the kits that follow. Many don't even require much time.

Furniture

Aldens, the huge Chicago mail-order house, has one furniture kit for a *pine rolltop desk* on trestle-type base that would be good for a corner of a country-style kitchen or a child's room. Measures 18" x 39" x 42" high. There's adequate surface area for bill paying or most homework. About $75.

If you have a taste for fine eighteenth-century American furniture but haven't yet inherited or made your own fortune, you may want to consider the magnificent kits available from the **Bartley Collection** of Lake Forest,

Illinois. Several of these kits are reproductions of pieces in the Henry Ford Museum furniture collection. They're infinitely less expensive than the originals and much less expensive than most quality reproductions.

Among the most interesting pieces offered by the Bartley Collection is their *Chippendale-style block-front chest-of-drawers kit.* The original, now in the Henry Ford Museum, was crafted in Massachusetts between 1760 and 1780. The cabinet of this chest is mortise and tenon construction, with dovetailed drawer fronts 2″ thick. The hand-cast brass has been precisely copied from the original. Solid Honduras mahogany, 31″ high, 36″ wide, 21″ deep. No tools required for assembly. The unassembled ready-to-finish piece sells for less than $700. Assembled and hand-finished price: about $1,800.

Another fine and practical kit available from the Bartley Collection is their *butler tray table.* This is the finest butler tray table kit available, selling for about $200 (assembled and finished price: about $450). This design dates from around 1720. The top has eleven individual pieces, not including the leaves. All eleven pieces are tongue and grooved together. Hinges are solid brass and hand-forged. No tools required. The table measures 18½″ high, 43″ x 31″ with sides down, 34″ x 22″ with sides up. Available in Honduras mahogany or cherry.

Bartley's *Queen Anne chair kit* is derived from an original chair made in New England between 1720 and 1740, part of the furnishings of the Secretary House from Exeter, New Hampshire. This excellent reproduction has a vase-shaped splat in the back of the chair and lovely cabriole legs. The seat would look wonderful with a needlepoint cover. These are very sturdy chairs and exceptional values: about $200 for the mahogany or cherry armchair, about $25 less for the side chair. Assembled pieces sell for more than twice the price.

Another incredible value from Bartley is their *Queen Anne drop-leaf table kit* (about $275 for the kit; about $500 prefinished). Available in either cherry or mahogany, the original of this table can be seen in the Decorative Arts Gallery at the Ford Museum. An excellent dining table for an apartment: 29″ high, 43″ long, 12″ wide closed, 46″ open.

Space here is too limited to describe other Bartley pieces. Suffice it to say that they have excellent kits available for a tip-top table; a brandy stand; a Queen Anne bench/footstool (this piece is *magnificent,* and less than $150); an old English muffin stand; a Queen Anne lowboy; a dining room table; a Queen Anne sideboard and cupboard; unusual Chippendale looking glasses; a pencil-post bed; a Windsor chair; and an extraordinary Chippendale corner chair, circa 1760–75.

Do send for their catalogue as soon as possible. Their prices seem to be rising at quite a clip; they do have sales, though, and once you get on their mailing list, you could save as much as $200 on special cuttings of, say, the Chippendale block-front chest.

Bedford Lumber Company has an enormous variety of kits available for practical, sturdy, inexpensive cedar chests. My own favorite is their plain *jumbo cedar chest*. This measures 46¾ " long, 24¾ " wide, 26" high. Considerably less than $100. An excellent place for storing your quilts, blankets, and out-of-season clothing.

Bedford Lumber also has nicely balanced, sturdy *Boston rockers* in sizes for adults or children. The adult's rocker is less than $75. The child's rocker is about $35.

Other interesting kits from Bedford Lumber include an *early American style drop-leaf table*, available in cedar, cherry, mahogany, maple, or walnut. A very nice end table, especially if you like the look of Country American furniture. This table measures 20" long x 20" wide x 29" high with leaves down. With leaves up it measures 37¼ " long. Less than $90. Another interesting kit is for their cedar wardrobe, 36" wide x 23½ " deep x 70" high, for less than $150; this would be good for your log cabin.

Cohasset Colonials has an excellent range of kits for reproduction Colonial American furniture.

One of their most interesting kits is their *Shaker rocker* with web or rush seat. This beautiful rock maple chair is copied from the original in the Fruitlands Museum in Harvard, Massachusetts. The "ladle arms" of this four-slat rocker are characteristic of rockers made in the Shaker tradition around 1800 in the Harvard and Shirley communities. Less than $75, with the fiber rush seat, it's easily half the price of a similar quality chair.

Cohasset's *low bed* is a maple and pine version of the wonderful country bed one used to find at auctions in places like Bucks County, Pennsylvania, complete with rope mattress supports. My Aunt Anne and Uncle Jan had an old double low bed at their farm in Kintnersville, Pennsylvania. These Cohasset versions come with angle-iron supports to accommodate a standard box frame and mattress. This particular bed is a copy of one in the collection of the Metropolitan Museum of Art. The double size sells for considerably less than $200. A trundle bed is available, too, for about $100.

Their *Shaker dining tables* are beautiful copies of meetinghouse tables. Each comes with breadboard ends with hardwood pegs. Pine. The kits are available in two sizes, 82" x 30" x 30" high, seating eight, or 30" x 54" x 30". The larger kits sell for around $200, the smaller for around $150.

Cohasset has *many* other exquisite designs. Their Windsor armchair kit is a real beauty; their high chair, copied from an original in the collection of the Concord Antiquarian Society, is a marvelous gift for a family with a young child; their four-poster canopy bed is *superb* and costs only about $200 in double size. But that's not all; their other wonderful kits include: Shaker sconce; Shaker pegboards; drop-leaf harvest table; Windsor settee; and several other items.

Conran's, the trendy furniture and accessories outlet, generally has nicely designed furniture that costs too much for the less-than-perfect workmanship involved. What they do have that might interest you is a small but handy range of knockdown/kit furniture, including a tubular steel bed that comes in single and bunk models (about $110 for the single; about $245 for the bunk bed), canvas and pine love seat (around $225–$250) and, most interesting, a kitchen sink kit that comes with lacquered pine base and stainless-steel sink—about $350. Faucets are not included. Check with Conran's to see what kits they're carrying at the moment.

The first thing I looked for when I moved recently into my new apartment was a wall unit to accommodate my books, my folk doll collection, and my little Meissen figures. But decent wall units can cost more than all the moving expenses combined. Luckily, the brothers of a friend were able to build exactly what I wanted and at a price I could afford. But if I hadn't found the Cammarota brothers, I'd have gone to **Custom Art Furniture,** for one of their exquisite *wall-unit kits.* Custom Art Furniture has more than fifty different kits available, in beautiful veneers, with a wide range of combinations of bookshelves and storage units for use in the den, bedroom, or living room. Some even come with mirrored surfaces, perfect for expanding the look of smaller rooms. Savings are, of course, *very* considerable.

Within the past few years, **Emperor Clock Company** has expanded its line of kits to include several very attractive solid ¾" cherry-wood furniture kits.

Their *Queen Anne secretary* is a particularly attractive drop-front desk. It has four drawers of dovetail construction, a compartmentalized interior with three small drawers behind the drop-front and brass-finished hardware. The drop front and top drawer are provided with locks. As the drop front is lowered, the writing surface supports extend automatically. The kit sells for about $375. Completely assembled and finished, this secretary would cost well over $500.

Their *Queen Anne writing table* is another fine design. It measures 59¼" long, 29" wide, 30" high—a large enough writing surface for you to really spread out and get some work done. The ¾" cherry desk features a large center drawer and four side drawers with dovetail construction. It has cabriole legs. About $450—at least $150 less than the preassembled and finished version.

Other interesting designs from Emperor include their Queen Anne lowboy, Queen Anne double-drawer commode table, and their end table, all in cherry.

Garden Way Research offers an attractive *park-bench kit,* which comes with solid cast-iron legs and steel-rod crossbar, polyester coated for antichipping and sun-fade resistance. The 5′ park-bench kit sells for about $100. No wood slatting comes with this kit; you must provide it, but it should be relatively inexpensive. Available too in an 8′ version, no wood, for about $125.

They also sell kits for Old Charleston benches, authentically reproduced from the ones at Harbor Park in Charleston, South Carolina. These sell for about $100 in the 5′ version, just under $150 for the 8′ version.

Heritage Design of Monticello, Iowa, sells an Eastlake-influenced "Victorian" *upholstered or caned rocking chair kit,* which comes in walnut, cherry, or maple. The design looks very Middle American; it dates from around 1876. Just over $200.

Knot Just Another Knotter of Big Sandy, Texas, has an attractive macramé *gazebo chair kit* that hangs from the ceiling. Very nice for porch use. Comes in white, brown, or yellow. About $75.

They have other macramé furniture projects too, but none I like as well as their gazebo chair.

Nasco, the big arts and crafts supply house and catalogue, has two very inexpensive *footstool kits* that would make excellent first projects for your young ones. Called the Happy Landing Footstool Outfit, the kits will provide experience in decorative wood finishing, plus not-too-difficult seat-weaving techniques. Available in the three colors—natural, green, or brown-white. The $5.50 kit measures 11½″ x 11½″ x 9″ high; it comes with hardwood frame, four skeins of fiber for weaving a rush seat, plus instructions. The 11½″ x 9½″ x 9″-high footstool outfit comes with essentially the same materials, and it costs only $5.00 (even less if you buy twelve or more, say for a school or Scout project).

H. H. Perkins Company sells several very inexpensive chair and stool kits. All have paper rush or splint seats; they're very strong and sturdy, though they might not sound like it. The *ladder-back chair for adults,* for example, with hardwood frame and materials for fiber rush seat costs just over $20. The *ladder-back chair for children* costs well under $15! There's also a very nice *child's rocker kit* with either rush or fiber splint seat for about $20. *Bar stool* kits cost less than $20.

Rollingswood sells fine quality antique reproduction furniture kits, many of which are for pieces not offered by any other furniture kit company.

Most impressive is their *Queen Anne highboy,* measuring 39½″ wide, 23¾″ deep, 84″ high. Available in Honduras mahogany, Pennsylvania cherry, or black walnut. Comes with curved cabriole legs carved from solid stock; hand-carved drawer fronts; solid brass pulls and escutcheons; hand-turned finial; serpentine molding with mitered corners; curved, closed bonnet with shadow panel; floating construction for drawers, interior dust panels, oak interior drawer parts. Construction is entirely mortise and tenon, no dovetailing. You'll need a good set of clamps for construction. The mahogany and cherry kits sell for less than $1,500—less than half the preassembled price. Black walnut will cost a few hundred dollars more. Plan ahead for this piece because they have only one cutting per year, to advance orders only.

Their *Queen Anne display table* has carved cabriole legs, scalloped rails, and beveled plate-glass top. Relatively easy to assemble. 29″ high, 29″ x 18″ on the top, 5″ deep. An excellent way to display your treasured small collectibles. Especially nice for small silver items. About $200 in mahogany, slightly more for cherry, about $220 for black walnut. Preassembled display tables will cost more than twice the price.

A lovely small piece from Rollingswood is their mahogany or cherry *spoon rack,* reproduced from a very handsome early piece. The middle shelf is slotted for your coin silver spoons. The bottom shelf is a lidded compartment, originally used to store knives. About $50.

Rollingswood has several other kits that are beautifully designed and are good values. I'm particularly fond of their charming, graceful fern stand (about $70); their Chippendale mirror, with lovely moldings and scrolls (about $130), and their classic Queen Anne sideboard table.

Since I happen to love Shaker furniture, I'm very fond of the fine Shaker reproduction furniture kits in the **Shaker Workshops** catalogue. My own favorite is their *Shawl Back Rocker kit.* This is a faithful reproduction of the No. 7 rocker manufactured by the Mount Lebanon Shakers for sale to the "world's people." It's Shaker design at its best. It has a high back, with cushion rail, smooth turnings, and flowing curves. Rock maple frame, tape seat. About $110—and well worth it.

Another fabulous kit is their *Elder's Chair.* This exceptionally comfortable armchair has generous proportions and elegant lines. The slender finials on the rear posts and the "mushroom" turnings on the armrests are precisely copied from the original. About $100. Rock maple frame, tape seat. A preassembled and finished chair like this would easily cost more than twice the price at Bloomingdale's or Lord & Taylor.

I'm also crazy about their *Child's Rocker.* It's beautifully proportioned and fine for a child up to age nine. Rock maple. The back measures 29″; it's 15″ wide, and the seat is 11½″ deep. This is probably one of the finest gifts you can give a young child. I well remember my own little antique chair with rush seat; I was almost as fond of it as I was of my dog and my dolls. About $45.

Shaker Workshops has other interesting kits, too, particularly their handsome Shaker towel rack; the pine trestle table; and their high weaver's chair, suitable today as a high bar or kitchen-counter chair.

SMI is the only kit company I've seen with a kit for a *bentwood rocker*. Very easy to assemble, since it comes with only seven components. Complete with rattan seat and chair back. Less than $100.

SMI also sells kits for those *carved solid oak kitchen chairs* that have been bringing such high prices over the past few years. The cane seat is factory preassembled. About $50. A 10 percent discount if you order four or more chairs. These same chair kits are sold by at least one other kit company for almost $20 more each chair.

Yield House of North Conway, New Hampshire, has the most extensive line of kit furniture available. Most of their pieces are constructed of pine; they are rather "Ethan Allen" in style.

Among the many interesting pieces they sell is their pine *Queen Anne tea table*. It can be used as a high coffee table in front of a traditional sofa or as a sideboard or end table. Two pull-out trays and an arcaded apron. Measures 26″ high x 18″ wide x 30″ long. About $130 for the kit. This kit is quite easy to put together.

Their *Sewing/Hobby Center* is a handsome, tall, louvered pine cabinet that opens into a gateleg table and has compartments for most of your sewing accessories. Custom touches accommodate everything from pattern files to scissors to spools of thread. 70¼″ high, 36″ wide, 17½″ deep overall. Less than $400 for the kit; worth at least $200 more. But it's not a "starter" kit.

Their pine *home office three-drawer files* are extremely attractive, and they're less expensive than some metal file cabinets. About $130 each; about $240 for a pair.

The Yield House *glass-doored lawyer's bookshelves* are another nice addition to your home, and they're cheaper, certainly, than most antique bookshelves of similar design. Kits for three stacking shelves cost about $140. Their six-drawered 24½″ high x 27″ wide x 16¼″ deep *Treasure Chest* is the type of cabinet that used to be favored by shipmasters, amateur cartographers, and collectors of botanical prints. This would make a charming end table. Each drawer has a brass-finished plate for an identifying label and oatmeal-colored porcelain pulls. The kit costs about $120. Very attractive.

Yield House is particularly good with kits for wooden bathroom accessories, particularly mirrored or louvered *medicine cabinets*. The kit I'm about to order for my bathroom has two mirrors, two locked drawers, a rack for guest towels, and it measures 28½″ high, 29¼″ wide, 5½″ deep. The double-size medicine-cabinet kit sells for about $80, $30 less than the prefinished cabinet.

Two years ago, Yield House introduced a very interesting line of Shaker furniture reproduction kits. My own favorite here is their *Shaker Jelly Cupboard*. This lovely small pine cabinet measures 51¾″ high, x 22″ wide, x 12½″ deep. The kit version costs about $125, a solid $50 less than the assembled, finished version from Yield House. I recently saw this same piece in another mail-order catalogue, selling for $190 more than the Yield House assembled version. Other interesting Shaker furniture kits: a Shaker hanging cupboard and a quite attractive large Shaker Country Cupboard.

Rugs

I don't think anything adds to the richness and emotional warmth of a home as much as fine rugs. Unfortunately, rug prices keep climbing astronomically. The little thirty-year-old Afghanistani area rug I saw last week, which would have been perfect for the small foyer of my new apartment, cost $750; I didn't buy it. Luckily, some years back I spent awhile in Pippa Passes, Kentucky; it was right at the beginning of President Johnson's Great Society and dozens of local women were being trained to do rug hooking, a craft that once had been as common as children in that area. I sat in on classes, and before long I was creating my own patterns. So . . . as soon as I've finished writing this book, the little foyer will probably get a hooked or a needlepointed rug.

You don't need enormous skill to make your own rugs. With some of the rugs detailed on the pages that follow, you don't even need much money. You do need time and patience . . . and lots of it. Frankly, once I've worked out or started a pattern, I find rug making a rather mindless but soothing activity; it's a great accompaniment to TV.

Most of **American Handicrafts'** rugs are, to me, rather kitschy, but they do have a few, especially for children, that are quite charming. Their most recent catalogue, for example, had a 27"-diameter round canvas, with latch hook and acrylic yarn, in a *Peter Rabbit* design right out of Beatrix Potter, for under $25. White and gray background; Peter wears a blue jacket. Another nice design for a young child's room was an 18" x 24" *Superman* design, for only $13. Primarily shades of blue. Another very cute one is their pastel *sleeping kitten design;* it's Chessie, the kitten made famous as Chesapeake and Ohio Railway's symbol of comfort. This 34" x 24" kit with acrylic yarn costs just over $30. Another charming child's rug, this one for execution with a punch needle (my favorite—it's faster), has a *pastel alphabet block design* for less than $25, including yarn, base, and punch needle. Because most of these rugs are relatively small and not too complicated (or expensive), they'd make good first-time projects.

The **American Needlewoman** has some very nice hooked-rug kits. The children in your life might well enjoy their *Kermit the Frog* and *Miss Piggy* wall hangings or rugs. These are pretty small—18" x 24" and 27" x 20"— but they're each under $15, and they're amusing.

More suitable for grown-ups is their *Europa* design, measuring 26" x 48" finished. A Mediterranean floral scroll border, burgundy background, set against a white center design. Acrylic yarn, 4-mesh canvas. Just over $40.

Their *Monghue Hunting Scene* is also reasonably attractive. Five-mesh canvas, precut yarns, 27″ x 38″. The design, on a brown/beige background depicts exotic mongol-looking huntsmen on horseback, various leaf and branch designs, and a white ram. About $55.

The only other interesting rug designs are their "Oriental" florals and geometrics, each about $60.

Art Needlework Industries, Ltd., of Oxford, England, has some of the most beautiful hooked and needlepoint rug designs you'll ever see. Most are available as kits, but, frankly, I wouldn't begin one of these as a first-time project.

For example, recent catalogues (this one appears in brochure No. 18) have included a needlepoint *'Pasyrik' Hunting Rug,* an extraordinary design combining geometric center and border with semiabstract men on horseback that gently flow like a Muybridge study around the rug. The colors are shades of ochre, white, and black. Just over $200.

Another brochure, No. 19, included a fabulous *Anatolian Rosewood Prayer Carpet,* measuring 35″ x 51″. A nomadic prayer rug in floral geometric design. Done in yellow or red ochre, lamb's white, metallic blues, Mecca greens, roses, or gray blues.

Another brochure features fascinating embroidery rug kits based on designs of the "Salzay" tribe. ANI are specialists also in rugs featuring Florentine Flame Stitch designs—utilizing traditional color combinations that were bastardized and popularized here over the past few years as bargello.

ANI does not quote prices in their catalog. If there's a design that interests you, they will sent you a price quote. Also, many of these kits are done a bit differently from kits with which we're familiar here: You receive a large, very clear color-charted design, much as you would if you were knitting elaborate designs; colors and designs are not stamped or handpainted on your rug backing.

I'm very much looking forward to making the *Smyrna Hunting Rug.* If you're seriously interested in needlework and/or rugs, do send for their fascinating catalogues.

The least expensive solution for floor coverings are stenciled floor cloths. Basically, these "rugs" are created by painting stenciled designs onto various kinds of cloth backgrounds (detailed below) and varnishing them. I personally would not choose to use one of these in a heavily trafficked area, such as an entry foyer or a studio apartment, but these are great for bedrooms, guest rooms, dining rooms, almost anyplace else you can imagine. **Adele Bishop, Inc.** has four *floor-cloth stencil kits*—all of which sell for less than $15, paints and fabric not included. (The paints are not particularly expensive—an 8-ounce can costs $6.95.) The cloths are remarkably durable;

they can be swept, vacuumed, and damp-mopped. If you get tired of one cloth, just roll it up and put it away. Like floors, they may be easily refurbished or revarnished if the surface begins to wear. As a surface, you can choose heavy cotton duck, canvas, heavy linen, woven grass, or straw matting. Each requires two or more coats of varnish. Liquid rug latex is applied to the underside of the floor cloth to prevent it from slipping. Designs are distinctly country American.

Braid-Aid is the place to look if you're interested in *100 percent wool, reversible braided rug kits.* These are extremely handsome, traditional oval designs, in sizes from 2' x 3' to 6' x 9'. The kits come in ten color selections, and they are well worth the prices charged—about $44 for 2' x 3', $92 for 3' x 5', $200 for 5' x 7'. These rugs are virtually indestructible, and they should last you a good twenty years of constant use.

CUM Textile Industries of Copenhagen, Denmark, has marvelous *rya rug kits* in sizes from 2' x 4' to 6'9" x 10'. Pile measures ¾" to 1½". Designs are more subtle than almost anything you'll find already made up in American stores; they're very beautiful. These kits provide a nice break from conventional American hooked-rug patterns. If you thought you were tired of the look of rya rugs (and I thought I was), these kits will convince you that all you were reacting to was boring design.

Elaine Magnin of San Francisco, has some very beautiful all-wool *needlepoint rug kits* at quite hefty prices. A 42" x 54" rug, for example, can go for as much as $475. An 18" x 36" rug goes for about $110–$125. These are, though, distinctive contemporary designs, all potential heirlooms.

If you've been at all interested in knitting during the past few years, you undoubtedly know the **Mary Maxim** catalogues. But Mary Maxim has more than sweaters. Each issue of their catalogue includes at least a few hooked-rug kits, and these often include very nice rugs for children's rooms. One of their children's classics is their Raggedy Ann- and Raggedy Andy-influenced *Rag Dolls rug kit.* This comes in wool, 21" x 30", for under $40, or in acrylic, for under $30.

Surprisingly, some of their pictorial animal designs are quite nice. My current favorite in this category is their *Polar Bear* design, less than $55 in wool, less than $45 in acrylic. 30" x 50".

Mary Maxim also features some very nice traditional floral designs in various sizes and colors. They also have very attractive insignia rugs for club people who want rugs with an Elks design, a Moose design, or an Eastern Star or Masonic design. My own favorite of these is the moose; it's both attractive and amusing.

Lately, Mary Maxim has begun to offer some attractive geometric designs as well.

Mary Maxim kits are of excellent quality; my mother and her friends have been buying them for years. I particularly like the fact that they offer their rug kits in durable wool; it's more expensive than synthetic yarn, but I like my needlework to last as long as possible.

The **Papillon** catalogue always contains a few wool *needlepoint rug kits*. Most are attractive, but some are truly incredible. My own recent favorite was their *Flowerfield Bunny Rug,* two charming rabbits at play in a field of strawberries and spring flowers. A very nice design that sold for $315, in #10 or #14 mesh. The rug measured 28" x 40". This is one of those needlepoint projects that could take a year to complete (assuming you work on it a few evenings each week), but it's worth the effort and time.

Peacock Alley has another fine needlepoint catalogue that always includes a few wool *needlepoint rugs*. A recent favorite of mine was their ten-mesh, 3' x 4' *Wildflower Rug,* selling for just under $300.

Shillcraft is a major source of *hooked-rug kits*. Designs range from an ex traordinary *Donald Duck the Sailor* design for children's rooms to florals to geometrics to Oriental designs. The Shillcraft catalogue is an excellent place to look if you're interested in large room-size rugs. Their *Fresco* design, for example, a rectangular rug with floral border, is available in sizes up to 80" x 120". Available in acrylic, nylon/wool blends, and all-wool pile. The 100 percent wool 80" x 120" Fresco would cost less than $450, about half the price of a premade rug of similar quality. Their other prices are also very reasonable.

The Stitchery of Wellesley, Massachusetts, always has a few needlepoint items one wants to make up, and their needlepoint rugs are very beautiful indeed. You'll want to subscribe to their catalogues; they come out frequently and invariably include a few *needlepoint rug kits*. My own recent favorite was one called *Regency Carpet.* This 59" x 35" design comes with design hand-painted on thirteen-mesh mono canvas, with tapestry yarns to work the delicate floral designs. The kit costs $350, and one would have to order seventy-two additional skeins to complete the background. (They completed it in ivory and it looked perfect.) Background skeins for this kit cost under $75.

Stitchin' Time of Rochester, New York, acts as a clearinghouse for rug and other needlework items for manufacturers such as Bernat, Spinnerin, and Elsa Williams. They have a free ninety-day layaway plan, and they do not charge for delivery.

The *Spinnerin* catalogue, available from Stitchin' Time, contains one interesting *American Eagle* design, 34" x 84", which would be appropriate for a more traditional home: It's the best eagle kit I've seen. The acrylic kit sells for less than $55; wool costs less than $80.

There are several interesting "Oriental" designs here as well, especially their 58" x 84" Medallion and their 54" x 84" Kashmir. The Kashmir rug is *very* attractive, with a dark rose-color background; it sells for about $135 in acrylic and less than $200 in wool.

The *Bernat* catalogue contains several attractive florals, and one nice Oriental, but its best rug is called *Junior Babyland,* a 24" x 35" bear/flower/rabbit design, which would be lovely for the room of a young child. About $32.

Most impressive, though, are the *fabulous* needlepoint rugs from *Elsa Williams.* My own favorite is a truly extraordinary design called *Hatfield.* Finished size is 51" x 84". It's the kind of tapestry style popular in England at the turn of the seventeenth century. This magnificent wool rug has a wide border of detailed and beautiful leaves on a red field, with extremely complicated interior design of flower blossoms and leaves on a black field. But this rug is not exactly cheap: about $2,000. Yet it's worth it—a needlepointer's dream, if you can afford it.

Wool Design, Inc., has an extraordinary collection of tasteful, beautifully designed *latch-hooked-rug kits.* If you've seen other hooked-rug catalogues, you'll be genuinely surprised by this one. They're particularly good at Oriental designs—everything from long runners you can use to define a staircase to 93" x 131" room-size rugs.

Of their room-size rugs, my own favorite is *Large Turkmene,* available in red or gold background. This 93" x 131" size is worked in two halves, then sewn together; the seam in the middle is completely covered by the high pile. The design, despite its bright colors, is quite serene and beautiful. Less than $500.

There are many exquisite smaller rugs. I like their *Kerki,* a geometric floral in 34" x 72" size. Less than $120.

I can't urge you too strongly to send for this catalogue if you're interested in an Oriental design hooked-rug kit; Wool Design has the best of these.

Their Berber designs are quite good, too, with subtle coloring and very interesting patterns. Some of their rya rugs are nice, too.

Clocks

I love the sound of pendulum clocks. One of my uncles collected and restored American shelf clocks, most of which, I have to admit, kept rather approximate time: At Aunt Anne and Uncle Jan's farm, clocks struck the quarter hour or the hour often and not necessarily at fifteen-minute intervals.

Pendulum clocks seem to make time come alive; they're very soothing.

If you weren't lucky enough to inherit antique clocks, or if you don't have the budget to purchase antique clocks in working order, the kits that follow provide a viable, often relatively inexpensive alternative.

A word of advice: Many of the clock kit companies described below run sales just before Christmas. It might be worth waiting, if you can restrain yourself from ordering immediately; often, you can save enough to buy one or more decorative accessory kits with the difference.

Barap Specialties has some wonderful, inexpensive clock kits. Their *Salt Box Wall Clock* is based on a two-hundred-year-old New England design. Its design is very simple, and it integrates a nice little drawer, which provides handy extra storage for your country kitchen. Maple only. 8″ wide, 15″ high, 2¾″ deep. With 110 volt electric movement, the kit costs only $20. With cordless battery movement, about $30. Store-bought, this clock would easily cost $20 more.

Their *Colonial Spice Box Wall Clock* is another lovely kitchen clock. Under the movement is a 4″ deep, 3″ high shelf, perfect for tiny collectibles. Below the shelf is a handy drawer. Maple. 16¾″ tall. With electric movement, less than $25. With cordless battery movement, less than $35.

Their *Early American Table Clock* is very similar in line to a New Haven Clock Company shelf clock I inherited (and prize) from my Uncle Jan's collection. 9½″ high, 7″ wide, 3½″ deep. A major difference is that whereas my clock has lovely decals of roses on the door, this clock has a mirror. Cherry only. With electric movement, the clock costs just over $20. With battery movement, it costs just over $30.

Caldwell Industries of Luling, Texas, has two quite unusual *wooden gear clock kits* based on early wooden gear clocks from Germany. One kit has a hand in the center that turns; the other has a rotating dial (the hand stays in the twelve o'clock position, and the numbers turn in front of it). Both clocks are powered by weights not supplied with the kit but available separately from Caldwell. These are verge and foliot escapement clocks, like the first mechanical clocks. About $80.

Caldwell has other unusual clock kits, including an iron wheel clock with bell, an old Viennese salon clock, and a flying pendulum clock kit.

Craft Products Company has several handsome *grandfather clocks,* my favorite of which is their Cambridge model, available in either ¾″ cherry or walnut. The cherry version of this elegant hall clock, complete with triple-chime movement and moving moon dial is an excellent value at less than $600. Measurements are 77½″ high x 18⅜″ x 12¼″ deep. Easily worth more than twice the price. Furthermore, you don't have to be an expert woodworker to assemble it, since the most difficult parts have been pre-assembled.

Their *Richmond School Regulator kit* is another fine design and good value. Oak only. Comes with preassembled door, convex dial glass, "Regulator" door glass, and painted metal dial with brass-finished rim. Bim-bam battery movement. Relatively easy assembly. The cost is less than $75.

Craft Products has other excellent kits as well, including one for a very beautiful reproduction of an Eli Terry shelf clock in cherry or walnut. Their Country Store Regulator is a fine design and good value also—about $50 (half the price of comparable clocks recently seen at Gimbel's).

Craftsman Wood Service Company has several very attractive reproduction American clocks. Perhaps the most attractive is their 26″ high, x 17½″ wide x 7″ deep *Regulator clock*. The kit is light-colored hardwood, and it includes a battery pendulum movement, dial, hands, glass, and hardware. Just over $90.

If you're more interested in a contemporary-looking clock and you don't care to pay those outrageous department store prices, you may like Craftsman's very simple and clean-lined *butcher-block clocks*. These come in three styles, 12″ square, 12″ diameter round, or 12″ octagon shape. Comes with stencil for painting the numbers. About $13 for the kit and about $11 for the movement.

Craftsman Wood Service has several other very nice kits, including ones for an elegant walnut English bracket clock, an American school clock, and a charming Victorian cathedral clock.

Edmund Scientific Company has a surprisingly modern-looking school clock, which is, in fact, based on an 1832 design. This kit comes with a quartz pendulum movement. Cased in solid pine with brass pendulum, 26″ x 15″ x 5″. Under $70.

Emperor® Clock Company is one of the largest manufacturers of grandfather clock kits. It really pays to get on their mailing list if you're at all interested. But wait a few months before you make your decision, since they regularly run sales that can save you about $100 off the prices quoted below.

Emperor® Clock Company has several handsome *grandfather clock kits*. Model 3001C, their most expensive, measuring 82″ x 19½″ x 13″ comes in oak, cherry, or black walnut. The oak case without movement retails for around $210, but if you wait for their sales, you should be able to buy this case for around $180. Similar savings are available, during sales, for the cherry case, regularly about $250, and black walnut, usually about $300. Movements will cost you between $250 and $240. Their lyre pendulum costs about $40 more. Assembled clocks in this model range between $1,000 to $1,200; therefore, these kits represent savings of at least 40 percent to 50 percent.

Emperor also sells a handsome *black walnut school clock kit* with key-wound eight-day striking mechanism. It's usually priced at about $180, but if you wait for their sale flyers, you should be able to buy one for about $125.

Heritage Clock Company has several grandfather clock kits, most of which are a bit too elaborate for my taste. But their *Lexington grandfather clock kit,* 81″ x 26″ x 14″, is a rare beauty. In solid oak, the case alone costs just over $400. Walnut runs about $70 more. A simple movement and dial can cost an additional $250 or more. But since the least expensive assembled Lexington, in oak, costs about $1,100, this kit should save you at least $500 or more.

And Heritage has more than just grandfather clock kits. Several of their wall clocks, including a red oak schoolhouse clock, and their oak railroad regulator clock are among the most attractive reproductions available. But kit savings are so insubstantial ($20–$25) over preassembled prices that I am not going to go into detail here. But if you're interested in fine reproduction wall clocks at fair prices, do send for their catalogue of varied and unusual clocks.

Kuempel Chime Clock Works and Studio is a most unusual company. First of all, it was founded in the mid-1920s by one of the first designers and manufacturers of kits of any types, Rueben Kuempel. In 1913 Kuempel, a trained engineer, founded a company to manufacture kits to convert Model T's into sports cars. He later produced hope chest kits and, finally, grandfather clock kits with excellent German movements.

The Kuempel workshop is staffed almost entirely by retired craftsmen, with ages well into the upper eighties. Reuben Kuempel was also a pioneer in the use of flex-time, an arrangement in which workers set their own hours of work—a perfect arrangement for retirees. Each clock kit is attentively hand-built to order by these senior craftsmen.

Kuempel has several fine grandfather clock kits, all of which are available (at slight extra charge) with hand-painted moon wheel depicting your home or any other scene you might want. One of the nicest clocks is their *Spirit of Canterbury* kit, with choice of mahogany, cherry, red oak, or walnut case. The case is 84″ high, 19¼″ wide, 11⅜″ deep, with delicate crown arches. Less than $900 for the walnut version (about $50 less in mahogany). Assembled, this clock would go for about $1500 or more.

Mason & Sullivan Company has been selling an unusual variety of fine-quality clock kits for well over thirty years. Their styles range from school clock kits, to carriage clock kits, to grandfather and grandmother clock kits with handsome, simple lines.

One of the people who tested kits for this book, Diane Cleaver, put together and finished Mason & Sullivan's *Shaker Wall Clock*. This fine-looking clock was originally designed by the master clock-maker Isaac N. Youngs (1793–1865); the original is in the collection of the museum at the Hancock Shaker Village in western Massachusetts. The kit Diane Cleaver chose, in cherry, sells for just over $100 without the movement (pine would be slightly less). The equivalent finished and assembled clock sells for more than twice the price; in fact, I've recently seen a copy of this clock selling for $565.

Diane's background as a woodworker is limited: She once built her own bookshelves. She reports that making the cabinet was straightforward; the pieces were numbered very carefully and the instructions were very clear. Mason & Sullivan recommended the use of clamps for this project, but Diane managed to work well without them and in a very small workspace.

Still, Diane reports that Mason & Sullivan's emphasis was on the *cabinet* not on the installation of the clockworks. She had trouble figuring out exactly how to install the clock face; she says it was, without the necessary instructions, very complicated. Also, they didn't say anything about installation of the hands; she didn't know whether the minute hand went on top of the hour hand or vice versa. Furthermore, there were insufficient instructions about how long to hang the pendulum; a friend of hers had to figure that one out. Then, she discovered that there was no key sent with the works. She called up Mason & Sullivan, who were, she says, extremely nice and accommodating; they sent the key. But she wound it, and the clock's still not ticking. Diane says she's frustrated.

Diane told me she thinks Mason & Sullivan (and other clock kit manufacturers) ought to dedicate more effort to explaining how the clockworks ought to be installed and how they work. The interesting thing is that, despite the frustration, Diane seems truly pleased with her clock. It is, in fact, the most beautiful Shaker reproduction clock kit on the market.

I think Diane's experience with this clock was *not* typical (I'm sure Mason & Sullivan would agree). Their clock kits are among the finest on the market. If you're interested in fine clock kits, do send for their catalogue.

If you're looking for a relatively inexpensive case/grandmother or grandfather clock, by all means send for the **New England Clock Company**'s kit catalogue. These clocks are available only with oak or pine cases, but prices include all brass German movements, and they run very much less than any other such kits I've seen. For example, their good-looking #K-269 *Grandmother clock kit,* with striking train with full Westminster chime, strikes on the quarter hour and counts the full hour. About $400. Cases on the other grandfather clocks are a bit elaborate for my taste, but they might suit yours.

Their *oak Regulator clock kit* is quite nice too, with a dial that shows the hour and the day of the month. About $175.

There are very few Victorian reproduction clock kits available—pretty surprising, since even relatively unattractive antique gingerbread shelf clocks are commanding surprisingly high prices, particularly in the Southeast and Northeast. The **Viking Clock Company** has at least three such reproduction kits, the most interesting of which is their *Victorian Teardrop shelf clock*. The original of this clock is actually post-Victorian, dating from about 1880, but the hanging filials on each side, plus other detailing, make this clock truly "Victorian" in style. This case is solid black walnut, with gold silk-screened glass door. The kit comes with the door preassembled, and the glass is included. Comes with eight-day German movement, which counts the hour and strikes on the half hour. 23¼" high, 13" wide, 5½" deep. About $200, but this past Christmas I received a sale brochure pricing it at about $170. The assembled clock sells for about $250.

Viking also has kits for a *Bavarian Regulator clock,* a *Vienna Regulator clock,* and several grandfather clocks.

Westwood Clocks 'n Kits is good if you're looking for a rather monumental *oak grandfather clock*. Most of their cases come in cherry as well, but oak somehow seems more suited to these styles.

Perhaps more interesting are their smaller clocks, especially the unusual *Vienna Regulator*. Based on a classic European design, this clock measures 36" long, 14" wide, 8" deep. Available in oak or cherry, in Westminster chime, or as a plain regulator clock. The case is a clean-lined wooden frame, with front glass panel extending almost from top to bottom. Also available with hand-beveled glass at a higher price. This clock is listed in their catalogue at about $380 for oak, Westminster chime, but their Christmas sale catalogue had it for $60 less.

Westwood has several other attractive clock kits, including their school clock (one of the nicest around), their Dutch wall clock, and their carved Vienna Regulator.

Decorative Accessories

In addition to the kits that follow, you'll find many decorative pillows, samplers, tablecloths, and bedspreads in *chapter 7: Needlework*. Model sailing ships make nice accessories as well; you'll find these in *chapter 6: Toys*.

If you have a taste for country American accessories, or if there's a sportsman or sportswoman in your family, you'll probably be interested in the **Bay Country Woodcrafts** catalogue. Bay Country is particularly good for easy-to-do decorative duck decoy kits at about $20 without paint. Joel Siegel tested their *Wood Duck kit* and reported that the only problem he had was that the body of the duck, where it joins the neck, was not flat as it appears in the catalogue. He had to flatten that area. But he enjoyed the kit very much. Each kit, by the way, comes with very specific and easy-to-follow instructions for painting.

Bay Country also has *lamp kits,* which can be used with any of the many decoy kits in their catalogue. These make charming accent lamps, and they are very similar in appearance to the very expensive decoy lamps one finds, for example, already assembled in the Orvis catalogue. The lamp kit, with base and hardware, sells for about $25 without decoy or shade. A nice coordinating burlap shade is available for $15. With the decoy and shade, it's still about half of what you'd pay Orvis.

They also have a duck coatrack kit for a child's room, rather expensive at $27.50 but worth it, perhaps, if it gets the little ones to hang up their clothing.

Adele Bishop has an extraordinary range of beautiful *stencil kits,* which can provide you with the means to stencil primarily eighteenth- and nineteenth-century designs on fire screens, walls, floors, pillows, mantels, decorative tinware, trunks, wastebaskets, antique bathtubs, and furniture of all kinds. If you like the American country look, here is an inexpensive way to achieve it; her stencils are a particularly fine alternative to costly wallpaper. Designs range from an extremely charming primitive pussycat design, to a rose with tulip design copied from an eighteenth-century American quilt.

Here's a possibility if you're looking for unusual porch or balcony party lighting and you don't mind spending almost $45 to achieve it (high, of course, but less than you'd pay in Bloomingdale's or Hammacher Schlemmer): **James Bliss & Co.** has a kit for a replica of a *Swabian Stable lantern* used until the middle of the nineteenth century. This attractive and intriguing wood, glass, and tin lantern is the kind one would have carried before the days of electric lights or Duracell batteries, and it is powered by one candle. The finished lantern measures 13″ high x 5½″ wide x 5 ½″ deep.

If you're looking for quick and inexpensive ways to effectively frame photographs or prints, you might be interested in **Brookstone's** *all-in-one picture framing kits.* The kit includes mat board, backing board, glare-free plastic "glass," hanging hook, and four see-through corner mounting brackets. The mat board is reversible, white on one side, off-white on the other. Prices range from $6 for 8″ x 10″, to $8.25 for 12″ x 16″.

Are the seats of your caned chairs torn and shabby? You needn't pay outrageous prices to have them professionally recaned if you send for **Cane & Basket Supply Company's** *hand caning kits.* These are available in various cane sizes and cost about $6.50 for one or two average chair seats.

Conran's has a *shade-making kit,* which contains everything for making your own roller blinds. You supply your own fabric. For windows up to 36″, the kit costs under $8. For windows up to 49″, under $11.

Constantine's has chair-caning kits for even less money than Cane & Basket Supply—about $4. The kit includes 250′ of cane, 12 wooden caning pegs, a small awl, and 12′ of binding cane. Professional chair caning could cost you a minimum of four times the price.

Constantine also sells decorative *duck decoy kits* in four styles for about $17 each without paint. Available in mallard, green-winged teal, wood duck, and pintail duck. Each comes with instructions for painting.

Here's a very inexpensive and quite attractive lamp kit, which is particularly suited to country American interiors: **County Loft's** *Boston bean lamp kit.* The base is a heavy large Mason jar, about 20″ high, which you fill with colorful layers of beans, seeds, corn, and grain, or shells, sea glass, or small pinecones. The kit comes empty and without a shade, but it's predrilled and wired. This is a terrific-looking lamp when finished; you should be able to find a nice, inexpensive burlap shade to complement it in the five-and-ten. The kit is less than $17.

Craftsman Wood Service Company sells *duck decoy kits,* which look very similar to those offered by Constantine. About $19 without paint.

Wall murals can be quite effective if they're tasteful in design—a rarity unless they're planned and executed by an artist or architect. Frankly, I can't stand their murals for adults, but **Double M Marketing Company** does have a few *wall mural kits* that offer an inexpensive and attractive solution to brightening up the walls of a child's room. If you have a child who's interested in racing cars, you might be interested in their Formula I mural—about $30 in 6′ x 2′ 6″ size. (Other sizes are available as well.) For younger children's rooms, they have a wonderful locomotive mural, 14″ x 8″, for only $10. The kits come with paint, brushes, and transfer pattern. Also available at similar prices, a rag doll mural and a funny clown mural.

Imaginations of Framingham, Massachusetts, offers *fabric wall mural kits,* two of which, their Duck Pond and Teddy Bear murals, make up into charming accents for a young child's room. The Duck Pond mural, 24″ x 44″, costs less than $20. The more elaborate Teddy Bear, 32″ x 46″, costs about $25.

Lyme Crafts, a tiny mail-order company, has an easy-to-assemble, inexpensive Shaker-type wooden *peg rack kit,* useful for hanging up clothes in the bedroom or mugs in the kitchen. Money-back guarantee. Six pegs.

$8.95, postpaid. Write to them before you place your order; I haven't been able to reach them by phone, and they *are* operating out of a post office box.

Handsome, accurate barometers can be very expensive. **Mason & Sullivan's** *barometer kits* are not exactly cheap, but they're less certainly than barometers with similar workmanship and quality components. Their handsome barometers come in 31″ and 35″ sizes; they range in price from just over $80 to just over $90. Faithful replicas of Sheraton antiques, the wood is solid preshaped cherry, and the hygrometer, barometer, and thermometer are German-made. The larger piece has a lovely sunburst wood inlay beneath the thermometer.

Early American spinning wheels, if you can find them, are a prized decorative accessory; if you can find one that works, that's even better. **Nasco** has an excellent *Early American reproduction spinning wheel kit* for about $160. This was the style popular in the Northeast and Southeast one hundred fifty to two hundred years ago. It has twelve spokes, and it is made of fine-grained solid maple. This is a working wheel, which can be used to spin. The wheel itself comes completely assembled. All fittings are solid brass and wrought iron. Construction is uncomplicated. Once completed, the wheel should run true and free of wobble.

The Museum Gift Shop at Old Sturbridge Village has a wonderful *spinning wheel kit,* which is easy to assemble. This "sitting wheel" was used, they say, primarily for flax and is available with a distaff, but it is equally useful for spinning wool. Without distaff, about $160. With distaff, about $180. I called them to ask what kind of wood they use for the kit, but the two people with whom I spoke had no adequate answer. I suggest you write to them to inquire.

Babies and their parents seem to love mobiles. **Patch-It** of Waitsfield, Vermont, sells a very attractive, inexpensive *bird mobile kit* which makes up into a mobile about 24″ x 24″; it comes with materials for five calico birds.

If you'd like an old-fashioned mail basket but don't particularly care to pay the going rate, $17-$19, for one, consider the *reed mail basket kit* offered for $4 by the **H. H. Perkins Company.** This is a fine project for a beginner, and the pretty basket is worth the effort.

Pickwick Lamps has *lamp base kits* for about $20, which enable you to display favorite photographs, needlepoint, decoupage, or other craftwork on the lamp base. The kit can be assembled in just a few minutes, and it makes up into a surprisingly handsome lamp.

Baskets have become surprisingly expensive over the past few years, especially the antique baskets we used to pick up at country auctions for practically nothing. But if your taste runs to accessorizing with baskets, here's a way to get some handsome ones at ridiculously low prices. **Savin Crafts** offers several attractive easy-to-make basket kits. Most intriguing are their *magazine basket kit* ($5.25), their *utility (wastepaper) basket kit* ($2.75), their *sewing basket kit* ($3.50), and most especially their handy *knitting basket kit* ($3.75), a 6″ wide x 15″ high cylinder with cover.

I've already listed two lamp base kits; here at last is a *lampshade kit*. **Shades of Olde** of Lyons, Colorado, is now manufacturing and wholesaling lampshade kits in pagoda, round, cuff top, and gooseneck round shapes. These retail for about $7–$15. These shade kits enable you to use your own fabrics for a custom lampshade look, and they come with instructions for lining. With these kits, fabric is not bunched on top; rather, it's stretched tautly over the frame (an old lampshade-making technique). Frames are zinc-plated so that you can wash the shades if you have the need to do so. These are very old-timey-looking styles; they're very nice.

Stained-Glass Accessories

It's true that elaborate stained-glass hanging lamps are not the world's easiest kit projects. But the popularity of stained-glass accessories (as well as their prices) seems to grow as every year goes by, and more and more people are taking up the craft.

My downstairs neighbor, Judd Gabey, took an inexpensive night class in stained glass three or four years ago, and she has since filled her windows and those of her friends with beautiful pieces incorporating shells and beach glass. The tables in her house are covered with beautiful stained-glass boxes to hold just about everything conceivable—and at Christmastime family and friends wait for little stained-glass fancies from her worktable. The reason I bring up Judd here is that her worktable is set up in a corner of her bedroom; you don't need a home workshop to do some of the projects that follow—just a fair-sized area where you and your materials won't be disturbed, and time.

Mary Maxim, the great needlework kit catalogue house, usually includes a few reproduction *Tiffany-type lamp kits* in their catalogue. Their kits contain precut glass pieces, copper foil, brass parts, solder, soldering flux, antiquing solution, and very good instructions. You'll need to supply your own small 50-watt soldering iron, wire clippers, pliers, and screwdriver. At least three styles are available, an 18″ rose design, a 20″ geometric design, and an 18″ fruit design. All are very attractive, and they sell for less than $135. An excellent value.

Spector's Stained Glass has kits for a wide variety of stained-glass accessories. One of their simpler projects is their 8″ diameter *Windjammer mirror kit,* with precut glass pieces and all material except soldering iron. This is a lovely small mirror, and it is an excellent project for beginners. About $10.

Studio Design, Inc., has so many exciting stained-glass designs that it would be impossible to describe even a representative sampling of the best of them here. If you're at all interested in stained-glass kits, I urge you to send away for their catalogue.

Their hanging lamps come in 16″ x 30″ pool table sizes, as well as shallow domes and deeper domes of all shapes and sizes. Designs run from traditional floral or geometric motifs, to an oblong old-time train design, to Disney characters for children's rooms. Table lamp designs range from plain, tasteful stained-glass "pleats," to elaborate Tiffany reproductions. They also have a fascinating variety of kits for suncatchers, terrariums, wall mirrors, clocks, and ceiling panels. But be careful as you go through their color catalogue; many of the pieces illustrated are available in assembled form only—pretty disappointing once you've made up your mind to buy one particular lamp kit.

If I were compelled to select the one shade of theirs that I'd most like to make and own, it would probably be their red, green, or amber #D2424 24″ *Conical Geometric Design;* this is a fascinating, art-nouveau-influenced design, which looks superb as a floor lamp. The dome kit, with 265 glass pieces, sells for about $160; the lamp base runs about $90 additional. Preassembled, this floor lamp would cost almost $500.

Whittemore-Durgin caters to more sophisticated stained-glass craftspeople, but they do have a few *Tiffany reproduction lamp kits.* Most spectacular is their 26″ Grape Trellis shade, very close in effect to the Tiffany original included in Egon Neustadt's *The Lamps of Tiffany.* Shadings in this lamp kit are most unusual, achieved by "plating" (using two layers of glass, which combine the desired colors and densities). This is a very difficult and time-consuming kit because the glass is furnished in sheets. This shade kit sells for about $120, and it's well worth it if you have the skill and space to accommodate it. (Perhaps, needless to point out, this is not the kind of project you could successfully complete in a corner of your bedroom.)

H. L. Worden Company also caters to more sophisticated stained-glass craftspeople. They call their kits semikits because you cut your own glass. They have more than 75 antique designs, many of which are truly fabulous. Each kit comes with a special Styrofoam form that makes construction easier. If you feel you're up to complicated stained-glass work, do look at their catalogue.

2

Kits for Musical Instruments

Dulcimers and Hammered Dulcimers

Alpine Dulcimer Company of Boulder, Colorado, sells two fine dulcimer kits.

Their *Valentine Dulcimer Kit* has body and fingerboard of variegated gum, soundboard of Sitka spruce. The flat peg head and heart-shaped sound holes accentuate the simple integrity of clean folk design set off by ebony tuning pegs, silver frets, and bone nut and bridge. They use no plywood. All special machining has been done, including accurate placement of fret slots in the fingerboard and proper tapering of the tuning peg holes. The kit includes all the necessary parts, including strings and tuning pegs, and gives clear instructions. You provide glue, sandpaper, finish, and a few tools, such as plane, chisels, files, and C-clamps. Both this and their Little Melvina Kit are about 38″ long, 5″ wide, and 1⅜″ deep. Each is available in three and four strings. By constructing your own Valentine dulcimer Kit, you save over $100 off the preassembled price.

Their *Little Melvina Model* is a fine teardrop dulcimer, crafted of solid walnut and Sitka spruce. Ebony tuning pegs and German silver frets. Bone nut and bridge, which produce a clearer sound than that found on dulcimers with wooden bridges. Carved peg head scroll, F-shaped sound holes, and graceful contour. The peg head scroll is precarved and ready to install. The kit is also available with blank peg head, which you can carve yourself.

This is a magnificent dulcimer; the kit, under $90, should save you about $125 or more.

Left-handed dulcimers are available in each model at about $5 extra per kit.

Black Mountain Instruments produces fine mountain dulcimer kits in combinations of spruce/mahogany, spruce/cherry, and spruce/walnut. My mother, who has done very little woodcrafting, built their spruce/cherry model in five evenings (about fifteen hours) with almost no difficulty. (She said the sanding alone took her three or four hours.)

These kits are of traditional hourglass shape, with scrollhead, quality mechanical tuning machines, four-string setup, heart-shaped sound holes, nickel-silver fretted fingerboard with a strum hollow, and solid wood top and back. They have a lacquered, hand-rubbed finish.

Their most popular model, the spruce/cherry combination, costs about $60—a savings of more than $30 over the preassembled version.

Country Ways of Minnetonka, Minnesota, carries some intriguing musical instrument kits. Three Appalachian dulcimer kits are available: K-101 is a three-string model, teardrop shape, in mahogany. At less than $30, this is a fine first dulcimer, especially for families with children. Easy to change the tunings. K-121 is a four-string model, teardrop shape, of fine butternut. About $40. K-141 is a four-string traditional hourglass shape, in butternut, with prebent sides. About $45.

The Dulcimer Shoppe of Mountain View, Arkansas, has two styles of *dulcimer kits*. Each style has scroll-peg head, fretboard, and tail block of solid black walnut. The face, back, and sides are laminated walnut plywood. All parts are precut and lightly sanded, with the fretboard slotted to ensure accurate fret placement. The nickel-silver fret wire is cut into individual frets. Each kit contains four black-buttoned Grover pegs and four strings.

Their M-K4 kit makes a slender hourglass dulcimer. Kit comes with prebent double-curve sides, plus four precut heart-shaped sound holes. About $40.

Their T-K4 kit makes a teardrop-shape dulcimer. Sides in this kit are not bent, but they say no special tools are needed to shape the flexible plywood. The two F-shape sound holes are precut, but they do need some hand trimming. Also about $40.

Elderly Instruments has several dulcimer kits available, including kits by R & J, and Here, Inc. The R & J kits are made with laminated woods for the backs and sides, and they are available with laminated mahogany or solid spruce tops. Their sound box is quite deep, 2½", creating a full bass sound. Their dulcimers measure 36" from scroll to tailpiece and are all four-stringed. Kits include all materials except glue and finish. The laminated sides in the kits are not prebent, but they are very flexible, so you can build them as either hourglass or teardrop shapes. A little more challenging than most dulcimer kits. Available with laminated mahogany back, sides, top, for about $35. A version with mahogany back and sides, solid spruce top, is under $40—less than half the preassembled price.

They also carry a kit for a *hammered dulcimer*. The kit makes an instrument 40" x 3" x 18" x 18" (it's a trapezoid). It has twelve treble courses of four strings, the longest of which is 35", the shortest 16". There are eleven bass courses of two strings each. Kit includes all parts except top and bottom. A tuning wrench and hammers are also included. All difficult cutting and drilling is already done. Apparently they're about to switch the brand of hammered dulcimer kit they carry, so contact them for more complete and up-to-date information.

Guitars Friend has many fine kits. Their dulcimer kits look particularly interesting. All pieces are precision-milled. Directions are easy to follow. All solid-wood construction, not laminates.

Their *Appalachian dulcimers* are nut- and saddle-notched, with prebent fingerboard sides. The kit includes strings, Sta-tite metal friction tuners, sound holes left uncut. Prefretted. Maple sells for about $65. Walnut/spruce: under $80 (about $70 less than their preassembled model). Koa/maple fingerboard: less than $75 (half the price of their preassembled model). Cherry/maple fingerboard: just under $70 (almost $60 less than their preassembled model).

Their *Panhandler dulcimer kits,* teardrop shape, with loud, distinct bassy sound, come with prefretted fingerboard, notched nut and saddle, and includes strings. Sound holes left uncut. Maple: less than $60. Walnut/maple fingerboard: about $65 (about $55 less than their preassembled model). Cherry/maple fingerboard: about $60.

They also have unfinished *Huckleberry Mountain hammered dulcimers* for about $100 less than finished models. You put in pins and do all finish work.

Here, Inc., has several dulcimer kits. Their standard mountain dulcimer sound box is a little more than 1¼" deep. You can order 1¾" sides for a nominal extra charge. All kits include all parts with all crucial sawing and drilling done. But no drilling is done in their lower-priced hammered dulcimer kits. When ordering you might keep in mind, as Here, Inc., points out in their catalogue, that dulcimer shape affects sound. "Teardrop shapes tend to have a more mellow sound . . . the hourglass shape sounds somewhat brighter, suggestive of a mandolin. The teardrop dulcimers are probably a little louder overall. Contrary to popular rumor, both shapes are traditional, along with several other shapes."

Their most popular, inexpensive dulcimer kit is their #20K. *Modified teardrop shape,* with three strings, 27" fret pattern, laminated Philippine mahogany body, spruce soundboard, lacquer finish. Available in four-string version. Less than $30 (a savings of about $40 over preassembled model).

Kit 35K is an attractive *hourglass-shaped dulcimer* with three strings, 27" fret pattern, solid cherry body, spruce soundboards. Available in four-string version; also available in walnut at extra charge. About $50 (at least $25 cheaper than preassembled model).

They also have an interesting *backpack version:* 26" long, 5½" wide, 2 deep. Mixed materials. Less than $30.

Their *hammered dulcimer kit,* #100HK, makes an instrument that measures 3" x 35" x 16" x 15". Handle extends 2" from 35" side. Horizontal pinblocks. The longest string is about 28"; the shortest about 11". The finished instrument weighs about 18 pounds. The standard version comes with butternut exterior; cherry or walnut are available as options. This model tunes well to "D" scale, starting at treble course #2 with "D" at #2, gives D, G, C, to F scales on treble, and chromatic octave in bases. All maple laminated pinblocks, individual bridges for more accurate tuning and ease in stringing or replacing strings, 14 treble and 13 bass courses for a large range of notes. Piano-grade spruce soundboard. Comes with tuning wrench and hammers. Two string per treble course model: about $100 (one-third the price of their equivalent preassembled hammered dulcimer). Three-string model: just over $100, less than one-third the equivalent nonkit instrument.

Hughes Dulcimer Company has a fascinating variety of kits from folk harps to dulcimers. They carry five different styles of dulcimer kits. Their best *hourglass dulcimer kit* costs about $60 (more than $30 less than their comparable assembled model). It's solid walnut and spruce, has four strings, and measures 34". The *church dulcimer,* with six strings and a deep rich bass sound, comes in two versions: one (walnut) for about $40, the other (maple) for about $30. Solid spruce tops are available for $8 more. The $40 version, measuring 39", should save you $30 over the assembled model.

Hughes also carries a walnut kit for a *double or courting dulcimer.* This one, with eight strings, costs $50 for the kit—about $26 less than the preassembled model. Solid spruce top, $8 more. Their *musicians dulcimer* comes in six versions, with machine gear tuning like a guitar. This is a good starting dulcimer for most people. Top of the line, four strings, 37" walnut, costs about $30 (saving you about $20 over the assembled price). A smaller, simpler version, good for the children, costs less than $20; this one is maple and has three strings.

Their *hammered dulcimer (psaltery)* is a very good buy in kit form: about $90. The assembled version costs about $200. Available in walnut, it tunes to A, D, G. The hammered dulcimer is, of course, played with wooden hammers. If plucked with the fingers, it becomes a psaltery.

International Luthiers Supply, Inc., carries the Folk Roots *mountain dulcimer kit.* This is a four-string hourglass-shape dulcimer with spruce top, walnut laminate back and sides. Comes with semifinished solid walnut scroll, fingerboard, and tailblock. The fingerboard is slotted, ready to receive nickel-silver frets. Nickel-plated individual tuning machines, steel tailpins. Kit also includes nut, saddle, set of strings, and instruction manual. At $40 this is an excellent buy.

They also carry a *hammered dulcimer kit,* which sells for around $70—another excellent value.

Banjos, Violins, Mandolins, Guitars, Balalaikas, Lutes, and Cellos

Constantine's has four guitar kits available in rosewood, mahogany, maple, and walnut. Each kit includes all fittings except tuning machines. All kits contain soundboard, back, sides, neck. (Wood for laminated construction is standard; if you wish a solid-wood neck, it's available for $7 extra.) Kit also includes: rosewood fingerboard, interior blocks, lining, struts, bracing, rosewood stock for making bridge, bone saddle nut, bone top nut, nickel-silver fret-wire set, end pin for attaching strap, wood purfling, rosette materials, plus glue, five sheets of sandpaper in three grades, plus filler. The soundboard in each kit is fine Alaskan hard spruce. Prices range from about $65 for rosewood, to less than $60 for walnut, to under $50 for mahogany and maple.

Country Ways has two *mountain banjo kits.* These are replicas of the traditional handmade mountain banjo, and they come in black walnut. The resonance of the wood and the natural head provide an "old-time" sound and are good for frailing. The central body has been laminated, shaped, and rough-sanded, and the fret positions cut in the fingerboard. You glue the rest together, shape the neck and peg box, and sand. The kits include all wood and metal parts—tuners, strings, bridge, etc. Available in authentic but hard-to-learn fretless model, and five-string with fretted neck. About $110.

Country Ways also has a very nice *mandolin kit.* It's all walnut, with contrasting cherry stripe on the back. The soundboard is spruce, with the hole already cut. The fret pattern (14″) is precut in the rosewood fingerboard. Sides are prebent, and all parts, including tuners, metal tension rod, strings, etc., are included. Since the kit calls for a slight arching to both top and back, it's not really for beginning kit makers.

Elderly Instruments has both *Saga* and *Eagle banjo kits.* The Saga kits are made in Japan and are available in open-back and resonator models. The open-back model features a cast rim with integral arch-top tone ring, a pre-shaped neck with adjustable truss rod, fretted rosewood fingerboard, "Granada"-shaped peg head, plastic inlays, tension hoop, armrest, adjustable tail-piece, 24 nickel-plated bracelet shoes, hooks and nuts, four 4:1 ratio offset geared pegs with a friction fifth peg, plastic head, strings, bridge, small screwdriver, and bracket wrench. Less than $100.

The Resonator model comes with all the above, plus laminated mahogany resonator, which is routed for binding, ivoroid plastic binding, 24-piece flange, and two thumbscrew attachments. Under $120.

Their *Eagle banjo kits* are made in the United States; and they make slightly better instruments than the Saga kits. Left-handed kits available at no extra cost. Available in open-back and resonator models. The open-back model has shaped mahogany neck with steel reinforcement bar, rosewood fingerboard, and peg head overlay, 18 percent nickel-silver frets installed, shaped peg head with drilled peg holes and installed lag bolts. Maple and ebony bridge. Pearl inlays. More fine-quality details in all than the Saga kit. The open-back model sells for less than $150 in kit form; resonator costs just under $200.

Guitars Friend has, believe it or not, a *guitar kit by Martin Company.* All the wood is Martin solid wood, either A or B grade (the latter means wood that's slightly flawed but with no structural problem). Tops are spruce already joined, with the sound hole and rosette routed out. The back is joined and braced, sides already bent, and the neck rough-shaped with the reinforcement rod in place. The fingerboard is slotted. Included are inlays, bindings, fret wire, bridge pins, Grover Rotomatic machine heads, instruction book. Available with mahogany sides and back, around $200. Also available in rosewood for $30 more.

Guitars Friend also carries *Saga Electric Guitar Kits.* These go for under $150.

In addition, they carry two *banjo kits.* One, *the original Stewart-MacDonald kit,* will be described further along in this section: Look under the Stewart-MacDonald entry. Guitars Friend also carries *banjo kits by Saga.* These are cheaper versions of the kits by Stewart-MacDonald. Of the seven Saga models they carry, Guitars Friend recommends the Standard Model with Resonator—about $150. Guitars Friend has some words of caution in their catalogue: If you're thinking of buying a cheap preassembled banjo, *don't do it.* You're much better off, they say, putting the same money into a kit and building it yourself. Cheap preassembled banjos don't have a good sound.

Guitars Friend also carries the fine *Stewart-MacDonald Eagle Mandolin kit.* The fingerboard is fretted, and the top is joined to the sides. Top and back are carved and just need final sanding. F-holes are precut. A fine quality instrument, at around $135.

Here, Inc.'s *Mandolin kit,* designed by Craig Pederson, comes with flat back with symmetrical bracing, making it adaptable for left-handed playing.

Body and neck are walnut with mirror image back; prebent sides; rosewood fingerboard; 15:1 ratio tuners; 14″ fret pattern; precut sound hole; spruce soundboard. Slight arch in top and back (created by bracing) for good sound. This is an advanced kit for people with previous instrument building or woodworking experience. About $140—more than a hundred dollars less than equivalent preassembled model.

They also sell a *banjo kit* that comes in three different woods: maple, cherry, or walnut. All are fretless, but you can get the kit with frets cuts into the neck for less than $8 extra. Prices range from just over $80 for the maple kit (a savings of over $60 over the preassembled price), to just over $90 for the walnut kit (a savings of almost $70 over preassembled price).

International Luthiers Supply, Inc., has eight *violin kits,* three of which come with partially carved top, back, and neck. One of their top-of-the-line kits would come with partially carved, very white, straight-grain, European silver-spruce, Stradivarius pattern top; select, fine old European maple back and sides, naturally seasoned; well-flamed European white-maple neck; European spruce end block, quarter-sawn straight grained; spruce corner block; spruce lining (also available in white linden wood); straight-grain silver-spruce bass bar; already rounded silver-spruce bass bar; very flexible three-ply black-white-black wood fiber purfling for inlaying around the edges of top and back; finest-quality semifinished, select ebony fingerboard, very black and evenly textured; ebony string nut and saddle; finest ebony tailpiece, finished ready for use; retractable end pin, plated steel rod, rubber tip, ebony sleeve; ¾ or ¼ size finished European maple violin bridge; nickel-plated E-string adjuster; nickel-plated piccolo; large Bakelite chin rest; ebony mute, ebony ¾ or ¼ pegs; varnish; strings; and instructions. A very impressive kit, which sells for just under $100. An *excellent* value.

International Luthiers Supply also has comparable quality *violin bow kits,* ranging in price from $28 to $46, and quite an interesting *violin graduating caliper kit* (less than $10).

They also sell six *guitar kits,* including kits for classic, acoustic, and jumbo guitar. Their *acoustic guitar kit,* for example, includes a European silver-spruce top, best quality matched rosewood back and sides, mahogany neck wood, beautifully grained rosewood peg head veneer, white linden lining, ebony fingerboard, and other elements of similar quality. The acoustic guitar kit sells for about $125, another exceptional buy; an acoustic guitar of comparable quality would probably sell for at least twice the price.

International Luthiers Supply also carries the Japanese-made Saga *banjo kits,* previously described in the entry for Elderly Instruments. International Luthiers' prices are quite good, so before buying one of the Saga banjo kits, I recommend that you compare prices.

If a *mandolin kit* is what you have in mind, International Luthiers should have one to suit you; they sell five different mandolin kits, in both "flat" and "arched" styles. A typical top-of-the-line "arched" mandolin kit would come with: very fine, old wood European spruce top; fine old European maple back and sides; well-seasoned, rough-sawed European white-maple neck wood; white-maple peg head veneer; gold-plated two-piece Kluson tailpiece; best-quality ebony fingerboard; and other parts of similar quality. Price is just over $100—again less than half of what you'd pay for a preassembled instrument of comparable quality.

The **International Violin Company** of Baltimore, Maryland, sells two *classical guitar kits.* Guitar Kit #1 comes with fine-quality spruce top; maple neck spliced, with ebony fingerboard and German silver frets; fine-quality rosewood back, and other high-quality materials. This is a fairly expensive kit. Their pricing policy is confusing. This kit is listed at almost $400, but a stamped notice on the front of the price list says that dealers and instrument makers receive a "confidential 50 percent discount." Frankly, it sounds like any kit maker qualifies for the discount.

International Violin Company also sells three complete *violin-making outfits/kits.* Each has excellent top-quality components and prices (assuming you get the 50 percent discount), which range from around $100 to $140.

Perhaps most interesting in this catalogue is their complete *cello-making outfit/kit.* The only cello kit I've seen, this outfit comes with better-quality spruce top (their grades are "usual quality; better quality; fine quality; selected spruce, old wood"); slightly flamed maple back with sides, corner blocks; set straight sides; cello neck with scroll; bottleneck stain; fingerboard; set fiber purfling; ebony top nut; ebony saddle; cello end pin; bridge; tailpiece with gut attached; bass bars; pegs; peg soap; violin glue, etc. This unusual kit sells for less than $400.

Stewart-MacDonald Manufacturing Company recently introduced an excellent-quality mandolin kit: the *Eagle Style 7 Mandolin Kit.* This design has very good tone, and it incorporates several desirable features, including accurately carved, aged spruce top and long-scale fingerboard. This is a relatively easy kit; the adjustable truss rod and fingerboard have been installed, and the neck has been shaped (you can still thin the top, shape the tone bars, decide on degree of inlay, etc.). Basically, with this kit, you have to sand and inlay the neck (available with or without frets installed) and glue the neck to the body. You also have to sand the top, shape the tone bars, glue the back to the body, and glue a strip of binding in place. Easy to finish. This kit sells for just over $150; it's one of the best mandolin kits available.

Stewart-MacDonald is also known for their excellent *banjo kits,* of which they manufacture six. Their most popular banjo kits are their Style Numbers 3 and 3R; these feature laminated beech wood rims and bell-metal flathead tone ring, individually matched to its wood rim. (For tonal quality, wood-rimmed banjos are considered the most desirable.) Prominent features of these kits include their geared Five-Star planet tuners, their Five-Star head, notched tension hoop, adjustable tailpiece, and scroll peg head. The neck is fitted with two-way adjustable truss rod and is made of kiln-dried Honduras mahogany. The Style 3 makes a fine open-back instrument, to which you can later add a resonator. Style 3R comes with the resonator and all fittings, and like Style 3, it is available with a five-string left-handed neck, tenor neck (19', 22⅞" scale, 3RT) or plectrum neck (22', 26³⁄₁₆" scale, 3RP). The Style 3 kit sells for under $250; 3R costs less than $300. These both represent hefty initial investments, but most assembled wood rim instruments go for well over $500.

Harpsichords, Spinets, Pianofortes, Clavichords, and Virginals

Burton Harpsichords of Lincoln, Nebraska, offers exquisite harpsichord, spinet and clavichord kits. Their kits come in two styles: a Basic Kit, for the builder with some woodworking sophistication and access to a radial arm and/or table saw, and a drill press. Perhaps more interesting to most readers are their Complete Kits. These involve assembling and finishing precut parts. No clamps are needed for the Complete Kit. Charles Burton estimates completion time at between eighty and two hundred hours for most of their instruments.

The case and framework of each Burton harpsichord, spinet, and clavichord interlock under the tension of the strings, yielding built-in stability and strength. Wrestplanks are cross-laminated hard rock maple, to hold the tuning pins firmly and prevent warpage; and the use of parallel-laminated cherry ensures strong bridges of constant shape. Strings are rust-resistant steel music wire and spring-temper phosphor bronze.

They offer two ⅛"-thick soundboard materials. Laminated basswood is their standard soundboard material. With its crisper tone, it might be best considered for continuo uses, and it is unquestionably better, they point out, in most institutional settings by virtue of its stability. Quarter-sawn Sitka spruce, available as an option, is considered to be the finest of soundboard materials; it produces a full, rich tone. Spruce is probably best for solo and concert uses or places where humidity can be maintained at a reasonable (25 percent to 65 percent) level. Since it is somewhat more sensitive to humidity changes, the Burton catalogue states, plan on somewhat more frequent tuning and maintenance.

Clavichord Kit. This is an extremely handsome solo or practice instrument with a very soft tone. It is single-strung for ease in tuning; the scaling and string gauging give this clavichord exceptional clarity, uniformity of tone color, and responsiveness through all five octaves. The instrument measures 59¾" long x 18½" wide x 30" high. This is a wonderful instrument to have if you live in an apartment and must keep even your music rather quiet. Complete kit sells for less than $400 (the finished instrument sells for over $900 more).

Spinet Kit. The Burton spinet was developed in response to requests for a smaller-size harpsichord suitable for continuo work with small ensembles or for apartment dwellers with space problems. It has a five-octave keyboard and a round delicate tone. 47″ long (across keyboard) x 29″ wide x 35″ high. Complete kit sells for less than $600 (the finished instrument sells for over a thousand dollars more). This is a *very* beautiful instrument.

One Manual Harpsichords. There are three of these kits. The Burton 8′ x 8′ harpsichord has two stops tuned to 8′ (concert) pitch. The stop whose jacks are closest to the nut has a bright tone color; the other has a darker, rounder tone. This difference in tone, along with that offered by the buff stop, allows five variations in volume and character of sound.

The Burton 8′ x 4′ harpsichord also has two stops, but one sounds 4′ pitch (an octave higher). When combined with the 8′, the 4′ stop increases the brilliance of the instrument. Played alone, it is a delicate and unique solo stop. For further tonal modification, the 8′ is provided with the buff.

The Burton 8′ x 8′ x 4′ harpsichord combines the tonal possibilities of the 8′ x 8′ and 8′ x 4′ dispositions in a single instrument. Two stops sound 8′ pitch, one stop sounds 4′ pitch, plus 8′ buff stop.

Prices for the three range from around $900 to just over $1,000. The 8′ x 8′ harpsichord kit is about $1,800 less than the equivalent finished instrument; the 8′ x 8′ x 4′ kit should save you almost $2,000.

Two Manual Harpsichord. This is an 8′ x 8′ x 4′ instrument on which one 8′ has its own (upper) manual, adding the possibility of dialogue between voices to the 8′ x 8′ x 4′ disposition. The upper manual can be played independently or "coupled" to make 8′ x 8′ x 4′ available on the lower manual. The buff stop can be applied to either 8′, yielding fifteen possible stop combinations. This magnificent instrument measures 95″ long x 39″ wide x 36¼″ high. The complete kit sells for just under $1,600—a savings of almost $3,000.

Frank Hubbard Harpsichords, Inc., was the first company, they say, to provide kits for historically accurate harpsichords. Their kits are available in several stages of roughness or completion. The Basic Kit requires the builder to make all the straight parts of the instrument from his or her own materials and to cut, fit, and join all of the components of the harpsichord. Anyone considering the Basic Kit ought to have available a circular saw, a drill press, a complete set of chisels, planes, clamps, and other hand tools. Construction time: usually 500–600 hours.

The Dimensioned Kit comes with case and frame materials thickened and cut to width, but it leaves to the builder the work of mitering, rabbeting, shaping, and joining. Same tools required as for the Basic Kit. 400–500 hours to complete the instrument.

They also have a Precut Kit available. Each part is accurately dimensional, shaped and tapered as appropriate, with miters, dadoes, rabbets and mortises cut, and joints prepared for gluing. Requires normal handworking tools, about a dozen clamps, and a solid bench on which to work. About 300 hours (four or five months of spare-time work).

Another option: the Precut Kit with case assembled. In this one, the rim of the instrument (spine, cheek, bent side, and tail) is glued together. The belly rails, wrest plank, name board, and cap molding are fitted and glued in, the bottom is installed and trimmed, and the reinforcing keys are cut and fitted into the bent side joints. 250–350 hours to complete.

French Eighteenth-Century Single- and Double-Manual Harpsichord Kits. The prototype for this kit was an instrument made in Paris in 1769 by Pascal Taskin, possibly the most famous of all eighteenth-century French harpsichord makers. There is nothing in the harpsichord literature, they say, that cannot be successfully performed on an instrument of this type. Completed range is five octaves and one note, FF-g ′ ′ ′ (sixty-three notes). There are three ranks of jacks and three choirs of strings, 2 x 8′, 1 x 4′, with a buff stop, which can be installed on either the back 8′ choir or the upper manual 8′. An additional *peau de buffle* register with leather plectra can be added to the lower-manual 8′ if the builder chooses. The keyboards are replicas of Taskin's keyboards whose lower-manual key levers are guided by pins running in a rack at the rear of the keyboard. This method eliminates the use of a front rail and permits the use of thin key levers, resulting in the light action favored by eighteenth-century composers. There are no cloth bushings used in the keys, the octave span is 6¼″, and the key heads are 1⅜″ long, conforming exactly to the original French practice. The key fronts are finished with pearwood arcades, the ebony key heads are rounded and scored with decorative lines, and the sharps are tapered in height and width. The single-manual version of the French Kit is identical to the double from the name board back. Prices of the French Double-Manual Harpsichord Kit: Basic Kit, about $1,700; Kit with Dimensional Parts, $1,900; Kit with precut parts, $2,200; Precut with assembled case, $2,490. A completed kit costs over $1,000 more than the Precut version.

Single-manual prices range from about $1,500 for the Basic Kit to just under $2,300 for Precut Kit with case assembled. Fully assembled price would be about $1,300 more.

Single-Manual Flemish Harpsichord Kits. This kit is a reproduction of an instrument built in Antwerp in the year 1584 by Hans Moermans. It has a distinct Flemish sound, unusually large range, and relatively simple construction.

The keyboard has a range of four and one-half octaves, extending from BB to f³ (fifty-five notes), an unusually large range for an instrument of its period and one that allows it to be used for much eighteenth-century music. It was typical of earlier harpsichords to achieve an expanded lower range by retuning some of the notes in the bottom octave. The low BB on this instrument is meant to be tuned to GG. The C# is then tuned to AA and the D# to BB. Much seventeenth-century music assumes this "short octave" tuning, but other scores require the chromatic notes. The kit instrument may be tuned either way, according to the player's preference.

Available as a kit with Dimensioned parts for about $1,400. Kit with precut parts, about $1,600. Kit with case assembled, about $1,900. The completed instrument would cost $1,100 more.

English Bentside Spinet Kits. The bentside spinet is distinguished from the harpsichord in that the strings and spine run transversely to the player and are not parallel to the key levers. The strings are plucked much closer to their center points than are the strings of a harpsichord. As a result, the spinet produces a strong and sustained tone, but one that is darker and less brilliant than the harpsichord. Bentside spinets almost invariably had only one choir of strings at 8' pitch.

This particular bentside spinet is a nearly exact reconstruction of one made in 1765 by Baker Harris of London for John Collins of Newport in the colony of Rhode Island.

Kit with precut parts, just over $1,300. Kit with case assembled, just under $1,600. Kit assembled and veneered, leaving only musical assembly and voicing to the builder, about $3,100. Completed instrument, $4,700.

Viennese Pianoforte Kits. This kit is based on the Johann Andreas Stein pianoforte of 1784. Stein's instruments were particular favorites of Mozart and the young Beethoven. This instrument can open to you the brilliant keyboard literature composed between 1765 and 1825 by Clementi, Hummel, Field, Hässler, Méhul, Paesiello, and Cherubin; the true color and brilliance of these composers really comes through only on the pianoforte.

Basic Kit, less than $1,800. Kit with Dimensioned parts, about $2,000. Kit with precut parts and assembled case, about $2,500. Assembled and veneered kit, $4,200. Totally completed instrument with veneered case, $9,-600.

The Instrument Workshop of Seattle, Washington, has been marketing *harpsichord, clavichord,* and *fortepiano kits* for the last decade. Their kits come in an advanced state of completion, wherein all the woodworking has been done, the soundboard has been tapered and glued in, the bridges and nuts are in place with their pins installed. The kit builder has only to paint, oil, or varnish the case; glue, shape, and polish the key covers; string the instrument; and assemble the action. The jack slides and stop levers are installed. All gauges and hand tools (except hammer and paint) are included.

One Manual Flemish Harpsichord. Designed after the seventeenth-century instruments by Andries Ruckers and Hans Moermans. Range has been extended to five octaves. By loosening two bolts, the back of the keyboard drops below the action so that the keyboard can be shifted sideways by the space of one semitone. This permits the instrument to be played at modern pitch, as well as one half note lower without retuning. Kit to be painted, about $2,000. Kit to be veneered, about $2,400. Finished instrument is about twice the price.

Two Manual French Harpsichord. Based on eighteenth-century instruments by Pascal Taskin. The *peau de buffle* is an additional row of jacks with soft leather plectra, which produce a subdued singing sound, a sharp contrast to the crisp tone produced by the delrin quills, which are used for the other stops. The back 8', the *peau de buffle,* and the 4' are played from the lower manual, and the front 8' from the upper manual. The two keyboards can be coupled by pushing in the upper manual. The two keyboards can also be shifted sideways as a unit by the space of a semitone (by loosening bolts as on the Flemish model), which allows the instrument to be played at the pitch of A 440 as well as A 415. Kit to be painted, about $2,300. Kit to be veneered, about $2,800. Finished instrument, with stand, $5,400–$6,200.

Two Manual English Harpsichord. Based on the large instruments of the late eighteenth century by Shudi and Broadwood, it has all the features of the Two Manual French Harpsichord and in addition the typically English cut-through lute. It also incorporates a *peau de buffle.* Kit to be veneered, about $3,100. Finished instrument would be at least twice the price.

Available too from the Instrument Workshop are kits for a *One Manual Italian Harpsichord,* an *English Virginal,* an *English Bentside Spinet,* a *Double Strung Clavichord,* and a *German Unfretted Clavichord* based on an instrument by Johann Hass, and a *Fortepiano,* based on an instrument by Jean-Louis Dulcken.

All **Williams Workshop** kit instruments (small Ruckers harpsichord, spinet, and clavichord) were designed to use the same keyboard; it has a four-octave compass, C-c^3 with 6⅝" octaves, 1½" keyheads, and 2¼" sharps. These keys are supplied bare and must be covered.

Their *small harpsichord kit* (52" long x 30" wide) is modeled on the 1627 Andries Ruckers in the Gemeentemuseum at the Hague. It has been enlarged slightly to accommodate a full chromatic compass. There are two versions of the instrument available: 2 x 8' lute; and 1 x 8', 1 x 4'. Basic kit, requiring woodworking background and tools, less than $400. Semikit form, with all basic casework complete, the soundboard installed with bridge in place, wrest plank drilled, with nuts in place. The builder will only have to weight and ease the keys, put them in place, assemble and voice the jacks, install them in their guides (which must first be installed), and string, after pinning from a supplied dimension-stable Mylar template. Hitch-pin-holes are predrilled and guide pinholes can be factory-drilled, if desired; see their price list. The lid must be fitted and its edges banded and various small parts installed, legs attached, etc. This version is intended for people either who do not have extensive woodworking experience and tools or who want to get on to the playing in as short a time as possible. Voicing time will be the same as for the basic kit builder, but all construction will have been avoided and the owner of the semikit can be certain of the structural integrity of his/her casework at professional standards. Price, less than $900. Comparable completely finished instrument, at least $1,800.

The Williams Clavichord Kit. The kit consists of a sturdy oak frame, hard maple pin block and hitch pin rails, a ¾″ fir plywood bottom, birch plywood lid, a complete keyboard, string wire, brass tangent rod, hitch, tuning and guide pins, weighting lead, veneer edge tape, square-tapered legs with mounting plates, soundboard supports, key retainer, pressure board, sample tangent, lid flap, the soundboard, brass rod for the bridge, all small hardware such as screws, glue, etc. Even the special drill bits needed for the guide and hitch pins are provided. Basic kit price, about $260. Semikit price, just over $400. Finished price, ready to play, about twice the price of semikit.

Italian Virginal. Compass CC-f³. This is the easiest Williams Workshop kit to build. The virginal is 65″ long x 22″, exclusive of the keyboard, 9″ deep. The keyboard is supplied ready for covering. The soundboard is quartered spruce, the sides precut basswood. The interior parts such as pin blocks, hitch-pin rail, guide supports, braces, and liners are all precision-cut for easy assembly. Moldings of typical contours are supplied for both interior and exterior, precut music desk parts, lid flap, scrolled cheek blocks, key door, and key-bed supports are included. Also supplied are cut and sanded bridges and pizzicato strip, a molded jack rail and blocks, 24″ square-tapered legs and mounting plates, punched jack guides, felts, delrin jacks and plectra, various sizes of music wire with additional spares, all hardware such as three sets of brass hinges, brass and wood knobs, screws, hitch, tuning and guide pins, lead weights, tuning hammer and fork. All parts are fully guaranteed. The illustrated construction manual is written in clear easy-to-understand style, describing the thirty-six steps needed to complete the kit. A parts list, tuning instructions, and a full-scale plan drawing are provided. Basic kit price, less than $500. Semikit, less than $1,000. Equivalent finished instrument, $1,800.

Organs, Guitar Amplifiers, and Synthesizers

My friend Salavatore Raciti had an organ in his little house in Pepperell, Massachusetts. Instead of waking to the sound of birds there, one woke to Bach, and it was very *loud*, but nice.

Frankly, I was surprised at how many organ kits there are. **Devtronix,** for example, of Sacramento, California, sells kits for at least five. Their most popular model is the *Paramount Electronic Organ Kit,* and it looks as fancy as its name. It has voices equivalent to a mighty three-manual 16-rank Wurlitzer, and, in fact, it closely resembles a Wurlitzer pipe organ. Unlike most electric organs, the Paramount has stop keys that change before your eyes, as they do on theater organs. Features include one hundred fifty stop keys, twelve couplers, two expression pedals, a crescendo pedal, capture type combination action, thirty-four preset thumb pistons, choice of French-style or standard scroll, full sixty-one-note manuals, full thirty-two-note AGO pedalboard, second touch on accompaniment, authentic metal bar glockenspiel, Wurlitzer-style engraved stop keys, independent tremulant for each rank, five sets of independent tone generators, one set of divider-type tone generators. The organ measures 35½" deep, 60¼" high, 62¼" wide. The starting kit is less than $12,000. An entire kit with capture-combination action sells somewhere around $20,000. A comparable preassembled organ could cost you as much as $30,000 to $40,000 more, Devtronix informs me.

The **Heath Company,** those masters of electronic kitmaking and marketing, sell a *computerized HeathKit®/Thomas Troubador Organ* for under $2,000; that's a saving of about one-third over preassembled price. It's microprocessor-based and comes with preassembled and tested modular circuit boards, wiring harnesses with built-in connectors, and no complex tuning procedures. Assembly time is estimated at about thirty hours. The cabinet has a glass music rack and comes fully assembled; it is made of furniture-grade hardwoods. The kit even comes with matching padded bench.

The HeathKit® line of music makers also includes a *25-Watt Guitar Amplifier Kit,* which features a full-control amplifier and speaker system with two heavy-duty 12" woofers. It also has double-spring variable reverb and tremolo, dual foot switches, 28" wide x 19¾" high x 9" deep. For 120/240 VAC, 60/50 Hz. About $200.

PAIA Electronics' *Proteus I®* *Lead Synthesizer Kit* features two exponential VCOs; triangle, ramp, square, and modulated-pulse waveforms; sync provided on oscillators; noise source; exponential 24 dB/octave pass voltage controlled filter; wide-range low-frequency modulation oscillator; wide-range ADSR envelope generator; three-octave encoded keyboard with computer port; sixteen programmable presets with battery backup; preset data and address port provided; liberal patch-over hardware on rear panel. Plus minimum point-to-point wiring for easy kit assembly and high reliability. The kit costs around $400; it saves you about $100 on the assembled price.

Radio Shack has a *Tunable Electronic Organ Kit* for children who make music. Less than $15. You build it in the 15" x 5⅞" x 1½" box in which it comes. No soldering necessary. Plays two octaves of major scale.

Schober Organ Corporation has kits for a *recital organ,* a *theater organ,* and an *automatic electronic organ.* The basic recital organ, about $4,000 (perhaps half the price of a comparable preassembled organ) features: sixty-one-note manual keyboards with standard pipe-organ shape and dimensions, the upper overhanging the lower for easiest playing; thirty-two-note concave, with radiating pedal clavier that conforms to natural body motions; adjustable expression shoes; eighty-five basic tone pitches, produced by a tone-generator system that never needs to be tuned; library of stops that give infinitely changeable voicing; walnut solid and veneer console.

Wersi Electronics, Inc., has many organ kits, the newest of which is their *concerto W3A* model. This traditionally styled organ features sixty-one keys on upper manual, C to C (five octaves) with twenty-two fixed stops; functions for all footages; sixty-one keys on lower manual, with seventeen fixed stops in kit pack #7. Many different options are available, too complicated to detail here. For more information, write for their catalogue.

Folk Harps, Kalimbas, Lyres, and Other Instrument Kits

Country Ways, Inc., has several kits for simple folk instruments, including one for an *Aztec Drum.* Built of butternut and oak, this unique rectangular drum makes a different resonant sound for each of the wood tongues struck. About $25.

The *Bones* is one of the great country rhythm instruments. Cut from cherry wood, these just need finishing and sanding. Less than $3.

Their *Limberjacks* (also known as lumberjacks), a type of instrument at least four hundred years old, are in the shape of a little person dancing a "clog" beat at the end of a board. About $5.

They also have a kit for *Thumb Pianos.* This is a simple version of the African mbira. Very easy to play. Children like it. You've probably seen these and not known what they were; each looks like a flat, rectangular wooden box with small round sound hole in the middle. Over the sound hole is a line-up of little metal spokes, which you pluck with downward motion. About $9.

Rumba Boxes are giant mbiras; they are the standard "bass" in most calypso bands. Very simple construction. About $20.

Here, Inc., of Minneapolis, sells an *Ambira*® Kit (*thumb piano*), which measures 5″ x 6½″ x 2½″. It is a westernized version, with notes ordered from high to low. The kit can also be assembled in the African way. Less than $10.

Here, Inc., also has a *Bass Ambira*®, twelve reeds, measuring 19″ x 10″ x 5″. It can be tuned to give all common backup notes in keys of A, D, G, and C. Pine-and-lauan plywood box and hardwood bridge. About $30, half the price of their assembled bass ambira.

Here, Inc., also sells kits for one-hold, two-hold, and three-hold *kazoos,* all considerably less than $10.

Hughes Dulcimer Company sells some very unusual musical instrument kits. Among the most interesting is their set of three *tomato box instruments,* which look rather like very primitive and boxy bass viols. Their version is a nesting set of three—soprano, tenor, and bass—for about $40 for all three. Nice for family music-making. Completed instrument set sells for double the kit price.

Hughes also has *folk harp kits*. These look something like concert harps, but they're smaller. The Irish and Celtic harps are small enough to hold on the lap, while the Bardic harp sits on the floor or a low stool. These harps are walnut, with light, contrasting birch soundboards. The Bardic harp kit comes with turned pillar. The Bardic harp kit sells for a bit over $200; this is at least $200 less than a completed harp. The Celtic harp sells for around $100, which is $125 less than an assembled harp. The Irish harp kit is less than $60, about a 45 percent discount.

Available, too, are kits for ancient Greek-style *lyres*. Hughes sells the six-stringed version, which will play the I-IV-V chords of the folk song. It is used mainly as a simple accompaniment to singing. Assembly takes about six hours. Spruce soundboard. Walnut costs less than $25—half the price of an assembled walnut lyre. There's a maple version, too, which should cost you about $5 less than the walnut.

Hughes also has kits for *Lumberjacks,* in walnut and maple, and *Kalimbas,* the African rhythm instrument.

International Luthiers Supply, Inc., sells a *piano-tuning kit,* which comes with manual tuning hammer, tuning fork, four rubber-wedge mutes, two wire-handled stick mutes, plus two continuous-muting strips. These are high-quality tools; they cost about $26. If you can't get the hang of it within ten days, you can return the outfit for refund.

Lee Music Manufacturing Company of Culver, Oregon, has quite a nice gadget kit for people who own reed organs. It's called the Lee Silent Suction Unit, and what it does is give *effortless electric player operation for reed organs.* The unit can be mounted vertically or horizontally. The switch goes under the keyboard. No more foot pumping, if you're not in the mood for it. About $65–$75.

Rugg & Jackel Music Company has a *Mbira,* or African thumb piano, kit. A nice project for children or for shop classes. About $11.

3

Sporting Goods and Sporting Clothing

Backpacking, Camping, and Mountaineering Equipment and Clothing

Backpacks

The fully equipped outdoorsperson will probably want to own or have access to three sizes of packs: one large-capacity frame pack for journeys of several days or for winter weekends that necessitate more voluminous equipment; a more modest capacity frameless or internal frame pack for day hikes, weekend excursions, or long, technical climbs; and a small rucksack or belt pack for cross-country skiing. If you rarely walk into the wilderness for extended periods of time, you might not want to go to the expense of buying a large-capacity pack; many outdoor-equipment stores rent this kind of equipment (a complete guide to where you can rent equipment appears in *Backpacking on a Budget* by Anna Sequoia and Steve Schneider, Penguin Books, NY, NY 1979) or you may want to borrow the equipment from a friend. But a day pack is extremely useful to own, good for everything from weekend backpacking trips to a hard day's shopping in town. A good-quality presewn day pack retails for from $22 to $27; for $12.50 to $15, you can sew your own from one of the following kits. Belt packs, if you ski cross-country, are inexpensive and extremely useful, and they don't affect your balance on skis the way some heavier day packs may. You may be able to find one of these, presewn, retailing for from $12 to $17; if you make your own from a kit, you should be able to equal the more-expensive model for about $12.

Large-capacity Frame Packs

Country Ways, Inc., sells an interesting *kit for a pack bag with a capacity of 2,504 cubic inches.* The kit provides plans from Woodward Publications, with all the materials you need except grommets. It fits almost any "cruiser"-style frame (not included). The bag is one large, undivided main compartment, which is good if you're going to carry, for example, fly rod or saw, as well as your tent. There is a zipper across the front of the bag near the bottom for easy access to the lower area of the pack. The fabric is 8-ounce nylon pack cloth, urethane-coated and waterproof. Five outside pockets and Velcro-sealed map flap. Since there is a good deal of detail work involved, patience and/or sewing experience are necessary. The pack bag kit sells for around $30. Country Ways claims that it's the equal of a presewn bag, costing about twice as much. Perhaps, but before buying the kit, you might take a look at the current Recreational Equipment, Inc., catalogue; this excellent equipment coop has some large-capacity presewn bags for scarcely 25 percent more.

Frostline's *Hatch-Back Sack® Kit* is an interestingly designed *large-capacity pack bag.* The entire front zips opens for easy access. It can, of course, also open from the top or bottom. Three cinch straps adjust the weight closer to your back as the load lightens. It's constructed of 7.5-ounce urethane-coated nylon pack cloth. Four outside pockets. All zippers are covered by wide waterproof flaps. Capacity is 3871 cubic inches, and the cost is about the same as Country Ways' pack bag. Available in a choice of blue, green, or orange.

Frostline also carries a very nice kit for an *internal frame pack kit;* with it you'd need no additional pack frame. Many people find this style of portage more comfortable than using a separate pack-bag-and-frame combination. The internal aluminum molds to fit your body. With a total empty weight of 32 ounces, this pack could easily become your favorite for almost everything except week-long heavily loaded forays. Available in 8-ounce waterproof nylon pack cloth, with 10-ounce Cordura nylon wraparound bottom. This pack is a *very* good buy; you could save as much as 40 percent or more off the price of a presewn comparable-quality internal frame pack. Blue, green, or orange.

KlimaKraft, a small business in Oak Ridge, Tennessee, produces an extremely *inexpensive pack frame kit* suitable for Cub or Brownie Scout troops. Young Scouts will need help with its construction, but for $9.50 plus postage, this is the best your little Scouts can do.

Day Packs, Rucksacks, and Belt Packs

Altra has a very nice, *small day pack kit,* under $14, which is good for bike trips or as a lightweight cross-country ski pack. Their day pack has leather accessory hangers, two large zippered compartments, and padded shoulder straps. Coated nylon cloth. It's 30 percent to 35 percent less than a comparable presewn pack. It should require more than a couple of evenings of cutting and sewing. Green only.

Country Ways sells two kinds of day packs. Their Deluth model comes in two sizes, one measuring 24" x 29", the other 29" x 29". These are the *traditional packs for canoe tripping,* and there are no protruding frames or pockets to catch on branches or gunwales. They use 8-ounce waterproof pack cloth for each. The bottoms of the packs are double thickness, and the strap system surrounds the pack and bears the weight. Each comes with heavy-duty foam-padded shoulder straps. These are good utilitarian bags, at about $30 each. Hard to sew if you have a lightweight sewing machine.

Their *day pack* expands to 16" x 13" x 6"; it comes with a 9" x 5" x 1½" outside pocket with zipper and rain flap. The pack closes with a drawstring and cord lock, and it has a new quick-release fastening, which holds the outer flap and provides instant access. Constructed of waterproof nylon pack cloth, with wide soft straps and a carrying loop on top. A very good value at $12.50. This is a good "first-time" kit project.

Frostline has several day pack kits, the most attractive of which is their 18" high *teardrop-shaped Day Pack Model,* measuring 8" wide by 2¾" thick just below the peak, to 14" wide by 16½" thick at the base. It has two big pockets with a center opening and two-zipper accesses covered by wide protective flaps. It comes with foam-padded shoulder straps, ice ax carrier, and accessory strap holders. The waist strap has a snap and **D**-ring. An excellent value at less than $15. Available in blue, green, orange, yellow.

Their roomy *belt pack,* selling for around $12, has two zippered pockets, both covered with waterproof storm flaps. Easy to get off and on. The main compartment measures 4" deep x 16½" long x 8½" high at the back. The rear pocket is 1¾" deep x 12½" long x 5" high. Blue or yellow.

Bowser Bags

I've included bowser bags in each book I've written on outdoor equipment, but I've yet to meet a dog who will tolerate one; perhaps your dog will.

The only bowser bag kit still on the market is produced by Frostline, though I suspect even they don't sell that many. They call theirs the *Doggie Pack Kit* and sell it for just under $14. Constructed of durable 10-ounce water-repellant Cordura nylon, the contraption has zippered pockets on each side, covered by storm flaps. Instructions tell you how to size this pack for large- or medium-size dogs. Handy if you want Rover to carry his or her own food.

Sleeping Bag Kits

Country Ways, Inc., offers three weights of *PolarGuard-filled sleeping bags:* summer weight, with 4¼" of loft, comfortable in temperatures from the 70s into the 40s; three seasons, 5¼" loft, good from the 60s into the 20s; and extra warm, 6½" loft, good down to about 0 degrees. These come in a modified mummy style, or if you're one of those claustrophobic sleepers, a rectangular shape is available. Two of their bags will zip together.

PolarGuard, as you probably know if you've read anything at all about camping and outdoor equipment, is a continuous-filament-synthetic fill, which is a bit heavier to carry than down but which equals it in warmth per inch of loft. Yet it doesn't lose its insulating properties (i.e., loft) when damp or wet. PolarGuard is certainly easier to use as a kit fill than down; it comes in one piece and sews up quickly (estimated completion time for these bags vary between six and twelve hours per bag, depending upon how much sewing experience you have).

Each bag is available in four lengths, to fit folks from 4'6" tall (or less) to 6'8". Every Country Ways sleeping bag has a full hood and drawstring and a zipper that opens from both ends, for ventilation or to open the bag out into a quilt. There's also an insulted draft tube built into each sleeping bag kit.

These kits make up into very serviceable sleeping bags, and they should save you 40 percent to 45 percent off the cost of comparable preassembled sleeping bags.

Country Ways also carries nice, inexpensive "Sleep Sack" kits for children up to ages five or six. At $22 or thereabouts, these make wonderful gifts.

Frostline Kits sells at least four styles of sleeping bags, plus a down liner kit, which will extend the comfort range of your present sleeping bags by at least 20 degrees.

Their *Big Horn down mummy bag* sells for under $160, but it compares well with preconstructed bags for $100 more. The winter model is good to −10 degrees, is differentially cut, and has no sewn-through seams. The 70" zipper opens at either end; it is backed by a wide down-filled flap for warmth. Available for heights up to 6'5", this bag has 6" of loft in the regular model, 7" of loft in the winter version. Forest green or navy.

Their *Cougar kit* is a *combination of down bag and foam pad,* which weighs less than separate bag and pad. The foam pad is shredded open-celled polyether, which won't disintegrate with exposure to dampness or oxidation. Available in standard or winter models, these bags have either 3" or 3½" of loft, and they are supposed to be good down to −10 degrees. Forest green or navy.

The *Nimbus model* is for spring camping when the ground may be wet. Good down to 15 degrees, the bag is filled with four layers of PolarGuard, two on top, and two on bottom. The large size sells for less than $60. It zips together (as do all Frostline bags) with other Frostline sleeping bags, and it is excellent for campers who are allergic to down fill.

Frostline's *Northwoods kit* is their least expensive model—less than

$55—and it compares well with a $90 to $95 ready-made bag. This simple mummy-type bag is filled with PolarGuard, and it is a perfectly serviceable bag for three-season use. Forest green, navy.

Plain Brown Wrapper, Inc., offers *two models of mixed goose-down/goose-feather-filled sleeping bag kits.* Each is available in two fill weights. All bags come with a rectangular hood, which opens flat or closes with snaps and a draw cord. Since the two-way zipper along the side extends across the foot, you can use these bags flat as comforters. Prices range from under $85 for a bag with 6½″ loft, comfort range +10 degrees to +65 degrees, to under $120 for a bag that has 8″ of loft, measures 66″ long, 83″ wide, and is good from −10 degrees to +50 degrees. You should be able to complete one of these bags in fewer than five or six evenings.

SunDown Kits of Redmond, Washington, sells *two weights of prime northern goose-down-filled sleeping bags.* The Viking model, available in 5′10″ length, as well as 6′6″ length, has a comfort range of −15 degrees to 60 degrees. The Northwoods model, in the same lengths, is a three-season bag with comfort range of 0 degrees to 65 degrees. Optional fill is available to extend the comfort range of the Viking model.

These are both modified mummy bags, with V-tube construction that ensures even loft; there are no sewn-through seams. A full-length down-filled zipper tube insulates the zipper area. A pillow pocket under the hood can be stuffed with a jacket for extra head padding. Shoulder drawstring can be sewn into the hood to keep cold air from entering the bag without your having to close in the entire hood.

These are excellent-quality sleeping bags. But they're not particularly cheap: Prices, at this writing, range between $130 to $155, but they're a good $80 to a $100 less than prime goose-down-filled bags of similar construction and fill.

Sleeping bag liner kits are available for each; I strongly recommend purchasing these with your kit, as down bags are expensive to clean and quite a project to wash.

By the way, if you're taller than 6′6″, contact SunDown about a custom-cut kit at extra charge.

Tents

Just a few years ago, there were tent kits available from quite a few manufacturers. During the past couple of years, however, two major producers, Holubar and Eastern Mountain Sports, have discontinued their kit lines, and Altra, another fine kit manufacturer, has discontinued production of kits for tents. That narrows the market down to Frostline and SunDown kits. Luckily, Frostline still offers four elegant, cleverly designed tent kits, and SunDown continues to produce its roomy A-frame model.

Frostline's arched, *Quonset hut-type Trailridge II* tent kit weighs 9 pounds 8 ounces total; it can accommodate three adults, plus gear, or two adults and two young children. The tent body is 1.9 ounces rip-stop nylon, and the floor is waterproof urethane-coated nylon, which extends 10″ up the sides. There is a cooking flap sewn into the floor for use during emergencies. (I strongly recommend, however, that you not cook inside the tent; it's the most common cause of tent fires.) Both the front vestibule and rear are waterproof. Entrances at both ends come equipped with mosquito netting, and the side poles are shock-corded. A separate waterproof rain fly is included in the kit. This is a *most* attractive tent, reminiscent of styles by Early Winters, Ltd. and Stephenson's Warmlite; it should save you about $75 to $80 off the cost of a comparable presewn tent. Blue or yellow.

I strongly suspect that the manufacturer will not appreciate the following suggestion, but you might consider it if you need a tent for, say, a teen-age daughter or son, plus one for yourself: Before you assemble your tent kit, you might want to trace a duplicate pattern (everything except the rain fly), and cut a corresponding tent from Gore-Tex, the waterproof yet porous "miracle fabric," which is sold by the yard. (Suppliers of Gore-Tex by the yard appear in *Backpacking on a Budget* by this author and Steve Schneider.) You'll wind up with one attractive, standard tent—an excellent value—and one lightweight waterproof, rain fly-less tent for yourself—a *super* value (Gore-Tex tents still cost a fortune).

Frostline's *Kodiak* tent kit is a *classic British design,* reminiscent of tents by Blacks of Greenwich. It's an excellent starter tent, accommodating two adults. An expedition-type tent, the Kodiak incorporates a large sheltered cooking area, which is separated from the main tent by mosquito netting. This is a very attractive, practical tent, with no front guy lines. The tent costs about $110—less certainly than most presewn tents. But if you're lazy and don't feel that you need such a sophisticated design, you might consider looking at comparably priced presewn tents by Eureka.

Frostline's *Explorer* is a *two-entrance, two-person tent,* with mosquito-netted entrances at both ends, each unobstructed by poles or guy lines. The entrance vestibule has a floor and provides a good equipment-storage area. Total weight; 6 pounds, 8 ounces. Rain fly: 1 pound, 7 ounces. The Explorer stands up well under windy conditions. Available in blue or yellow.

Their *Crestview* tent kit is an *extraordinary free-standing wedge tent* with front and rear entrances. In case you've miscalculated and set the tent up in a rain gully, you can actually lift the assembled set-up tent and move it a few feet away. The rain fly has its own fiberglass ridge rod and is cut away over the entrance for ventilation. Like all Frostline tent kits, the Crestview comes with tent sack and tent pegs. Around $120.

SunDown's *Olympic tent* is a *roomy, two-person A-frame model* with roomy inside dimensions; 89″ long, 60″ wide, and 46″ high at both peaks. Side walls are permeable 1.9 ounces flame-retardant rip-stop nylon, and the floors, extending 11″ up the sides, are waterproof, urethane-coated taffeta nylon. The triangular entrance has two YKK Vislon zippers backed by fully zippered mosquito netting. The back of the tent has two 40″ zippers forming a large triangular window with a mosquito netting back. The kit includes tent, fly, shock-corded poles, cords, notions, seam sealer, sewing instructions, and nylon carrying case. Tent pegs are not included. Total weight is 7 pounds, which makes this an excellent tent for weight-conscious backpackers. With a price of around $85, this tent is a very good buy—at least $40 less than a comparable presewn tent. Comes with rust sidewalls, blue floor and rain fly.

Snowshoes are my own favorite means of winter travel. They're slow and more work, I suppose, than using cross-country skis, but travel by snowshoe satisfies my contemplative side. One doesn't have to be at all athletic to use them, and I can wander wherever I like. I'm not limited to narrow cross-country trails, which (in the Northeast, anyway) too often just lead from inn to inn. The catch is that snowshoes are expensive (if you don't make them from a kit), averaging these days about $70 a pair.

Snowshoe Kits

Country Ways, Inc., now offers a beautiful alternative to the high cost of good wood-frame snowshoes: Their *Ojibway Snowshoe kits* cost half the price of comparable preconstructed snowshoes, and they're not particularly difficult to make. The frames are made in Canada of straight-grain white ash, and they come already bent, shaped, and assembled, with rivets at each end. They need only light sanding before lacing. The lacing is tubular nylon webbing, flat-woven, and it should be covered after assembly with exterior polyurethane. This lacing is easy to tie and does not stretch when wet, does not ice up, and is not the kind of material mice like to eat. Once completed, Country Ways snowshoes are a pound to a pound-and-a-half lighter than either rawhide or neoprene snowshoes. Assembly should take no more than about three evenings. These are an excellent value, and they come in three sizes to fit everyone from a six-year-old child to a 240-pound outdoorsman.

Several years back, when my-brother-the-mountain-climber and I were doing equipment testing and comparisons for *The Climbers Sourcebook* (Anchor Books, NY, NY, 1975), the arrival of a package from **Sherpa, Inc.,** got my brother Steven so excited there was a total suspension of other work for two days: The package contained Sherpa® Snowclaw Snowshoes, and I spent the first day on my "old-fashioned" snowshoes, trailing well behind as Steven ran up and down steep iced-over, snow-covered hills in his "magic" snowshoes.

Sherpa snowshoes still offer a combination of lightness, traction, security, and speed unequaled by any other snowshoes I've seen. Frankly, I still happily use my fifteen-year-old Tubbs Bearpaws, but if I were regularly doing more difficult treks or if I finally made it to the Himalayas, I wouldn't consider *not* buying myself a pair of Sherpas.

The *Sherpa snowshoe kits,* (there are now two), like the regular Sherpa snowshoes, come with gold anodized aircraft aluminum frames. Laces have been replaced by a solid deck, which sheds snow quickly. Perhaps most important are their hinge rod and their binding with claws. The binding keeps your foot secure; there's no sudden ankle strain as your foot twists to the left and your snowshoe slides to the right. Thanks to the hinge rod, there's less leg strain because your gait on snowshoes more closely approximates snowshoe-less walking. Best of all, the claws act as built-in crampons, giving the most secure footing available without crampons. Like Steve Austin, you really are "faster and better" on these snowshoes.

A word about price: Because Sherpa snowshoes are, to some extent, replacing conventional wood-and-gut snowshoes, they're a "hot item" and are rarely put on sale. The kit offers a very small savings, but at the moment it's about the only way you'll be able to save much on these snowshoes.

Vermont Tubbs, Inc., is one of the oldest and most respected manufacturers of snowshoes in this country. They now offer kits in three of their most popular sizes, 10″ x 36″, 10″ x 46″, and 10″ x 56″. Each *kit* contains a pair of *steam-bent ash frames,* neoprene lacing material, neoprene binding material, and a clear instruction book. By buying the kit, you save 40 percent to 45 percent off the price of these classic snowshoes. And if you find you can't complete the kit yourself, you can return all materials, plus $25, to Tubbs, and they'll complete it for you. (As far as I'm aware, this is a unique service, except for SpeakerLab, the hi-fi speaker kit company of Seattle, Washington, who offers the service for free.)

Cross-Country Ski Kits

Bingham Projects, Inc., of Ogden, Utah, is owned by an industrial arts teacher; most of the excellent projects included in this catalogue (water skis, skateboards, bows and arrows, etc.) have to be bought in quantity and are most suited for use in the industrial arts classroom. But many of these projects can be constructed in a home workshop. Their kit #2291 for *wooden cross-country skis* includes ten hickory laminations, two pieces of core wood to act as stiffener, and toe bindings. The kit is under $30 (less, if you buy ten or more). A $30 laminating press kit is necessary for this project, as are cross-country toe bindings (about $7) and epoxy glue. Other combinations are available. If you'd like cross-country skis for, say, a family of four, and there isn't a good thrift shop in you area where you can buy second hand wooden cross-country skis, this is one excellent way to beat the increasingly high cost of Nordic skiing.

A ski bag makes traveling to snow country a lot easier, especially if you're going by bus, plane, or train. It's particularly handy for cross-country skis; you won't get mushy hard-to-get-out wax all over your best parka or sweater. Some ready-made ski bags are ridiculously expensive. A few are not: My own canvas ski bag comes from a mail-order catalogue, and I paid not much more for it assembled than what *Frostline* is charging for their kit. But in case you can't find what you want at a fair price, you might consider Frostline's new *ski bag kit* of Cordura nylon. Fits skis up to 215 centimeters. The bag is 85″ long, and 11½″ wide, with adjustable carrying straps (you may want to add shoulder straps), and cinch straps to secure your skis and poles. $19.50.

Ski Bag

Green River Knife Kits. Each kit contains a blade made at the famous Russell Green River Works in Southbridge, Massachusetts. The blades in these kits have already been hardened and tempered, and they have been finished and polished, with the tang drilled for rivets. Two styles are available from the **Atlanta Cutlery Corporation** of Conyers, Georgia: The Clip Point Blade kit contains a 5″ clip-point blade. Handle scales are made of Kingwood. $8.50. Their Green River Knife with Skinner Blade kit contains a 6″ long skinning blade, ³⁄₃₂″ thick, and 4½″ beachwood handle scales. A sheath kit is included. $9.35. Comparable quality knives, preassembled, go for twice the price.

Atlanta Cutlery also sells one- or two-blade *pocket knife kits* with Solingen made parts and jacaranda wood handle scales. The two-blade model costs less than $11, requires no power tools to assemble, and should take only part of an evening to put together.

Camping Knife Kits

Country Ways, Inc., sells an excellent *Solingen stainless steel two-blade pocket knife kit,* very similar to the one offered by Atlanta Cutlery, at exactly the same price.

Country Ways has, however, a much larger variety of lightweight and standard camping knives. The lightweight models have, on the average, 4″ blades, and handles that need no rivets. At this writing, comparable knives go for about twice the price. They also have four varieties of standard riveted carbon-steel knives, my favorite of which is their *5″ Buffalo Skinner,* an extremely sturdy old-fashioned knife, which should last a lifetime, at well under $10. All Country Ways camping knife kits use the renowned Russell Green River Works blades.

Custom Knifemaker's Supply offers an exquisite *classic boot knife kit* with 8″ x 1″ x ¼″ blade hand-ground from 440-C steel by Blackie Collins. The threaded rivets are custom-made solid brass, and the handle is black linen base micarta counterdrilled for rivets. Stag handles are available as well, as are maroon or bone-color micarta, plus nickel-silver bolts. The kits sell for around $30, but a comparable-quality knife would cost infinitely more.

Additional Sources of Camping Knife Kits

Bingham Projects, Inc. Hunting knife kits of German Solingen steel and of Norwegian laminated steel. Address appears in Appendix under *Sources of Backpacking, Camping, and Mountaineering Equipment and Clothing.*

Backpacking, Camping, and Mountaineering Clothing

Down Booties

I strongly recommend down or synthetic-fill booties if you're going winter camping. They're excellent, particularly if you're tenting in the snow and then going cross-country skiing; cross-country ski boots may be fine in cold weather while you're moving, but even the half hour of mucking about you do in the morning before going off on your skis can be enough to freeze your tootsies.

Altra sells *excellent down booties.* They have nylon taffeta uppers, elasticized ankles, and rugged Cordura bottoms for durability and traction. The kit usually sells for around $21, but in a mailing I recently received from Altra, the booties were on sale for $12.50. That's quite a buy.

Country Ways' *PolarGuard booties* are really intended for indoor use, but you can use them in place of your felt liners inside "Sorel" boots or mukluks. Less than $12 for the largest size.

Frostline booties are really your best buy (unless, of course, you too can get the Altra booties on sale). *PolarGuard booties* sell for less than $6; *down booties* around $10. If you intend to use these as camp gear, you ought to buy their overboots, with waterproof, replaceable Naugahyde sole, which looks like buckskin leather: another $9; unless your feet are extra large—then it's $10. Cheaper than frostbite.

Plain Brown Wrapper has a very nice kit for *lace-up prime-goose-down boots* with quilted body, Dacron II sole and tongue, tipped laces for tightening around the ankle, lace loops, and welt and toe insert. Very flashy contrasting colors. Sizes range from extra small to extra large (11½ " long). Well under $15.

SunDown *down booties* cost about $10; they are filled with 1.9 ounces of prime goose down, and their soles are made of fricton-resistant, water-repellant, nylon Cordura fabric.

Altra's *Insulated Coveralls* are beautifully proportioned, high-waisted, and slimming. They're available in blue, navy, or brown taffeta, and wheat or navy Taslan. The pants are fully lined and warmed by a layer of polyester needlepunch insulation. For either men or women, these insulated coveralls cost about $40 in taffeta, a bit more in Taslan. Each costs 40 percent to 50 percent less than comparable presewn gear.

Altra also has kits for insulted coveralls for children. In navy only, these cost about $25—half of what you might pay for a comparable presewn garment.

Frostline has one kit for insulated pants, available either in down or Hollofil II insulating material. These are tough nylon taffeta, with three-layer construction for extra warmth. Features include a full-length zipper so that you don't have to remove boots or skis to put them on. There is also an elastic waistband and abrasion patches on inside ankles. Less than $50 for down; less than $40 for the Hollofill version. These are not exactly *stylish* pants, but they do look warm. Available in navy or rust.

Country Ways has *PolarGuard mitten kits in both children's and adult sizes.* The children's size costs about $8; adult size is less than $10. Since mittens *do* tend to get wet, PolarGuard is a pretty good idea because it won't lose all its insulating properties when wet.

The palms are Cordura nylon, which will withstand everything except rope tows. The outer shell is breathable water-repellant taffeta. The lining is brushed nylon velour, which feels warm on contact and draws moisture away from your hand. Easy to sew.

Frostline has two different kinds of mittens. Their *Down-Filled Ski Mitts* feature 4½ " down-filled gauntlets with concealed nylon knit cuffs inside. Leather palms and thumbs are stitched to 100 percent nylon taffeta backs. These trim and handsome mittens sell for less than $20.

Their *Mountain Mitts* have a down-filled inner mitten with stretch-knit nylon cuffs. The outer mitten has leather palms, and thumbs with optional waterproof layer all around. Down-filled gauntlets. Just under $22. (Of the two, I think these are the better buy.)

Plain Brown Wrapper sells *prime goose-down-filled mittens* with inside knit cuffs at the wrist and elastic at the top of the gauntlet. The palms have an extra layer of Super K-Kote 200-denier nylon oxford cloth. Very nice color selections available, plus hand lengths ranging from extra small (7") to extra large (9½"). These can be machine-washed and tumble-dried. Less than $13.

Coveralls and Insulated Pants

Down- or Synthetic-fill Mittens

Down-fill Shirts

Frostline has an excellent *down shirt kit* with choice of regular or Western-style yoke, straight or curved shirttail, and diamond or square quilt pattern. It has snap closures on front, cuffs, and flap pocket. Available in rip-stop nylon or denim-blue chambray cloth. Nylon lining. In a medium size the shirt weighs 13 ounces. This kit is an excellent value at $29.50; a comparable presewn garment would cost a good $20 more. My mother, no master seamstress, has sewn together several down-filled Frostline kits. She told me that they're very easy, very simple to do. The directions are excellent. Even inserting the down fill was quite easy, she says. The project shouldn't require more than three evenings.

Plain Brown Wrapper's down shirts, with an average thickness of ¾″ loft, feature box quilting, interlined shirt cuffs, collars and placket. Western-style V-yoke fronts and back. Front and cuffs close with snaps. Single-ply pockets. Average comfort level is estimated by +15 degrees to +60 degrees. Less than $25.

SunDown's down shirt is a real beauty, filled with 3½ ounces of prime goose down (in the medium size). It can be worn by itself in the autumn, replacing bulky sweaters or jackets, or on cold, wet, windy days, it can go under your down parka for an extra layer of insulation. It has a front zipper with protective flap and Velcro closures, and one pleated cargo pocket with Velcro closure. The sleeves also close with Velcro fasteners. The outer shell can be either denim-blue chambray cloth or navy-blue rip-stop nylon. The alternate material is used as the inner lining. Diamond quilt pattern. The shirt is washable, or it can be dry-cleaned. Available in sizes extra small to extra large.

At $24.95, this is a crazy value—cheaper than a decent heavy wool sweater.

Down- or Synthetic-fill Vests for Adults and Children

There are more down- and synthetic-fill vest kits on the market than a country dog has fleas. What follows is a selection of kits representing substantial savings over presewn vests or vests that are so artfully styled that you couldn't buy comparable presewn items.

A word of caution about vest kits. Right now, there are too many manufacturers producing presewn vests. With a little patience and luck you might be able to find a presewn model on sale in the style and quality you want, at about the same price or just a little more than the kits that follow.

Currently **Altra** has six different vest kits, most of which have zip-on sleeves offered as an option (an option that increases the cost of the vest by $21 to $22.50).

Their *Down Vest* is a plain, handsome down vest filled with 4½ ounces of down. It has double hand-warmer pockets, Velcro front closures and durable 65/35 fabric. This vest is a classic, and it has been one of Altra's best-selling items since the company's inception. Currently priced at $39.50, the vest is worth another $20. Navy or rust.

Altra's *Western Vest* has more connection with the slopes of Aspen than a shoot-out at O.K. Corral. It's *extremely* fashionable and is an excellent buy at $36 (about 50 percent of what a comparable vest would cost at full retail price). It comes in combinations of navy/red, navy/yellow, and powder blue/navy. The shell is nylon taffeta, with down fill in the body, and Hollofil® in the shoulder and collar, where you're most likely to get wet. This vest kit is designed with inside pocket, adjustable hip tabs, and ticket ring. It comes in great color combinations: navy/red; navy/yellow; powder blue/navy.

Their *Poly Vest,* with colorful strips on each shoulder, is filled with Hollofil insulation, which will keep its loft and warmth even in damp weather. This is an easy-to-sew kit, with patch pockets and taffeta shell. A nice value at $29.50; a comparable presewn vest could cost up to $55. Blue or navy with red, white, and yellow or blue shoulder stripe.

Country Ways' vest kits are excellent values, ranging in price from $16 (children's sizes and extra small) to $23 ("windcloth" in extra large). Each vest can be made quite long to keep your kidneys warm, and is filled with 1½" of PolarGuard. Since PolarGuard doesn't have to be quilted to hold it in place, these vests have a smooth look. The vest is available in one-color or two-tone versions. Their model A-101 has taffeta throughout. The A-102 style features "windcloth" on the outside for a different look and for heavy-duty use. Vests are easily washable. The Country Ways booklet *Vest Customizing Ideas* comes with each kit; it details how to add stripes and trim, decorative quilting, yokes, etc.

Frostline has a large variety of vests. To me, the most interesting models are the ones that follow.

Their *High Country Vest kit* is a basic, traditional design, filled with either down or Hollofil insulation. The back has an insulted kidney flap. This vest can be constructed of either rip-stop nylon or denim-blue chambray cloth, a polyester/cotton blend. A heavy one-way zipper is protected by an ample insulated flap. There are two large cargo pockets, each with self-sealing flaps and hand warmers beneath. There's also an inside self-sealing chest pocket. A yoke pattern is included, in case you want to fancy up your vest. Down vest kit prices range from $27 to $29 for extra large. Dupont Hollofil II ranges in price from $21 to $23. My friend Rebecca Dominguez-Blum tested this kit in the down version. She said she hated having to sear the fabric edges, but that it made up into a fine vest. It took her about twenty-five hours, even though she's an experienced sewer.

Frostline's *Backpacker Vest Kit* is cut longer than most vests for extra warmth. The Backpacker vest has extra insulation in the collar and the hand-warmer pockets behind the two large cargo pockets. Available in 1.9-ounce rip-stop nylon or 2.5-ounce denim-blue chambray cloth (polyester/nylon blend). Sturdy one-way zipper. The vest comes with either down or Hollofil insulation. Prices range from $24 to $26 in down and $17 to $19 in Hollofil. This is an excellent kit, especially for your wood-chopping husband or for a woman who likes to keep her bottom warm (short vests have never made much sense to me . . .).

If, however, a short high-fashion vest is what interests you, you might consider Frostline's *Aztec Vest kit.* Although this is not very practical for backpacking or mountain use, the Aztec vest is fine for wandering around Stowe or Boston or for mild-weather skiing. The stand-up collar helps protect the wearer from high wind, and it looks very jaunty. The Aztec has two zippered close-to-the-body pockets, and it comes in either down fill or Hollofil II. Prices range from $28 to $30 in down and $21 to $23 in Hollofil. Savings should range from 40 percent to 50 percent. Several flashy color combinations, of which navy with bands of green and blue, and red with bands of navy and tan, are just two.

Children love vests, too. Frostline's *Child's Backpacker Vest,* an easy-to-sew kit, is a scaled-down version of the adult's Backpacker Vest described above. Choice of down or Hollofil insulation. Prices run from $14 for down, sizes 4 to 6, to $23 for down, sizes 12 to 14. Hollofil prices range from $10.95, for sizes 4 to 6, to $16.95 for sizes 12 to 14.

Plain Brown Wrapper sells six different vest kits for adults; two are available in children's sizes, too. Their handsomest vest is probably the *Prairie Wolf* model, with shell of 60 percent Dacron polyester, 40 percent nylon Antron. Collar and pockets come in contrasting colors; this gives this machine-washable prime goose-down vest an expensive custom look. Average loft is about 1¾". The child's vest costs under $17. Adult sizes cost well under $25.

SunDown has several interesting vest kits. Their *Down Vest* is cut long to provide patch pockets and warmth to the lower back. This vest has a down-filled stand-up collar, and Vislon zipper. The medium size contains more than 4½ ounces of down and measures 29" from base of collar to bottom of back. Available in rip-stop nylon or nylon taffeta in several attractive colors. At $21.60 this vest is an excellent buy. It comes in sizes up to extra large, at no extra charge.

SunDown's *Rugged Down Vest* is the same as described above, except that the outer fabric is tough, water-repellant, 60/40 cloth—much more practical if you want it for hunting or rugged backpacking. About $2.50 more than the Down Vest.

Their *Child's Down Vest* is identical to the adult's version. A size 8 to 10 contains about 3½ ounces as down, measures 21½" from base of collar to bottom of back, and weighs about 8½ ounces. $15.95—another excellent value.

Allen J. Valero vests are not down- or synthetic-filled, but they're too attractive not to include here. Valero vest kits are constructed of soft, deliciously smooth *shearling*. My favorite vest, their *Rigger Long Vest*, has deep fleece-lined pockets and either toggle or button closings. An excellent vest for either men or women, it is available in white only. Best of all, these vests are washable! At this writing, the kit sells for just over $75—about a 40 percent to 50 percent savings off the cost of a comparable garment (if you can find it). Other vest models are available as well.

Altra gaitors come to just below the knee, giving protection from both snow and brush. Fully lined, these gaitors have easy side-entry zippers plus Velcro and front lace hooks. Around $15.

Gaitors

Frostline produced both *anklets and gaitors*. Each attaches to the boot lacing with a small hook or elastic cord for added protection, and each is constructed of water-repellant mountain cloth lined with nylon to breathe. There is a separating zipper in back covered with self-sealing flap. Anklets have elastic top and bottom. Gaitors have elastic at bottom and ankle and drawstring at top with under-boot cord. Anklets are 6½″ high and cost less than $8; the gaitors are 16″ high and cost around $11.

Knickers are, generally, ridiculously expensive. If you're big or well muscled, you probably have a hard time getting the right fit. My own too-expensive presewn wool knickers pull at the thighs, bag at the derrière, and itch. Right now only one kit company, **Frostline,** has knickers in its catalogue; they look just fine, and you can have a friend pin the pattern to you before you cut them out, so you can make minor alterations before it's too late. Available in either mountain cloth (a blend of cotton and polyester) or wool and nylon. Each has four zippered pockets, and closures at the knees are adjustable with self-sealing tabs. Each comes in men's or women's sizes. The men's knickers cost $20 in gray wool and less than $15 in mountain cloth, in either navy or rust. Women's knickers are the same price, but the mountain cloth version comes in rust, medium blue, or navy. The Frostline wool knickers are *much* cheaper than most comparable presewn versions.

Knickers

There are even more parkas and down- and synthetic-fill jacket kits available than there are down vest kits. What follows, therefore, is a partial survey of the best of the market. Unfortunately, most kit manufacturers have been lax about classifying parkas according to warmth, the way they

**Parkas and Down-
and Synthetic-fill
Jackets**

do sleeping bags. If you have questions about how warm these items will keep you, write to the manufacturer; if the manufacturers don't respond adequately, you won't want to buy from them anyway.

Altra has more jackets than anything else. Their *Down Parka*, less stylish than most of their jackets, is nevertheless an outdoor classic. It is relatively easy to sew, and it is constructed of sturdy 65/35 fabric. It has raglan sleeves, cargo/hand-warmer pockets, waist drawstring, and it is filled with about 10 ounces of down. Available in navy or rust at about $70—probably $25 to $35 less than a comparable presewn garment.

Their *Western Parka* is a short, very stylish ski jacket with contrasting yoke and collar. The yoke and collar are insulated with Hollofil for rain-resistance, and the body is down-filled. Details include hip tabs, chest pockets, and front zipper pockets. About $65—40 percent to 45 percent less than something off the rack. Available in navy/red or rust/wheat.

Altra's *Warmcoat* is a smart-looking, warm, city-slick jacket with 65/35 shell. Filled with Hollofil, this extra-long jacket has a smooth outer shell backed with needlepunch and with insulation quilted in the lining. A *very* attractive jacket for the man in your life—and a good buy at $50 (about $25 to $35 less than a comparable jacket). Tan only.

Frostline has several medium-weight parkas available, but perhaps most interesting are their parkas for cold weather conditions. Their *Tundra Jacket kit* for extreme cold weather conditions is good for winter mountaineering, cold weather camping, or any activities in the North Country. They don't specify how much down goes into the jacket (write and ask), but it certainly looks as though it has good loft. Outside shell is 1.9-ounce rip-stop nylon. The heavy-duty two-way front zipper is backed by a down-filled flap. The collar is large and ample. Nylon knit cuffs. Average thickness is 1¾". Less than $70. About thirty hours of cutting, searing, stuffing, and sewing. Available in navy, royal blue, or rust.

Their *Polar Bear* parka kit is very good indeed for wet, cold weather conditions. The parka is insulated with two layers of PolarGuard to keep you warmer when wet (warmer than down anyway); but I've been caught in downpours in my PolarGuard parka, and it's darn cold and clammy, despite its "miracle" fill. Less than $40.

Frostline's *Backpacker Jacket,* an easy-to-sew project, is shorter and lighter than the other two parkas mentioned, but it's a fine general-use parka for the teen-agers in your family. Available in either down or Hollofil, this parka costs less than $40 in down, less than $30 in the Hollofil version. The down version should save you about $25 off the cost of a comparable ready-made down parka.

Frostline's *Child's Crestone Kit* is a very nice down or Hollofil II tough-wearing parka for children. Available in 100 percent nylon taffeta or mountain cloth, a blend of cotton and polyester. The taffeta Crestone in down costs under $30 in sizes 4 to 6, under $45 for sizes 12 to 14. Hollofil and taffeta ranges from around $20 to under $30. The mountain cloth versions range from just over $30 in down, sizes 4 to 6, to just under $50 in sizes 12 to 14. The Hollofil version is $5 to $10 less.

Plain Brown Wrapper has several down parka kits. Most impressive (and warmest) are their *Eagle* and *Hawk* parkas, with 2″ average loft and comfort ranges of from −35 degrees to +50 degrees. These parkas come with tubular quilting, raglan sleeves, permanently attached hood with draw cord and hook and loop closing, down-filled head warmer and cargo pockets, and inside map pocket. Draw cord around bottom. The Eagle Shell is 60 percent cotton, 40 percent nylon. Hawk fabric is lighter, less durable 1.9-ounce rip-stop nylon. The Hawk costs well under $60; an excellent buy for that kind of warmth. The Eagle sells for well under $65. The Eagle model is also available in a goose-down/goose-feather blend, for about $55. It comes in navy, light blue, red, cedar.

SunDown's *"Superdown" Jacket* comes with either a rip-stop nylon or nylon taffeta shell. It contains 10⅓ ounces of prime goose down (in the medium size; large sizes weigh correspondingly more), with more down placed in the critical upper body areas. A medium size measures 32″ from base of collar to botton of back. It has a 3″-high down collar and down-filled hand-warmer pockets. With a selling price of less than $50, this is one of the best values available in outdoor clothing. For about $3 more, Sun-Down will provide you with the same jacket kit, with rugged 60/40 cloth shell (best for hunters, ranchers, or workers who are hard on their clothing). Available in sizes extra small to extra large. A down hood kit costs $10 more; the added warmth is worth the additional money. Wide color choice, depending upon the fabric you select.

Foul-Weather Gear, including 60/40s

There are trends in outdoor clothing, accessories and equipment, just as there are trends in other types of clothing and equipment; the difference is that outdoor clothing trends seem to have a longer lifetime. Take 60/40s, for example, the distinctive outer garment that Carl Sagan wore in all the outdoor scenes of *Cosmos* and that one sees several times a day on city streets and practically all the time on college campuses. About eight years ago, when my brother and I were working on *The Climbers Sourcebook,* a 60/40 was *the* badge of the outdoorsperson; walking around with a Chouinard ice ax couldn't have broadcast one's interest better than those early 60/40s. My brother wore his North Face 60/40 all the time; he wore it to shreds. Frankly, for years I didn't see the point of them, and I didn't buy one: It's true that they looked great and that the pockets held a lot, but they were too expensive. They kept one dry only in a *light* rain, and since they weren't lined, they weren't warm. The lightweight, inexpensive nylon wind shells sold for sailing at the time provided about the same wind protection. Eventually, wool-lined 60/40s came out, and the garment made a bit more sense to me; they were still too expensive, I thought, but at least they were warmer. But then, about four plus years ago, Early Winters, Ltd. of Seattle came out with a Gore-Tex 60/40, offered me one at wholesale to test for *Backpacking on a Budget,* and I was hooked.

Gore-Tex is, of course, the polymer film developed by W. L. Gore & Associates for use as arterial wall replacements in heart surgery; used as a laminate in outdoor clothing, it allows air in (you perspire less) but keeps rain out. A comparable product, Klimate, has also recently appeared on the scene, offering properties similar to Gore-Tex. The only difference between the two in terms of performance is that garments sewn of Klimate laminates can be dry-cleaned or washed; one does not dry-clean Gore-Tex garments.

You'll undoubtedly find the following section slanted toward Gore-Tex and Klimate kits; that's because I personally wouldn't bother constructing rain-gear kits anymore if they're made of conventional nonporous fabric. (It is true, however, that if someone gave me a presewn Plain Brown Wrapper Muskrat jacket, I wouldn't turn it down.)

Altra's only rain-gear kit is for a mountain parka (60/40 type) constructed of tough 65/35 fabric. Available in three attractive colors, for about $40 (half the price of a comparable presewn garment).

Their *Deluxe Mountain Parka,* with wool plaid lining, sells for less than $60; it's attractive and is a good buy.

Country Ways has kits for parkas, anoraks, and rain pants of conventional rainproof fabrics, but their best values are their Gore-Tex kits.

The *Gore-Tex parka kit* can save you about 30 percent off the cost of a comparable presewn Gore-Tex 60/40-style parka. This is a great-looking jacket, about twenty times more windproof than the usual sailing jacket or mountain parka, and it *breathes.* An excellent value, in sizes to fit your preteen or he-man. About two evenings worth of sewing. Available in rust or orange.

Gore-Tex Anorak. Slightly less expensive than the parka kit; the savings are comparable. This pullover style jacket is much favored by both sailors and mountain climbers. Available with PolarGuard insulated handwarmer kangaroo style front pocket. Rust or orange.

Gore-Tex Rain Pants. These cost at least a third less than presewn Gore-Tex rain pants, and they're *terrific.* The high waist is held up by quick-release suspenders. Cuffs adjust and close with Velcro tabs. Both seat and knees have reinforcing patches for extra strength.

Country Ways also has Gore-Tex kits for rain chaps; for a nice, handy, simple rain shell; and for an insulated sea jacket.

Frostline has pioneered so many outdoor clothing kits, it amazes me that at this writing they're offering only one Gore-Tex kit. The kit they do have, their *Zephyr Gore-Tex Parka kit,* is beautifully designed, if a bit more expensive than Country Ways' 60/40-type Gore-Tex jacket. But you'll still save at least $30 off the price of a comparable preconstructed garment.

Plain Brown Wrapper offers the best-looking conventional fabric rain-gear kits on the market. Their Muskrat rain jacket with navy body and contrasting bright yellow yoke is one of the all-time most attractive rain jackets I've seen, either in kit or preassembled form. And it's so cheap . . . well under $35.

SunDown has a very good, attractive line of rain-gear kits constructed with breathable Klimate cloth. I'm particularly taken by their rust-colored *Klimate Rain Parka kit.* About the same price as Frostline's Gore-Tex parka kit, this parka is nice and long and comes with a visored hood with drawstring, seamless shoulders (*very* good!), three large patch pockets with Velcro closure flaps, hand-warmer pockets, a waterproof weather flap inside the two-way front zipper, interior waist drawstring, and cuffs that can be made either adjustable or elastic style. Another excellent feature of this parka is its 10″ underarm zippers, used to increase ventilation.

A word of caution about Klimate and Gore-Tex rain gear: You *must* periodically renew the seam sealant, especially if you've rolled your rain parka or pants into a backpack. This past spring, after lecturing a group of co-workers about the glories of Gore-Tex, I happily walked off into a heavy rainstorm, a little more than two miles from home. By the time I arrived I was soaked through to the skin, and the lining of my blue blazer had faded all over my favorite silk blouse. It was my own fault; lazybones Sequoia hadn't resealed the seams in almost two years.

Fishing Tackle and Accessory Kits

Rods and Racks

The Angler's Supply House, Inc., of Williamsport, Pennsylvania, has a stunning variety of fly rod and spinning rod kits. Their rod kits contain all the parts and supplies necessary to finish the rod. All parts that require special skill and/or machinery, such as ferrule, top, cork grip, and reel seat on fly rods are already mounted on the rod so that there is no chance of damaging the blank or the part. All that is required to finish the rod are the winding of the guides with thread—a job that, they say, can be done in an evening.

Angler's Supply House's real strength, it seems, is that they are willing to create a custom-designed rod for you. For the *spinning rod kits,* you get to pick metal or fiberglass ferrule; colors of thread; whether or not you want bright tungsten steel guides or other choices; and what kind of spinning grip you'd like.

When you buy one of their *fly rod kits,* you get to pick: metal or fiberglass ferrule; standard or two-tone cork grip in one of two shapes; choice of reel seat; color of 2/0 silk thread; black nickel or bright chrome snake guides, top, butt guide, and keeper. Kit prices tend to be under $35. This makes a marvelous gift.

Bedford Lumber Company, Inc., makes an attractive, inexpensive *fishing rod rack,* which would look great in your log cabin, finished basement, or rustic den. Made of solid cedar, except for the back, which is constructed of cedar plywood. Displays three to five rods, four reels, hooks, lures, etc. Extra drawer for storing accessory equipment. 21½″ wide, 6″ deep, 38¾″ high. Less than $40.

Coren's Rod & Reel Service has a large selection of rod kits; at last, even if you're a rank beginner, you can create a fine custom rod that is relatively inexpensive, and it will last for years. Components include choice of Fenwick or Lamiglass rod blank, fitted with either a species cork handle with Varmac hardware or a Fuji pistol grip. Guides are either Fuji, Perfection, or Foulproof. Also included are spools of thread, varnish, color preserver, a hook keeper, epoxy, and instructions and spacing sheet. If you wish a specific combination of components or a specific blank, they will create a kit for you. Just a few of their kits include:

Ultralite #RK621. Fenwick 5′ ultralite (1⅙–⅜-ounce lures and 2#–8# mono line), two piece. The kit contains a prebuilt cork handle with sliding rings, a set of 1′ Fuji ceramic guides and tip, thread, epoxy, color preserver, etc. Excellent for bluegills to walleyes. Less than $25.

Salmon Rod #CRK965. 8′ medium-heavy, two-piece ferruled (¾–1¾-ounce lures, 10#–30# best line), reddish brown Lamiglass blank. Prebuilt hypalon grips with Varmac fixed reel seat, Fuji ceramic guides and tip-top, thread, epoxy, etc. An excellent salmon rod for lures, and it can be used for snagging. Under $30.

Baitcast #RK626. Fenwick 6′ bait-casting worm rod for ½–1-ounce lures and 12#–25# mono line. Comes with Fuji pistol-grip handle and butt adaptor, Fuji casting guides and tip, thread, etc. A great rod for bass, powerful yet with a sensitive tip. Just over $20.

Fly #RK84-5. Fenwick 7′ ultralite fly rod, two piece, AFTMA #5 line. 7″ prebuilt cork grip, Varmac fly reel seat, black Fuji tip and stripper guide, and six black snake guides, varnish, etc. An excellent rod for brook trout to bluegills. Just over $20.

Netcraft has *extremely inexpensive rod kits*—about $9.75 to $15.00. These are nice kits for your young folks to build themselves or to give as inexpensive gifts. They're fun.

Their 5'8" one-piece *casting rod kit* has a medium-heavy action, suitable for bass, pike, walleyes, etc., using plugs and spoons ½ to ⅝ ounce size. It has a collet-type take down handle with nylon core. Price: only $12.50.

Their 7½' two-piece heavy, duty *spinning rod kit* is for heavy freshwater fish or medium saltwater. It has a good action for a nice size scrappy fish (like the coho). The handle with fixed reel seat is 16" long. Takes reels using 12-to-25-pound line. Price $13.75.

Netcraft also has three models of solid glass boat rod kits. Their 6'6" *heavy-duty offshore rod,* one piece, is good for coho, big kings, barracuda, sailfish, and marlin. The kit contains: blank, three stainless-steel guides, tip-top, detachable hard-wood handle (21" overall), plus heavy-duty 1" reel seat, butt cap, hosel, thread, cement, and instructions. For $1.50 more, they'll add a roller tip-top. Price $14.25.

Orvis rod kits are for the perfectionist with more than a few dollars to spend. They have kits for four general types of rod. Their *Madison and MCL Impregnated Bamboo Fly Rod kits* come with Madison MCL bamboo blanks with ferrules mounted, formed cork grip, all hardware (comparable to their finished catalogued single-tip rods), supplies and instruction booklet (including diagrammed guide spacings). Kits come with single tip in sack and aluminum case. Prices range from just under $200 to just over $230.

Their *Orvis Graphite Fly Rod kits* include Orvis unidirectional graphite blanks with self-ferrules, shaped and bored cork grip, and reel seat. All hardware included. Prices range from around $140 for their Trout Rod, 7½' two pieces, 1¼ ounces for 6-weight line with cork and ring steel seat, to just over $230 for their Two-Handed Salmon Rod, 13½', three pieces, 9¼ ounces, for 10-weight line with cork reel seat.

Orvis Graphite Spin Rod kits include graphite blanks with self-ferrules, cork grip in two sections shaped and bored, reel bands (or fixed metal reel seat), all hardware, and supplies. These kits come in sacks; they range in price between $115 to just under $175.

Orvis Fullflex A Glass Fly Rod kits include amber glass blanks with self-ferrules, shaped and bored cork grip, reel bands, all hardware, and supplies. Kits come in polyurethane bag and generally cost under $60.

Their *Fullflex A Glass Spin Rod kits* come with glass blanks and self-ferrules, cork grip in two sections shaped and bored to fit blank, reel bands, all hardware, supplies, and instructions. Their 8' kit has fixed reel seat and foregrip. These kits come in polyurethane bags and range in price from around $45 to under $55.

Gander Mountain's *Fenwick Rod Building kits* can save you up to 50 percent on the cost of a factory-built Fenwick rod. Their kits use the same Fenwick blanks found in factory-built rods. Available in fiberglass or graphite rod kits. Fiberglass rods range in price from around $20 to a high of just under $30. The graphite kits range in price from just under $35 to about $85.

Steckler-Tibor Fly Rod Kits contain the same blank as used in their popular "Angler's Series," reel seat, shaped and bored cork grip, all hardware, finishing material, thread, instructions, and fancy poplin rod bag. Their graphite 7' fly rod kit for 3 or 4 weight line sells for less than $85—a good $35 less than their preassembled model. Their 9' graphite rod for 7-or-8-weight line costs under $105—about $45 less than their comparable preassembled model.

In their *S-Glass Fiberglass Fly Rod Kits,* an 8' model for 6-weight line would cost you less than $40 in kit form; preassembled, it would cost about one-third more. The 8½' model for 7-weight line, under $40 in kit form, would cost $25 more preassembled.

Fly-tying Kits

Hille's Fly-Tying Kits from **Angler's Supply House, Inc.,** are designed for beginners. They are, however, not the junk kits one sometimes sees in discount or even sporting goods stores. These kits come with or without tools, and all material included is usable. Their inexpensive kit for trout and panfish, for example, costs only $7, and it contains thirty-five hooks for dry and wet flies in assorted sizes, thread, wax, lacquer, cement, peacock tail feather, golden and amherst pheasant tippets. Also included are assortments of chenille, body floss, crewel yarn, raffia, duck side feathers, paired duck wing quills, selected hackle of the proper sizes for the hooks and special hackle for tails, plus instruction sheet. They offer the kit in another version, which comes with 011 Vise and Hackle pliers. About $5.50 more.

They have several other interesting kits, including their K6 model for streamers, bucktails, bass, and trout. Less than $14, this kit contains forty streamer hooks in assorted sizes and styles, two spools of thread, lacquer, cement, wax, two colors of lacquer enamel, two cards of tinsel, and peacock sword feather. Plus assortments of chenille in two sizes, floss, wool yarn, saddle hackle marabou; also deer, calf, and squirrel tailpieces—each with assorted colors.

Buz's Fly and Tackle Shop carries two fly-tying kits for beginners. The Budget Assortment, $24.95, will tie at least thirteen different patterns, comprising eight dry flies, three wet flies, a nymph, and a streamer. The Deluxe Assortment, $59.95, will tie at least twenty-four additional patterns and includes two steelhead patterns. In all, more than one hundred flies can be tied with the Budget Assortment, and more than three hundred flies with the Deluxe Assortment. The tools in the Deluxe Assortment are professional quality, as are all tools except the vise in the budget assortment. Hooks are not included in either version to allow you freedom of choice in size, style, and quantity.

Gene's Tackle Shop in Rochester, New York, carries three fly-tying kits. Their least expensive kit, just under $10, contains twenty tying hooks, hackle pliers, a fly-tying vise, and unspecified materials for tying many different flies.

Their $20 Deluxe Assortment contains materials for tying a wide range of patterns of dry flies, wet flies, nymphs, bucktails, and streamer flies. Also contains sixty fly and streamer hooks, hackle pliers, fly-tying vise, sample of a completed fly, and a forty-eight-page *Guide to Trout Flies*.

Lure-Craft sells worm-making kits for just under $25. The kit comes with six different molds, one pint of #536 Super-Super Soft Plastic, three 1-ounce bottles of plastic coloring, 1 ounce "Lunker Lotion" flavoring, 4 ounces "worm oil," two pouring pans, plus stirring sticks.

Netcraft of Toledo, Ohio, has several fly-tying kits. Their basic $11 fly kit includes tying vise, one bottle fly head cement, thread, varicolored chenille, tinsel, assortment of quill pieces, one pair dark quills, dyed and natural Impali tailpieces, saddle and neck hackles, dyed grizzly hackle assortment, deer hair, mallard plumage, fancy feather assortment containing marabou, imitation wood duck, dyed and natural duck breast, peacock herl, and twenty assorted hooks. Materials included for tying about 245 flies. They recommend that their $1.25 booklet *Practical Flies and Their Construction* be purchased as well.

Netcraft also carries a bass bug and fly-tying kit, a deluxe fly-tying kit, a spinning fly and lure kit, a worm-making kit, a cherry bobber kit, a spinner kit (50 percent savings), French-style lure kits (60 percent savings), a jig-tying kit, a cork kit for lining your tackle box, two net-making kits, and others.

Fish-mounting Kits, Landing Net Kits, and the Best Fishing Vest Kit You've Ever Seen

The Angler's Supply House, Inc., is a distributor for Meyer *fish-mounting kits*. The kit, about $15, contains enough materials for a fish up to 10 pounds. The process takes up to three hours. All materials are nontoxic. Each kit contains a skinning knife, scraper, preservative, filler, eyes, needle and thread, paints, varnish, brush, and detailed instruction booklet.

Cascade Lakes Tackle has extremely handsome *landing net kits,* ranging in price from just under $25 for one 18½" long, with 11½" x 6" bow, 7" handle, 17" bag, to $26 for one 23" long, 15½" x 8½" bow, 7½" handle, 21" bag. All of these require final shaping, assembly, and finishing, and they give the angler the opportunity to create a landing net that can be hand-marked or engraved. All are teardrop-shaped. The formed ash bows are already cemented to cherry handles. Proportioned nylon net bags, lacing cords, and French snap assemblies are included. About $10 savings per landing net.

Frostline has an excellent *fishing vest kit.* It has twelve pockets, including six gusseted cargo pockets down the front; the top two of these have artificial lamb's-wool flaps for hooking flies. On the back is a huge removable pouch, which snaps to the vest. Beneath it is another large zippered pocket, which is actually the entire back of the vest. There are also two inside front pockets. Made of durable mountain cloth with front zipper. Tab on the front for your rod, an epaulet on the left shoulder to secure your creel, a hook in back of the neck for your net, and D-rings on the top front pockets for cutters and knives. Less than $25. A comparable vest would cost about $15 more preassembled.

Netcraft carries the Meyer 10-pound-capacity fish-mounting kits—for a good $4.50 less than The Angler's Supply House, mentioned earlier.

In addition, Netcraft has the Meyer *Bird- and small-animal-mounting kit* for less than $11. Essentially the same components detailed under The Angler Supply House entry.

Black-Powder Firearms Kits

Black-powder firearms are classed as nonguns by the federal government, since they don't fire a self-contained cartridge. You need no license or permit for them, and they can be shipped by mail right to your home.

The Armoury, Inc., of New Preston, Connecticut, is a respected manufacturer of muzzle-loading rifle kits. My firearms consultant, Norm Brilliant, a member of the National Muzzleloading Rifle Association and the Second Regiment, Middlesex Militia, New Jersey, has chosen the following kits as the best values for the money.

Kentucky Rifle kit. This is a moderately priced, one-piece full-length Kentucky Rifle kit, fully sanded, expertly inletted, available in .45 or .50 caliber. Previously, kits were available only with two-piece stocks; only expensive custom stocks were available with a one-piece stock. Norm says this rifle is good for big game. It has accurate flight with almost any kind of sights. About $135.

Hawken Rifle kits. .45, .50, and .54 caliber. Walnut stock with cheek piece. The patchbox and forend are fitted; the wood requires finish sanding and polishing of metal parts only. Brass furniture; fully inletted patchbox. This is a fine-quality kit, with many good features, including hook breach. About $140.

Flintlock Kentucky Pistol Kit. This can be used for target shooting, although, considering its primitive sight, it's really not a target pistol. It's a replica of an old-time piece, not really for precision shooting. A truly authentic pistol with precision-rifled barrel, authentic-style lock, bolstering on the percussion exactly like the original. Beautiful inletting, with parts that go into place with very little effort. .44 caliber. About $75.

Revolver kits. The Armoury was the first to offer a revolver kit for the famous Remington New Model Army .44 Caliber Revolver. All parts of this kit are completely machine-finished and require only polishing and a small amount of fitting. An accurate kit, good at the range. This is an exact replica. About $90.

Dixie Guns Works, Inc., of Union City, Tennessee, has an extraordinary variety of black-powder firearms kits available; we've never heard anything bad about any of their own brand kits. Generally, their kits are very inexpensive, and their rifle kits are particularly good. Norm does, however, suggest that you steer clear of the CVA kits in this catalogue.

Hopkins & Allen Arms carries an extensive line of black-powder firearms kits. Many, if not most, of their kits have hardwood stocks, not the walnut stocks one might prefer. Most of their muzzle loaders have the action underneath—underhammers; these are unusual, but they've been around for years and are quite reliable. Most Hopkins & Allen pieces are suitable for range shooting and for hunting.

Hopkins & Allen has *many* attractive kits. Their *Heritage Model Rifle,* about $85, is a replica of a New England Sporting rifle, circa 1830. It has a fast lock time, uninterrupted sighting plane, and underhammer design. The octagonal barrel is 32″ long, and the gun has an overall length of 49″. Choice of .36 and .45 caliber. This one does have a walnut stock; it weighs 8½ pounds. Preassembled price is about $115.

Their *Kentucky Flintlock Pistol* kit is another attractive item. It's nicely balanced, has an overall length of 15¼″, and weighs 41 ounces. The kit, about $56, should save you about one-third the price of a preassembled piece.

Other fine kits from Hopkins & Allen, at similar savings, include their kits for the Brown Bess Musket, Hawken Rifle, English Belt Pistol, Traditional Deluxe Kentucky Rifle, and Minuteman Rifle.

Lyman Products produces good kits. Their *Great Plains Rifle kit* is particularly interesting. It features an American walnut stock and choice of barrel designs, which gives you a choice of round-ball or conical-bullet gun. The lock is a fully-assembled color case-hardened percussion lock, featuring tumbler fly and lifetime coil mainspring. All hardware, including a double-set trigger and an adjustable rear sight, is provided ready for final polishing and finishing. Additional barrels are available in kit form for direct interchangeability. The percussion kit model costs $249.95; preassembled price is $339.95.

Navy Arms Company produces an excellent line of kits. These are fine shooting weapons with beautiful actions. Especially interesting is their *New Orleans Ace pistol kit,* the "original gambler's companion." This pistol kit is entirely American-made, with solid brass frame. It's .44 caliber, 9″, and weighs 1 pound. With smooth bore, the kit costs $39.95. Assembled, the pistol would cost $54.95.

Other interesting Navy Arms kits: the Ethan Allen Pepperbox ("fore-runner of revolving handguns"), the triple-barreled Duckfoot pistol, and their tiny Classic Twister.

Bicycle Bags, Tennis and Running Clothing, Gun Racks, Trampolines, Crossbow Kits, and Other Sporting Goods Kits

Bedford Lumber Company, Inc., sells a most attractive, very simple, inexpensive *archery tackle rack,* constructed of cedar. About $20. Holds up to four bows and about eighteen arrows.

Bedford Lumber also has several *gun rack kits.* Their Triple Gun Rack comes in cedar or walnut; cedar costs under $15 and walnut just over that. Their Handy "4" Gun Rack has a decorative pull-out drawer with brass pulls, holds four rifles, and comes in cedar or walnut. The cedar version costs just over $30. Their Saf-T-Gun Rack holds four rifles or shotguns, but the mechanism permits removal of guns only when the drawer is opened. The drawer has built-in lock and key. Cedar only. About $50.

If you have children in the house, you might be more interested in Bedford Lumber's *Sportsman's Gun Cabinet.* Available in walnut or cedar, this good-looking cabinet holds eight guns, and it has a large storage cabinet for ammunition and accessories. Glass not included in the kit. Locks and hardware included. The cedar version of this cabinet is just over $120.

Bingham Projects, Inc., has kits for hunting bows, arrows, hunting knives, water skis, and skateboards. One of their most interesting kits is a very inexpensive *Bow and Arrow Rack.* Made of redwood, the simple, attractive rack holds three bows and twenty-four arrows. About $10.

Frostline has several different kinds of bicycle accessories, but most interesting is probably their *Panniers kit.* These have a low center of gravity and stiffening plate in back for rigidity. They will fit any standard bike luggage rack, without swaying, flapping, or catching in the spokes. Waterproof. About $30—perhaps $15 less than comparable panniers.

Frostline has also been adding running and tennis gear to its catalogue. Of particular interest are their *Warm-Up Suit kits.* Easy-to-sew, so you should be able to make these in one evening. The suit is made of stretchable, absorbent 60 percent polyester/40 percent cotton. Completely washable. These come in three attractive colors, with front zippers, elastic waistband, contrast stripes, pockets in pants and jacket. Less than $30.

Gander Mountain, Inc., has an inexpensive *Buck Horn Mounting kit.* For well under $10, you can mount your prized antlers on this "teakwood"-finish plaque with red or green velvet covering.

Golf Day Products has an interesting *golf woods refinishing kit,* which does four to eight woods. With this kit, less than $10, you can save up to $70 on the cost of refinishing your favorite woods.

Doug Kittredge Bow Hut has several top-quality arrow kits. All kits sell for a few dollars less than their full retail cost; they represent considerable savings over buying preassembled arrows. Their *Professional Cedar Arrow kit,* costing about $10, contains thirteen cedar shafts, factory-finished in color of your choice; thirteen speed-type nocks, thirty-nine die-cut feathers, 4″ or 5″ shield shape; thirteen field or target points; fetching and nocking cement; one set number decals; plus booklet. Does not include broadheads. You select bow weight and arrow length.

Gerald D. Miller sells kits for the *"Jayhawk" Crossbow.* About $20, this kit consists of one 75-pound aluminum-alloy bow, one steel-cable bowstring, one trigger assembly, one hanger-bolt assembly, two alloy strips, one peepsight, pin safety, trigger guard strap, and instructions. All parts of the kit, except the bowstring, are guaranteed against breakage as long as you own the crossbow.

Patch-It of Waitsfield, Vermont, sells most attractive, inexpensive patchwork tennis racquet covers. Precut calico patches, plus lining, batting, and instructions included.

SMI sells an attractive *gun cabinet kit* designed to hold six guns up to 51″ long. Designed for a full-length mirror back, this kit features two full-length viewing doors, full-length side-view panels, and two base front doors. The kit comes with all mortises and tenons precut, all pieces presanded, all hardware, plus glass and mirror. Available in oak for about $155; mahogany costs about $20 to $25 more. Since SMI occasionally runs sales, you may want to get on their mailing list; the wait could save you $25 to $30 more.

Teco makes a *trampoline kit,* which sells for about $200. The trampoline frame, of treated wood, will stand up indefinitely in contact with the ground. The flat wood surface can easily be padded and covered with vinyl material. The Teco mat is a standard 6′ x 12′ size; it will usually last about four years with home use. Construction takes about four to five hours, they say.

Trampoline Kits and Supplies, Inc., has several professional-quality, wood- or metal-frame trampoline kits available. These are *above-ground trampolines* and do not require a pit, as do Teco trampolines, mentioned above.

These are easy-to-construct kits, available in a variety of sizes; their Globe Master professional-quality trampoline kit could save you about $180 to $200 off the price of a comparable trampoline.

4

High Technology and Scientific Kits

This chapter is for those of you who need new stereo speakers, an alarm system for your car, even an automatic timer to turn on the air-conditioning in your house before you get home. Of course, *you're also a person who wants to save 30 percent to 50 percent* on the cost of the "high technology" items you want.

This chapter is also for young people (or friends and parents of young people) who want to build your/their own AM radios, a home weather station, a giant hot-air balloon, or small solar-energy panels. These kits go beyond toys; they teach good, solid science, and they're fun.

If you have a yen for your own home computer, you'll find some direction, too. Plus electronic strobe-light kits, a soil-test kit, a surf-synthesizer kit . . . and more.

If dulcimer or clock kits are not sufficient challenge for you, you might want to consider **ATV Research's** *Solid-State TV Camera kit*. Designed with switchable RF and video outputs, the Model XT-1A can be either connected directly to the antenna terminals of a regular TV set or used to feed an industrial video monitor or any standard video tape recorder. With Vidicon, the kit sells for under $200—about $80 less than the exact assembled TV camera.

Bigelow Electronics offers an inexpensive way to improve the reception on your AM radio. Their *Philmore Aerial kit,* less than $6, is good for radios with external antenna connections. To properly accommodate this long wire antenna, you need at least 50 feet clear between two fixed buildings or poles, away from electric wires.

Bigelow also offers kits for solid-state diode *crystal radios.*

Burstein-Applebee sells a *solar-energy lab kit* for the young scientists in your family. Experiments include building a solar-powered radio, a sun-activated clock, sun-beam communicator, solar-heating system, a solar oven that boils water, solar cigarette lighter, solar-powered electronic circuit, and many more items (one hundred and twenty in all). About $20.

Chaney Electronics, Inc., offers a kit that is particularly good for boaters: an *electronic warning flasher kit.* This battery-operated device continuously emits bursts of intense light, which can be seen at great distances. Very easy to construct. Uses a high-output xenon flash tube, which flashes two times per second when batteries are fresh, then automatically slows down to one flash every five seconds as batteries grow weaker. Operates continuously for twelve hours on two C batteries. This kit is a potential life-saver; it costs less than $8.

Coulter Optical Company has a marvelous kit for constructing your own 4¼" *lunar-planetary telescope.* The kit consists of a Coulter 4¼" f/12 Pyrex paraboloidal mirror, null-figured, coated. Coulter 0.75" x 1.05" Pyrex elliptical diagonal flat, ± 1/10-wave, coated. Black phenolic tube 5½" diameter x 55" long, 1¼" I.D. drawtube focuser, two coated lenses to make a Ramsden eyepiece, and hub for diagonal. Does not include the cell, spider, mount. 6-mm, 12-mm, and 20-mm 1¼" O.D. Kellner eyepieces available from Coultner. With eyepieces and instructions for mount, the kit should come to under $50.

Edmund Scientific has a marvelous selection of science kits designed to expand young people's and adults' understanding of electronics, solar power, astronomy, and anatomy. The following is just a sampling of what they have available.

Deluxe Solar Cell Kit. Created by the co-inventor of Bell System's solar battery. Contains all material needed to turn silicon slabs into working solar cells. Accompanying text explains principles and theory of solar energy and its application in solid-state physics. Less than $40.

Solar Oven Kit. 6" high. Comes with 6¾" parabolic reflector, support stand, test tubes, and holder. About $5. A good science project for your precocious preteen.

Kaleideoscope kit. Build your own kaleidoscope. Includes color disk with two optical lenses, novelty shapes, colored twists, etc. Less than $10.

8X Refractor Telescope kit. Powerful enough to view craters on the moon. Finished telescope measures 18″ long x 1¾″ diameter. Less than $10.

Operate Your Own Optics Laboratory kit. One hundred and thirty-five experiments in optics and photography. Assemble, with this kit, your own 35-mm reflex camera with an interchangeable lens system, or reinvent the periscope, telescope, microscope. Ages twelve and up. This kit is an excellent investment, at less than $30.

Hot-Air Balloon kits. When assembled and inflated, these 9′ tall, 5′ wide paper balloons rise up to 200 feet. Very inexpensive (about $5) and easily repaired.

Soil-Test kits. These are excellent for science projects, but they're good, too, if you want to test the soil in your garden. Test for nitrogen, potassium, and phosphorus. About $5.

Economy Weather Station kit. For less than $30, you or yours can build a complete weather station, which gives you the know-how to check your predictions against TV and radio "experts." Features remote reading anemometer with wind vane and indoor indicator board, which flashes neon lights to show wind speed and direction. All connections are safe. Kit includes sensitive air-tank barometer with 2-foot indicator column for checking air pressure, sling psychrometer to measure relative humidity, rain gauge with calibrated tube, etc.

Edmund Scientific also sells kits for clocks, sextants, shortwave radios, astrolabes, a sundial, etc.

Educational Design, Inc., sells relatively simple and inexpensive science learning kits for home or schoolroom use. Among the most interesting being sold at this writing (their line changes periodically): Their *Crystal Radio* kit comes with germanium-diode crystal and tuning-coil antenna. Less than $6. The *Electric Bell kit* enables students to construct a variety of devices using an electromagnet: bell, buzzer, telegraph. Less than $6.

Their *Metric Balance Scale kit,* about $4, makes up into a double-platform balance scale with factory-accurate gram weights, which teaches the elements of weight measurement plus the basics of the metric system. More fun than science, their *Fingerprint kit* contains everything necessary to bring out, identify, and catalogue hidden fingerprints. Less than $5.

Graymark sells kits for such technical equipment as a *volt-ohm-milliampere-meter* and a *siren/code oscillator.* They also have automotive, clock, and radio projects at levels from beginning to advanced.

A nice project for a beginner who wants to learn the basics of semiconductor and radio-reception theory is their *2-Transistor Radio kit.* This kit features a reflex circuit, RF transformer, PM speaker, Hi-Q ferrite antenna, and twenty-four page student manual. Well under $15. For more sophisticated radio builders, Graymark has a *6-transistor kit* for under $20 and an *8-transistor kit* for under $30.

Also available from Graymark is an advanced kit for a *digital alarm clock,* plus kits for a *tachometer* and a *radar sentry.*

The Heath Company of Benton Harbor, Michigan, is one of the oldest and best-managed kit companies in business today. International in operation, Heath sells reliable, well designed kits for dozens of items you'll eventually want for your home—everything from hi-fi systems to garage-door openers. Many of their kits require little technical sohistication, and all of their kits will save you at least 30 percent to 40 percent (sometimes more) off the preassembled purchase price of all items mentioned below.

Heath has a truly stunning range of kits. The items that follow are meant to whet your appetite; if you send for their catalogue, you'll find scores more.

A great advantage of building your own technical amenities from a Heath kit is that you can *fix them yourself* should anything go awry (not a reflection on Heath quality; you and I know that machines break—especially, it seems, in my house).

A note for my nontechnically-oriented readers, especially men and women who've been trained to be afraid of anything involving electricity or circuitry: Heath has a nice range of relatively simple kits designed for one-evening assembly. Invest in one; most are relatively inexpensive. They're a good way to overcome one's fear of trying.

Two-Way Freezer Alarm kit. This is extremely valuable if you're one of those people (like me) who's been known to leave the freezer door slightly ajar. It signals if the door is left open or if the freezer temperature reaches 20° F, even though the door is closed. About $15, this easy-to-assemble kit could save you hundreds.

Low-Cost Photoelectric Lamp Switch. Turns lights on in the evening, off in the morning. Helps protect against burglars and makes sure that you don't have to walk into a dark house or apartment when you get home from work during the winter. Well under $10. Very easy to assemble.

Heathkit Casablanca® Ceiling Fan kit. An excellent and attractive way to cool your home in summer or to bring heat down from ceiling areas during the winter. Chain-pull switch operation, 52″ blades (tip to tip), plus variable-speed adjustment from 145 to 180 rpm. A light kit is optional (under $20), which makes this fan even more practical and charming. A very good buy at well under $120.

Solid-State Heat/Cool Setback Thermostat with Twelve Periods. Can save you up to 20 percent on your heating bills, and it provides automatic control and energy savings with your air-conditioner too. A programmable clock provides you with up to twelve setback periods each day for both heating and cooling. In the heating control, setback temperatures range from 2° to 15° F. The heat thermostat has a built-in light switch, which indicates that setback is operating properly. The cooling portion of the setback lets you completely shut down your cooling system when your home is unoccupied and turn it on at a preset time. Designed for use with electrical cooling systems, in combination with gas or oil furnaces. Works with either four- or five-wire furnace control systems. Very easy to install. Less than $50, this invaluable kit should more than pay for itself within the first few months of winter operation.

Ultrasonic Automobile Intrusion Alarm. If you ever park your car on city streets, you probably need this low-cost alarm system. When unauthorized entry occurs, the machine waits ten seconds, then begins sounding the horn, frightening off your unwelcome guests. This kit is very easy to assemble, and installation requires just three connections. Operates from your car's 12-volt battery. An excellent investment at less than $50.

Highway Emergency Strobe Light. With adaptor plug that fits into your car's cigarette lighter. Comes with a 12' cord, which lets you put the flashing light where you need it. Highly visible flashing strobe with flash rate of better than one per second. This important highway safety kit costs just over $30.

Room-size Electronic Air Cleaner. This is great if you have people in your house with allergies, asthma, or sinus problems. Excellent if your home is well insulated and "sealed up" during winter months. The air cleaner, in an inconspicuous, handsome case, removes dust, dirt, and pollutants from any room, and it cleans and refreshes the air. Charcoal filter cleans up most household odors; it's excellent if you still have smokers in your home. Kit comes with fully-assembled variable-speed fan, and it requires no soldering. Well under $200.

Accutrac® 4000 Turntable. If you love both music and gadgetry, you'll adore this turntable. The Accutrac® gives you total "computerized" control over how you play your records, and you can operate it from its front panel or with its cordless remote control. This is the world's only totally programmable turntable. It plays individual cuts in the order you choose; it repeats what you want to repeat and skips what you want to skip. It has precision direct-drive; die-cast platter; tubular S-shaped tone arm, with electronically controlled cue, pause and muting, antiskate, and individual 5 percent variable pitch control for each speed. Many more features. Well under $400, this fabulous turntable kit requires no soldering, and it takes just two to three hours to assemble!

Heathkit "Modulus." A deluxe stereo AM-FM tuner with superb 2/4-channel preamplifier. This kit is one of the most technically advanced on the market. Features four ½" tall LED's, which display the broadcast frequency far more accurately than a conventional tuning dial. Two tuning meters; signal-strength for AM and FM, and center channel for FM to give you real tuning precision. It has phase-locked loop stereo multiplex circuit to ensure wide FM stereo separation of 40db at 1000 Hz. On high-level inputs, the preamp section reaches full output with a signal of 170mv, yet it doesn't overload until 5 volts. The phono amplifier can be driven to full output with as little as 2mv but does not overload until the input reaches 60mv. The "Modulus" has peak-responding output meters for each channel, full bass, treble, and balance controls, lighted function push button, and more. The "heart" of Heathkit's music systems. About $600.

Heath has a very extensive selection of stereo components in addition to the two described above. Prices of some individual components start hundreds of dollars lower than the fancy components mentioned, but they range higher, too. These are excellent components. Heathkits are fine, even if you just want to improve the quality of your speaker system; they have great speaker kits.

A special note about *home computer kits:* Heath has an astonishing and, to me, barely comprehensible range of computer hardware for personal use. These are are apparently not very difficult to assemble (the Heathkit H8 Personal Computer, less than $400, is labeled a "six-evening kit"), are relatively inexpensive, and are part of a well-designed system, which can expand as your problem solving and programming capabilities grow. Some of these kits, like the *DEC H11A 16-Bit Computer Kit,* can save you as much as $800 over the exact preassembled model.

Heath also sells kits for color TVs, digital clocks, just about anything you *must* have for your home.

Inter-Tronics, Inc., sells what may be the most sophisticated *automobile alarm system kit* on the market. Known as the Ultimate,® it operates with a number of sonic transducers, which are supersensitive to tampering, yet with minimum danger of false alarms. Any number of transducers can be added to protect window glass, antenna, skirts, gas cap, hubcaps, mag wheels, even hood ornament. Uses three separate detection circuits.

"Circuit 1 incorproates a memory switch which monitors the closed loop circuit with a green LED. The circuit has a 'shunt plug' so that if the circuit is disabled, the Ultimate® System's other two circuits will protect the vehicle. This closed loop circuit includes as many transducers as desired, wired to many sections of the vehicle. If any one transducer is broken, or wires are bad or broken, the operator is alerted. A self-checking feature that conventional auto alarm systems don't have.

"Circuit 2, a magnetic detection circuit, protects problem areas like the hood latch, that get too hot for standard transducers, or that might be opened too quietly to trip the alarm. Any additional, closed circuit alarm devices may be added to the circuit.

"Circuit 3, a voltage sensor circuit, will sound off if the battery cable is shorted or the battery is weak. Even if a thief crawls silently on top of a convertible, and slides in through the slashed top. The Ultimate alarm will sound when he tries the starter. Yet clocks or battery 'static' will not give a false alarm.

"A keyless accessory in second brain module turns the system on 75 seconds after the ignition key is removed and the exit delay switch is activated. A red LED indicates the 75 second delay is in progress.

"Reset is not thermal, and thus not affected by heat or cold. The electronic alarm duration timer can be set for exact time desired, from one to six minutes.

"Reentry is simple ... for the owner. He/she holds a small magnetic 'bag' in proper alignment. The Ultimate® System allows him or her ten seconds to open the door, place key in ignition, then close the door. The computer switch also offers 'panic' and 'permanently off' settings."

Amazing . . . .

Inter-Tronics also sells home alarm systems you can install yourself.

Paul MacAlister & Associates sell very beautiful kits for three working home time instruments: a *perpetual calendar,* a *nocturnal,* and a *sundial.* They also carry a kit for an *astrolabe.*

The astrolabe kit, about $20, is for those who want to study and use the early astronomers' and astrologers' computer, star-map, and timepiece. Although designed in the manner of exquisite Renaissance instruments, this is an original astrolabe, computed for modern star positions. The traditional parts of mother, rete, rule, alidade, and tympans are printed on gold metallic-surfaced cardboard, precision die-cut for accuracy. The parts assemble easily into a working 8⅜ " diameter astrolabe. The kit comes with twenty-four-page booklet written by Roderick S. Webster, curator of antique instruments at the Adler Planetarium.

Have you fantasized about having a *wall-sized TV?* If you really want one, you can buy one, of course, for over a thousand dollars ... or invest well under $20 in **The Macrocoma Company's** TV projector kit. Using Mr. Good's lens system and about two dollars' worth of wood, plus an inexpensive mirror, you can project any size picture up to a giant 5' x 6' onto a wall or movie screen. Great for sporting events or J. R. Ewing. The short focal length makes this kit fine for use even in small apartments.

PAIA Electronics has three environmental sound-effect kits, which help you bring the soothing sound of the surf or the wind into your home. All are designed for use with any hi-fi or musical instrument amplifier.

Surf Synthesizer kit. This amazing, very inexpensive kit (about $15 without case; about $20 with case), electronically synthesizes the sound of the ocean. Great for insomniacs or a couple recalling a honeymoon spent on Cape Hatteras.

Wind Synthesizer kit. Very realistic wind effects. Trimmer adjustments provide a range of effects from a moderate breeze to full gale. Same price as above.

Wind Chimes kit. This is a few dollars more than the two kits listed above. Select either the ring of brass chimes or the percussive resonance of bamboo rods. Very relaxing.

Radio Shack seems to be expanding the number of kits it carries. Most seem to be educational toy-type kits, but there are some nice Archer Kits as well for a few choice items.

Electronic Bike Speedometer kit. Features ½ ″ dual scale, which reads 0 to 60 kilometers per hour and 0 to 30 miles per hour. Easy to assemble. About $15.

Strobe Light kit. Just what you need for your home disco. Adjustable flash rate. For 120 VAC. About $30.

Pocket Lie Detector kit. Fingertip sensor electronically detects skin-resistance changes owing to nervousness. Some soldering required. Powered by 9-volt battery. Now you can play FBI at home. About $12.

Police and Aircraft Radio Monitor kit. Allows your youngsters to monitor police frequency and tune in on twenty-four weather reports. Tunes 108–135 and 147–174 MHz. Safe solderless connectors. About $15.

AM Pocket Radio kit. An excellent, inexpensive project for your precocious preteen. The kit radio has thumb-wheel volume and tuning, eight transistors, earphones; it requires some soldering. About $13.

Rocky Mountain Science Supply has a *miniature solar power plant kit,* which can be used to convert toys and novelties to solar power. Comes with instructions on how to power a toy truck or car, also how to make a solar-powered beanie. Less than $10.

Speakerlab of Seattle, Washington, sells an extraordinary range of *top-quality stereo/hi-fi speaker kits.* All can be assembled by beginners, since they require little more than a tube of RTV silicone rubber glue and a staple gun for attaching the grille cloth. Since the kits come with special clips on all color-coded wires, you needn't even use any solder. The cabinet comes pre-constructed with already cut-out speaker mounting holes. You supply only stapler or tacks and a calking gun. Their kits usually require about three hours to assemble (slightly more on the larger speakers). They even have a *toll-free hot line* (a fantastic idea, which ought to be picked up by other kit manufacturers) *in case you have a question or problem during assembly.* Kits are available in three ways: with speakers and crossover only, plus plans to make your own enclosure; complete kit, with walnut-grain vinyl bonded to particle board enclosure; or complete kit with walnut veneer enclosure. Their kits come with a fantastic guarantee: If you cannot successfully assemble your kit despite their help via the toll-free hot line, you can return the kit to Speakerlab, and they'll finish it for you, no charge. They'll replace any parts you've ruined. They say they can offer this guarantee because their kits are so easy to assemble it's a real rarity that someone has that much trouble with them. Note that if you use the Speakerlab speakers with musical instruments instead of hi-fi systems (and I can certainly see the temptation), you void your warranty.

Speaker kits range from small, powerful, and inexpensive (about $60) to large, loft-size mommas that go for more than $1,000 each (and are cheap at the price).

Do send for the Speakerlab catalogue if you're contemplating buying new speakers; these are great kits.

5

Homes from Kits: How to Save $10,000 to $35,000 on Your Biggest Investment

A year ago, armed with the first part of the advance money for this book and accumulated savings from my two previous books, I set out to buy a home of my own. I knew the area where I wanted to live: It would mean a long commute into the city each week, but I had a tiny, very inexpensive apartment in town, a secure, well paying job, and a dream of living—even for just a few days each week—near the ponds where Canadian geese find winter refuge. After all, I told myself, why not? I was thirty-four, single, in reasonably good health, and earning more than many men with dependent children.

But I found myself priced out of the market. The few houses I saw or heard about in my price range were ugly, badly built, in terrible condition from age and neglect, badly situated—or all of the above. It was depressing. The closest I came to what I wanted at a price I could afford was a tiny old farmhouse, a termite-ridden "handyman's special" on a quarter acre, in need of a new roof, new windows and frames, new kitchen, new wiring, possibly new plumbing—and God knows what else; while I was making up my mind, someone else snapped it up for $6,000 more than I had been quoted.

When I began the research for this chapter, I thought anyone who built a home from a kit must be slightly crazy—or handier than I could ever be. I knew there were fine kits available for furniture, sporting goods, and needlework of all kinds—kits for just about everything. But I couldn't have anticipated the range—or the beauty—of some of the kit homes available in today's market. And I was surprised, once I began speaking with people who had built their own homes from kits, at the relative ease of construction of many of them.

So, in the course of researching and writing this chapter, I've become a convert. . . . Kit homes make good economic sense, especially for people like me, who know what they want, who are on tight budgets, and who are willing to work hard for just a few months or even a year to build equity that will last a lifetime.

The home kit field is booming. More than 200,000 kits were sold last year. The biggest boom, clearly, is in log home kits, but there are a surprising number of less rustic kit homes too: dome homes, post-and-beam homes, even conventional ranch-style suburban homes of wood and brick.

The variety may at first seem bewildering. But you probably know your own taste. Once you've read through the descriptions that follow, you'll probably have a clearer idea of what you want—and you can proceed from there.

If you think you might like to build a home from a kit, send for as many of the brochures as you can afford. (Full addresses and brochure prices appear in the Appendix at the back of this book.) You'll begin to get a good sense of the many styles and sizes available. Once you've decided what type of home you want, you can start comparing relative prices, construction methods, and what components each kit contains. This last is very important in assessing the real cost of each kit: Every home kit package contains different materials.

Once you've narrowed your choices down to the kits of two or three or four manufacturers, you ought to start getting in touch with people who have built kit homes from each. You'll find the manufacturers *very* cooperative in providing you with the phone numbers of other kit builders. Most manufacturers are pretty low pressure. And they *want* you to successfully put up one of their homes: Every satisfied log home customer, for example, generates more customers. The kit home concept seems to spread like wildfire.

When you speak with other kit home builders, talk to them about money. They're invariably proud of how much they've saved. Some people spend less than $10,000 to completely finish their homes: foundation, wiring, plumbing, interior partitions, closets, and kitchen cabinets. Some spend more. Some kit manufacturers estimate two and a half times the base kit price to complete your home; some say more. You won't have a realistic idea until you've spoken with others who have already done what you want to do—and until you've *seen* what they've done for the money. *Do go see samples of the home kits you want to build.* Some manufacturers even have home-building workshops. Some actually offer a slight discount if you attend their free home-constuction courses.

Research is key ... research and sweat. But the potential savings are enormous, and so is the satisfaction.

Log Home Kits

Six years ago Gail and Paul Bendick were living in Pennsylvania, dreaming about and saving for the day when they could own their own home. By today's standards, they had married young (Gail was twenty-two; Paul was twenty-seven at the time), and they were not rich. Day after day Gail went to realtors and looked at homes. She was "getting disgusted," she said recently; everything was too expensive.

Then it began to occur to the Bendicks that maybe they ought to *build* a home. They investigated building from scratch, and they investigated building a home from one of the many kits available at the time. They felt they didn't have enough money to build a stick house; a log home kit seemed the cheapest way to do it.

They chose a modest-size white pine log home package; the 24' x 39' Chalet by **Alta Industries** of Halcottsville, New York. (The same log home kit today still retails for less than $15,000.) Though they had never built a house before, they decided to go ahead with it on land they owned in Binghamton, New York. They began in October. They hired someone to help them with the foundation and someone to help unload the logs, but aside from that, they did everything themselves. By the first of January the house was complete enough to move into. Gail estimates that beyond the kit price, the house cost them between $5,000 and $6,000 to complete.

"I have no complaints whatsoever," Gail told me. "There's no air coming through, even though we didn't calk it until the year before last." And the price was right. "I enjoy my home," Gail says, "but I don't want to live for it all my life."

The Bendicks added an electric heater, but they use mostly wood heat. Gail estimates their electric bill at about $100 every two months. "There's practically no maintenance," Gail reports. "Once in a while I vacuum the walls. My main complaint is that I have trouble reaching the cobwebs on the cathedral ceiling."

Gail's other complaint? When they first built it, crowds of people would come by to look at the house. Invariably, they wound up knocking on the door, "even on Sundays or evenings...." But, Ms. Bendick reports, now that happens only occasionally.

There is a staggering variety of log home kits available today. The thirty plus homes described in the section that follows are among the most interesting and among the best values for the money, but they're really just the tip of an iceberg several hundred strong.

A word about what log home kits contain and how much they cost: Every log home kit manufacturer seems to offer a different package of materials. Some include materials for the exterior skeleton only. Some provide interior partitions and subflooring. Some even go as far as providing roof shingles, insulation, and closet door hardware.

Even the types of logs used differ: cedar, white pine, yellow pine, jack pine, ponderosa pine. . . . The list goes on and on. Some kit manufacturers preassemble parts of the building. Some precut places for doors and windows; some don't. And some kit manufacturers have rushed to cash in on this lucrative market within the past couple years; they may not be around in three or four years, when you may need them.

I suggest you do at least three things before rushing out to buy a log home kit. First, you ought to study thoroughly the current *Log Home Guide for Builders and Buyers,* published annually by Muir Publishing Company, Ltd., Gardenvale, Quebec, Canada H9X 1BO. (It was $6, but check the current price before you send your money.) Keep in mind that this is not the most objective publication in the world; the Muirs seem to make their living and support their publication with log home kit company advertising dollars. It is, however, a good survey of the current market, and it contains articles on such subjects as insulation standards, insurance, and relevant legislation.

Second, send for as many of the brochures mentioned here and in the *Log Home Guide* as you can. It's worth the $40 or $50 to see what's available and to judge for yourself.

Third, for heaven's sake, speak with as many people as possible who have built log homes. Don't be shy. Ask the manufacturers to give you the names of log home owners in your area and *go visit them.* People are remarkably honest. Unless they're dealers themselves, they'll tell you about any problems they've had or about what they'd do differently if they had it to do all over again.

One more word about cost: the Bendicks, mentioned earlier, may have been able to build their house for just $6,000 over the kit purchase price. But it'll more than likely cost you more. Most kit companies estimate completion cost at between two to three-and-a-half times purchase price. It really depends on how much work you do yourself, on how much you contract out, and on how complete the kit was in the first place.

In any case, building a log home from a kit may be quite an undertaking, but it could save you *up to half the cost of a comparable home.* That's a lot of money.

Log Home Kits That Sell for Less than $15,000

The American, available from **Southern Log Homes,** is a small, neat country cabin, with Kentucky Cabin two-storied gable-roof line, and an 8' x 32' front porch. Constructed of hand-peeled Southern yellow pine, this shell kit has flat interior walls, which is fine if you think you'd like to Sheetrock the interior to accommodate wallpaper or wood paneling.

Southern Log Homes provides just the bare minimum: all logs for exterior walls, sixteen courses approximately 8' high; porch plates, sills, and posts; Poly-log gasket material ⅜″ x ⅝″; 10″ steel spikes, wood-frame colonial-design window units with screens; prehung exterior doors of natural wood and glass; three sets of plans; plus six hours of technical assistance. Southern Log Homes does not supply rafters, girders, joist systems, or other lumber materials, since they feel you can save money by purchasing these locally (to save on shipping costs).

This is an interesting, compact two-bedroom design for the resourceful builder. Cost: less than $7,500.

The Blackhawk by **American Log Homes, Inc.,** is a small (1,056 square feet), compact, very inexpensive two-bedroom home, which provides just about everything a single owner or small family could want—including two bedrooms, a generous-sized living room, and a price tag of less than $11,000.

The American Log Homes package includes precut 6″ dry pine or spruce logs, which supposedly require no calking (though calking is provided with each package), 6″ x 6″ corner posts and porch posts, 4″ x 6″ rafter ties, log cabin siding for exterior of box sill covering, double-hung wood-frame windows with ½″ insulating glass, removable grills and screens, prehung solid-core wood exterior doors with hardware, spikes, gasket, three sets of blueprints. The package does not include roof, ceilings, subfloor, foundation, plumbing, heating, electrical work, or interior partitions.

A nice feature of the Blackhawk is its semienclosed small front hall; it's nice, particularly in bad weather, not to have to walk directly into the living room, as one does in many log home kit designs.

The Bristol: If you're handy enough to take on a home kit that requires complete fitting and erecting on the site, the Bristol by **L. C. Andrew** of South Windham, Maine, is a tremendous value at just over $14,000. It's 24′ x 34′, has two good-sized bedrooms (10′4″ x 11′6″ and 11′4″ x 15′), a sleeping loft, and cathedral-ceilinged living room. A nice feature is its 20′ x 8′ front porch. The Bristol looks as if it would fit as nicely beside a pond in Water Mill, New York, as on a Vermont hillside. The kit is designed to accommodate a warming center chimney, and it could easily be heated by a good wood stove. L. C. Andrew home kits are constructed of Northern white cedar, and they vary from conventional log home kits in that they utilize frame construction, which lets you put additional fiberglass insulation in both ceiling and walls. It means too that if you don't favor the look of interior log walls, you can finish the inside with wood paneling or wallpaper.

The Bristol is available also as a prefabricated home kit for approximately $2,500 more. Material for their prefabricated homes include floor framing as for conventional construction. The walls are fabricated in panels with doors and windows installed. The standard windows are Andersen Permashield with insulated glass and full screens. Gables are built in sections and may include a window or a louver. In all buildings ⁵⁄₁₆″ CDX plywood and #15 felt paper have been applied to the wall and gable end studs under the siding. The panels are bored, and bolts are furnished for fastening. Rafters are precut for the prefab package. ½" CDX plywood is supplied for a single floor and roof sheathing. Included also are self-seal asphalt shingles with #15 felt paper and metal drip edge. Eave and gable trim is supplied.

Framing materials are provided for the interior partitions. In the Birstol, as in all L. C. Andrew buildings with a loft or a full second floor, material for the stairs, railing, and flooring is supplied.

Their prices include the material necessary to erect the complete exterior shell. Items *not* included would be mason supplies (for the foundation and the fireplace), plumbing, heating, and electrical work of any kind. Materials for the interior paneling, insulation, or kitchen cabinets and countertops can be furnished as options.

L. C. Andrew, Inc., has been in business since 1926. They offer a 5 percent discount when full payment accompanies your order.

The Chalet by **Alta Industries Ltd.,** comes in three different sizes and prices (24' x 35'—less than $14,000; 24' x 39'—less than $15,000; 28' x 43'—less than $17,500). Each has two bedrooms, a sleeping loft, open kitchen/living room, plus mud room and porch. Both the middle and larger sizes also have defined dining areas. This is an attractive, relatively simple design with gable roof and just a touch of gingerbread trim. Constructed of solid white pine logs, the interior is smoothly machined to avoid dust-catching interior log ledges. All Alta kits contain custom-laminated ridge beams; precut roof rafter, ceiling beams, and snow blocks; custom exterior insulated metal door with insulated glass, wood screen door and trim; insulated wood casement windows with removable screens; 12" log locking spikes; and calking. No interior partitions are included. Alta has a network of dealers who can construct as much of the package as you'd like. Of course, the more they do, the less cash you save.

Heritage Log Homes of Gatlinburg, Tennessee, produces some of the most aesthetic log home designs available. Their gambrel-roofed 1,900 square foot *Cumberland Plus,* as well as having an appealing exterior, has one of the most sensible and thoughtfully designed layouts I've seen. First of all, the living room, a generous 16'6" x 22'6", is big enough for a family to weather rainy days without becoming testy and claustrophobic. There are, in addition, two-and-a-half bathrooms—another feature that can considerably ease family life. The kitchen, 14' x 11' is large enough for comfort (and baking), and it adjoins a comparably-sized dining room, 13' x 11'. There is, in addition, a large utility area downstairs. Upstairs are three bedrooms: a master bedroom measuring 14' x 14', with its own bath and fabulous closet space, and two other bedrooms, measuring 14' x 11'6" and 14'6" x 11". These two have excellent closet space, with a full bathroom off the hall. There's also a large porch downstairs. The Cumberland Plus log and timber package sells for less than $13,000. If you estimate completion cost (doing it yourself) at about three times the log and timber package price, this still works out as an enormously good value for the money. Well worth looking into.

The Heritage Gambrel by **New England Log Homes,** is a two-storied, three-bedroom home, which is an extraordinary value at just under $15,000 for the hand-peeled log version (their Panelog®—machine-peeled, flat-log interior version is about $750 less). The standard package has an 8' dormer planned for the upstairs bathroom; it would probably make good sense to extend it to provide cross-ventilation for one of the upstairs bedrooms. But that's one of many options available, including an 8' x 16' dining or living room front extension, energy-saving insulated glass windows, family room, and two-car garage.

This home has really nice proportions, especially for the price: 14' x 24' living room, 14' x 14' dining room, plus three fair-sized upstairs bedrooms, nicely separated for a family with one to three children.

A larger, 24' x 40' version of this home is available for barely a thousand dollars more.

New England Log Homes is now offering passive solar designs, too—worth investigating.

The Ossipee by **L. C. Andrew** looks like a sophisticated North Country cedar log cabin. It's one story, warmed by a central chimney, and contains two bedrooms (11'6" x 9', 11'6" x 11'6"), which are separated by enough closets along the common walls to provide the noise proofing too often missing in a small home. Next to the 19'6" x 11'6" living room is a 20' x 8' porch, which could easily be screened or glassed in to provide an extra guest bedroom.

This is one of the handsomest inexpensive log cabin kits I've seen. Materials alone, for fitting and erecting on your site, cost under $13,000. Even prefab, the Ossipee goes for just over $15,000.

Built with frame constuction which lets you put additional fiberglass insulation in both ceiling and walls, the Ossipee would be an excellent retirement or first home.

The Ranch by **Green River Trading Co.,** is one of the more compact homes included in this chapter. At 24' x 34' it has 748 square feet of floor space, two bedrooms, a 17'5" x 11' living area, and a 14' x 11' kitchen/dining area. The basic log package for the Ranch costs way less than $7,000. It includes all exterior wall logs, including gable ends; porch posts and plates; second floor/ceiling joists, girders, posts and tie beams, porch rafters; balcony ridge posts and railings; blueprints; closed-cell polyethylene gasket material; 10" spikes and 40D nails; 15 gallons of clear wood preservative; four cartons of acrylic rubber calking compound. Offered as options for this design are a half loft, a full second floor, living room, bedroom, or full front-wall extensions into porch area, and additional length. Rounded interior logs cost 15 percent above the basic price.

Green River Trading has been in business since 1975—a relative new-comer to the log home kit business but they seem stable and settled. Their logs are uniformly milled white pine, and they use a system of interlocking, double-tongue-and-groove construction, which should further increase weather resistance.

The Richmond by **New England Log Homes** could be a hermit's back-woods retreat—or a small starter home for a couple. It would make a nice second home for retired people too.

There's no denying that it's tiny: 704 square feet, with 16′ x 16′ living room, one 11′ x 13′ bedroom, and additional 10′ x 11′ bedroom. But the Richmond is a very inexpensive kit. It comes in two types of pine log: hand-peeled or Panelog®—a machine-peeled log, which provides the owner/builder with flat interior wall surfaces resembling paneling or a flat surface that can be covered with wallboard and papered. The hand-peeled logs, at about $500 to $600 more, seem to me to be a better value for the money. This excellent kit, not so incidentally, sells for considerably less than $10,000.

The log package includes all precut wall logs; all precut gables, precut collar tie; all precut rafters; all precut hand-peeled log porch posts, plates, and sills; prehung solid-wood exterior doors (wood combination storm doors are available as an option); prehung picture window; wood double-hung windows with removable sash and grilles; ridge beam; 10′ ridge column supports; wind stops; ridge wedge; Triple-Seal System materials—foam gasket, calking, and hard-board spline (for the hand-peeled version); 10″ spikes; 5 gallons of wood preservative; blueprints; step-by-step construction guide; plus four hours of on-site technical assistance.

The Sportsman by **Bellaire Log Cabin Manufacturing Co.** is the smal-lest cabin included here. It measures only 22′ x 18′ total, but it's the perfect white cedar backwoods cabin for someone who loves to hunt, to fish, or to be alone. It's a nice solution, too, for a family with just-married youngsters or for an older relative who would appreciate some privacy.

The Sportsman is quite inexpensive: less than $6,000 for one of the most complete log home kit packages available. Even if you choose to spring for all available options, including wood floor, insulated walls, Anderson insu-lated windows, and 2″ insulated roof, the price comes to just under $10,000.

Bellaire, in business since 1945, has other interesting small, inexpensive log homes well worth considering. Particularly interesting for snow country is their A-frame model, as well as the Bellaire model with two bedrooms plus sleeping loft. Bellaire log homes tend to combine log cabin rusticity with "modern" design.

The Trapper by **Northern Products Log Homes, Inc.**, is a simple, attractive seasonal cabin, which is one of the best buys in the log home kit field. It comes in four sizes, and it ranges in price from just over $8,000 to well under $12,000. Model C is 625 square feet, with two 10'8" x 9' bedrooms, a 24' x 14'8" living, kitchen, dining area, plus 8' x 25' porch. Cost for a very complete package: just over $10,000. Model D, 725 square feet, has slightly larger bedrooms, plus a 24' x 17'8" living/kitchen area.

Northern Products Log Homes sells one of the most complete kit packages available in today's market—including everything from interior partitions to sliding-door hardware. They also offer a free design service, which can help you transform the Trapper, for example, into a year-round home, or modify any one of their interesting standard designs. Their logs—primarily Northern white pine, though they may use other local New England wood—are milled to produce a natural, rounded exterior and a flat interior, which eliminates dust and facilitates building interior partitions and hanging cabinets. Interestingly, Northern Products does not dip their logs in preservatives at the factory. They cite two reasons for this: First, "any good preservative is also poisonous, and it is both dangerous and unnecessary to preserve the *inside* of the log." Second, "a new log still has a good deal of moisture in it, and preservatives simply don't soak in well until the log has some time to age." They recommend that after the structure has been up for several months, only the outside be coated with a good preservative.

Log Home Kits That Sell for Less than $20,000

The Aspen by **L. C. Andrew** is a Swiss chalet-type 24' x 40' cedar log home, which just squeezes into the under $20,000 category. The prefab version of this kit would run about $3,500 more. The Aspen has attractive exterior details like diamond-shaped windows, small louvers, and an intricate deck—all of which give it unusual appeal. With two bedrooms (10'6" x 11'6", 14'6" x 11'6"), a 19' long x 23' wide living/kitchen/dining area, and spacious 20'6" x 24' sleeping loft, this is an ideal ski country or lakeside retreat.

The Barrington by **New England Log Homes** is a spacious 32' x 52' four-bedroom pine log home with cathedral ceiling, two porches, two baths, and as much country charm as a person can abide. It's really a lovely home, especially at the price: less than $19,000 for the hand-peeled log kit (about $900 less for the Panelog® version with flat interior walls). It's 1,760 square feet of living space, and it has an extended front and a rear dormer. A slightly smaller version, as well as four larger versions are available.

The Cape/Chalet by **Alta Industries Ltd.** is an ideal deep-woods hideaway—at less than $16,000 for the 24' x 38' version. (They have a 24' x 34' version, too.) Inside are two comfortable 11'4" x 11'9" bedrooms, one of which faces the 6' wide porch, which extends the full length of the house.

In addition to a large L-shaped living room/dining area, there's a huge sleeping loft. Exterior gables come prefabricated of tar paper and cedar shingles. Roof and porch rafters are precut Douglas fir, as are the loft beams and girder. The porch of this pretty, modest home is a particularly appealing feature: It looks like the perfect place to sit rocking as evening rolls in.

The Gambrel, Model A, by **Alta Industries Ltd.** is a lot of house for the money (less than $18,000). First of all, it's huge: two stories, 34' x 24'—with 16'8" x 23'2" living room, 12'8" x 11'6" dining room, a large kitchen with laundry area (a feature that is sadly missing from too many log home kits), three bedrooms, and two or three bathrooms. Unfortunately, the standard kit doesn't have enough upstairs windows to suit me. (The standard plan, as far as I can read it, has no window in the upstairs bathroom). But Alta, like most log home kit manufacturers, can modify the design to your specifications; I'd have a dormer added to at least one of the upstairs bedrooms, and certainly to the upstairs bath. Each would tend to lose heat during the day, but they could certainly be covered with insulating blinds or Styrofoam panels at night to keep in precious heat. Another thing that would keep the Gambrel from being my (and possibly your) ideal country home: There is no fireplace indicated in the standard plans. The Gambrel, however, has a great 34'-long front porch. Alta uses solid northern white pine logs.

The Monhegan by **L. C. Andrew** is the ideal second (or primary) home for a large family. The main floor of this 26' x 34' house contains a separate dining room, a 16"6" x 12'6" living room, kitchen, den (or bedroom), plus bath. Upstairs are three bedrooms (10'6" x 22'6"; 12'6" x 9'; and 11'8" x 11'), plus lovely closet space, and a second bath. The upstairs master bedroom is accented by a skylight, as is a front bedroom at the opposite end of the house. Included in the design is a warming center chimney, which, combined with the Monhegan's white cedar exterior and separate inwall and roof insulation, ought to make this a comfortable weatherproof home. While this is a log home, there's an up-to-date sense about its design.

The materials kit for this home is around $18,000. A prefab version is available at about $3,500 more.

The Sierra by **American Log Homes, Inc.,** looks, from the front, like a rather small home. But, like many old-fashioned American farmhouses, it's deeper and more commodious than it at first seems. The living room is rather small—15' x 15'—but a cathedral ceiling adds to a feeling of spaciousness. (If I were building this home, I'd extend the living room wall to further open up this room.) There is, however, an eat-in kitchen, plus separate 12' x 15' dining room; there's also a second small porch off the dining room, which would be a lovely place for breakfast. There are two bedrooms on the first floor, 10' x 15' and 11' x 12'. Upstairs are two additional bedrooms, 15' x 20' and 11' x 12', plus an attractive study, 8' x 12', which is open to the living room cathedral ceiling. The upstairs master bedroom features a cathedral ceiling, dormer, and a large walk-in closet. This is a very attractive home—and just under $19,000.

The Stowe by **Green Mountain Cabins, Inc.,** is one of the most attractive chalet-type log home kits on the market. The one illustrated has 24' end walls and 34' sidewalls. The gables are board and batten. The roof is conventional construction with a 10' pitch, and there is a full second deck of 2" V pine. A nicely proportioned balcony is built onto one end. A four-bedroom model with insulated windows sells for less than $11,000 for the log package; less than $16,000 for the full shell house price. Two of the upstairs bedrooms are extremely narrow (7' x 15'), but the living room has good proportion: 12' x 23'. Since the company produces only about one hundred home kits a year and uses no dealers, custom design is more usual than not. Their booklet *Designing Your Own Green Mountain Log Home,* can help you realize your own log home fantasy.

Green Mountain Cabins uses only spruce logs, never red or white pine, with custom-peeled logs that look hand-peeled. They say they use spruce because it is stonger than other woods used in log home kits, is more rot- and disease-resistant than pine, and will darken more slowly than pine.

Green Mountain will work with individuals interested in installing passive or active solar-energy systems in their homes.

Green Mountain Cabins' interiors, by the way, are among the most rustic and attractive I've seen.

Log Home Kits That Sell for Less Than $25,000

The Gloucester is **L. C. Andrew's** saltbox-design cedar log home, with windows designed to face south. As far as log home kits go, this one is palatial. Overall size is 26' x 38'. The downstairs space includes an 8'4" x 8'8" bath/laundry, 12'2" x 9' kitchen, 15'8" x 12'6" family room, 14'8" x 12'6" living room, and 12'6" x 12'6" dining room. The master bedroom (including a wall of closets) measures 12'6" x 16'6"; the other bedrooms measure 17'6" x 9'6" and 15'2" x 9'6". There is an upstairs bath as well. The design includes skylights.

The Gloucester would be as much at home in suburbia as a main residence as it would as a second home with paddock and lake on the property.

The materials kit for this fine home would cost not much more than $21,000. A prefab kit, with exterior walls sheathed, with logs installed, rafters precut, and windows and doors installed, would cost not much over $5,000 more.

The Greensboro by **Northern Products Log Homes** is a large (1,870 square feet), comfortable split-level log home designed for year-round use. It's beautifully proportioned and, like most Northern Products home kits, has excellent cross-ventilation downstairs and good storage (to this writer, important comforts). There are three bedrooms: the one on the first floor is rather small, 14' x 10', but it has a solid wall of closets. Upstairs the bedrooms are 16'6" x 17' and 13'6" x 17'. The living room, planned to accommodate a fireplace, is 13'6" x 24' long. There is only one bathroom—probably the most serious drawback of this pretty home. One other problem: Both upstairs bedrooms have windows along only one wall (it's probably hot up there during the summer); dormers might be a nice modification for this kit.

One Greensboro owner with whom we spoke, Merle Green of Milesburg, Pennsylvania, reports that, although he modified his home to include only two bedrooms and added an additional bathroom, the package came to $200 less than that of the standard kit. Mr. Green reports that he's completely satisfied with his home. (This is his second Northern Products project; he built their Penobscot model for his son.) He estimates his savings at between $20,000 to $25,000 off the price of a comparable house. Construction time, Mr. Green further reports, was just over five months.

The Hogan by **Wilderness Log Homes** combines the psychological warmth of log walls with striking contemporary design and a feeling of openness and light—something that too often is missing from log home kit design. The Hogan is hexagonal in shape, with large picture windows, which open the inside to the exterior landscape and view. It's available as a one-story model for just under $17,000 in the cedar full-log kit; but it really makes more sense, if you can afford it, to spend an additional $9,500 to add a full "basement"—and sleeping space for more guests than you may wish to accommodate. Another important addition to this home could be a porch/deck, which wraps around three sides of the house's upper story (and costs another $2,000). There *are* slightly cheaper versions of this house available, should you choose to build either with full pine logs or with pine or cedar half logs. Actually, you might want to seriously consider the half-log kits if you'd like to use this as an energy-efficient year-round home; half-log construction allows you to insert up to 9 inches of additional insulation.

Katahdin Forest Products Co.'s simple, four-bedroom *Moosehead* model can be built either of hand-peeled northern white cedar (at less than $22,000 for the complete package) or spruce (less than $20,000) for the complete kit. This is a fairly uncomplicated design, modest in appearance, but inside it has more practical, comfortable living space than most log home kits available for the money. Downstairs, there's an 18' x 11'2" kitchen/dining area, an 18' x 11'2" cathedral-ceilinged living area, one bath, plus two generous bedrooms, 15'8" x 11'2" and 17'8" x 16'8", plus plenty of storage area. There is no bathroom upstairs.

Katahdin's logs average 4½" in thickness; maximum thickness is 5½". This is not quite as thick as logs offered by many kit companies, but cedar is reputed to have better insulating properties than, for example, northern white pine.

Katahdin's complete building package contains more items than we can delineate here; it's definitely worth considering. They also market a shell package, which can cost as much as $4,000 less (a good deal, if you're friends with a local lumber dealer). Or if you're on a very tight budget but want to start construction anyway, Katahdin can provide a walls-only starter package at up to $10,000 less than the price of the complete package.

Rocky Mountain Log Homes of Hamilton, Montana, uses the "Swedish Cope" method of log home construction: Logs are selected from standing dry timber in Montana or Idaho, then machine-milled and grooved. Corner logs are notched. The logs are fitted together by a strip of insulation, then secured with spikes. Window spaces are to be cut out by you once the log walls are up. (Here's hoping you measure correctly . . . .)

Rocky Mountain doesn't name their standard models, but among the models designed for large families, *Plan RM 025* (2,920 square feet) really stands out; in fact, it's one of the most attractive and sensible plans I've seen for a three-to-four-bedroom home. First of all, one enters the house through an entry hallway—nicer, certainly, than walking right into the living room. This house is designed for comfort: There's a separate pantry and laundry room; a mud room; a kitchen (15' x 12'), large enough for someone who likes to cook; separate 16' x 12' dining room; step-down 30' x 16' living room with 32' x 10' deck outside; two 12'6" x 12'6" bedrooms; and an 11½' x 12½' den. There's one full bathroom downstairs. The upstairs belongs to Mom and Dad: 16' x 16' bedroom, full bath, 10'6" x 11' dressing room, plus a private balcony. Very nice.

Plan RM 025 is available in various log widths, ranging from 7" logs to 12" logs. Even if you choose the 12" log width, the kit cost is less (at this writing) than $21,000. Even if you spend twice as much again to finish the house, you'd be getting more house for your dollar than you might have thought possible.

Northeastern Log Homes, Inc., offers one of the more complete log home packages available; their kits include everything except foundation, basement support posts, and masonry; plumbing and heating materials; electrical materials; kitchen cabinets and counters; underlayment and carpets; nails and flashing; interior stains; roof insulation and soffit vents; and interior doorjambs. *The Rangely,* an interesting chalet-style house constructed of 6" x 8" milled eastern white pine logs and costing just over $21,000 is one of their best values for the medium-sized family. The Rangely has a particularly spacious living room, 26' x 14'3", which adjoins an open 11' x 9' dining area. One odd thing about this model: There's a 15'8" x 2'6" balcony above the first-floor deck—and no way to reach it. Silly.

The *Tisbury* by **Green Mountain Cabins, Inc.,** is a roomy, aesthetically pleasing peeled spruce log home with gambreled roof. Cost for the full shell is less than $21,000. Their log package price is under $14,000. (For full details about what the full shell package includes, write to Green Mountain Cabins for their brochure.)

Green Mountain Cabins, Inc., a member of the self-policing Log Homes Council, believes that the gambreled-roof home is the best value for the money. The Tisbury model has great flexibility, with three bedrooms and more living space, created by eliminating the partition between the den and living room or by using four bedrooms. The first-floor bathroom is very spacious, accommodating a washer and dryer and good closets. There is an impressive cathedral ceiling. The Tisbury uses Vellux® windows in the roof, full log gables, insulated glass windows, and solid pine doors.

The Willington by **Timber Log Homes** of Marlborough, Connecticut, is one of the most beautifully proportioned three-to-four bedroom gambrel-roofed log homes we've seen. The house is 24' x 40' long, with a 16' x 24' wing for the cathedral-ceilinged living room. Downstairs, in addition to the living room, the Willington has a den measuring 24' x 13', 11'9" wide x 24' long kitchen/dining area, plus a 13'4" x 10'3" guest room. Upstairs are two baths, a 12' x 20' master bedroom, plus two other bedrooms, measuring 12' x 12'4" and 12' x 18'10". There's an additional full bath downstairs.

At just under $21,000, the Willington kit is constructed of uniformly milled northern white pine logs, which are rounded inside and out and flattened top and bottom; these measure 8" thick and 6" high. The package comes with 4" x 6" porch rafters plus 6" x 8" post, sill, and plate; double-hung, single-glazed windows; 1¾" fir doors in special spline grooved frames; 6" x 6" hewn ceiling joist system over first floor; 6" x 6" hewn cathedral rafters and 6" x 6" wall ties; spline, 10" spikes, colored window flashing, sealant, joist brackets, two sets of blueprints, and construction manual.

Log Home Kits Costing More Than $25,000

The Abraham Lincoln by **Liberty Log Homes** of Centreville, Alabama, has just about one thing in common with Honest Abe's home: It's built of logs. If you told Mr. Lincoln about this home, he would probably have thought you were lying: It's 2,690 square feet, and in kit form it sells for over $26,000 before energy-saving (money-costing) options. Actually, it's a great-looking 7"-log pine house, with gambrel roof and traditional T-shape design. You'll have to send for the floor plans yourself to appreciate this one. Downstairs, the living room (Liberty Log calls it the great room) measures 14' x 22'5", the kitchen is 8' x 11', dining area is 11'5" x 13'. A 6' x 28'4" porch runs along one wall. There's also a downstairs bedroom, 11' x 16', with very good closet space. The upper floor has four bedrooms, the largest of which is 13′5″ x 17″, with two large walk-in closets. Unfortunately, there's only one bathroom upstairs, but there's undoubtedly a way to modify the layout to accommodate one more; one bathroom shared by the occupants of four bedrooms must be rather like a college dorm.

Many options, such as hurricane safety cables that lash the house to the foundation, are available. If termites are a problem in your area, you might consider another option: kiln-dried logs treated with a special preservative.

Apparently, owner-construction is the exception rather than the rule with Liberty Log Homes—so I'd investigate.

The Arundel by **L. C. Andrew** has a gambrel roof, attached two-car garage, covered entry porch, and front deck. The L-shaped kitchen is nicely situated between the family room and the dining room. The downstairs of this 24′ x 34′ home kit is designed for a 23′4″ x 12′6″ living room—one of the largest available in a log home kit—a nice 12′ x 6′ porch, and an 8′ x 32′ deck. Upstairs bedrooms are 11′6″ x 20′6″, 11′6″ x 11′, and 8′8″ x 12′. There is, of course, a bath on each floor.

This is a phenomenal suburban or country home, and it costs less than $27,000 for the materials kit and less than $33,000 prefab.

The Hocking by **Bellaire Log Cabin Manufacturing Co.** of Bellaire, Michigan, is the kind of house one could settle into and stay in for the rest of one's life. First of all, with its vertical white cedar shell and 32′ front porch, it looks like a secure, cozy farmhouse. Inside, it has two full bedrooms with cathedral ceilings, 13′ x 17′9″, and 13′ x 15′, plus upstairs sleeping loft (12′ x 18′) overlooking and tucked under the living room kitchen/dining area and utility room, not directly over the bedrooms; your guests are not compelled to listen to private conversations. The utility room/pantry is one of the largest we've seen in a log cabin kit home: 6′9″ x 15′. The country kitchen and dining area open onto (but are distinct from) the nicely proportioned living room, 23′9″ x 17′9″. There are two bathrooms, one of which adjoins the master bedroom.

This house is a darn good value. Assuming you wanted every option, including wood floor, insulated walls, Andersen insulated windows, and 2″ insulated roof, the price would be just under $34,000.

Wilderness Log Homes of Plymouth, Wisconsin, markets an interesting log home kit for people with a large family and a fair-sized bank account: *The Nantucket*. The standard Nantucket has four bedrooms and two full bathrooms upstairs, plus a mud room, powder room, smallish kitchen, 19′4″ x 13′8″ family room, 13′ x 23′4″ living room, and 10′2″ x 11′3″ den downstairs. As the plans now exist, there's no dining room—an important room in a house this size with only a 10′6″ x 8′ kitchen. Wilderness Log Homes will, of course, modify the kit for you if you so desire.

The Nantucket kit is quite complete (write to Wilderness Log Homes for full details); it is offered in either pine or cedar—both in half-log kits or full-log kits. The full-log wall would naturally provide its own insulation; with a half-log kit, you could insert up to 10 inches of additional insulation in each wall, plus use whatever interior finish you wish—even additional half logs, available at extra cost for this purpose. The basic prices for this large home vary quite a bit: A pine half-log kit would run just over $25,000; the cedar full-log kit could run a good $35,000 or more, especially if you decide to add cedar shake shingles, a porch, dormer, or a garage. It adds up, but it certainly makes more sense than going out and buying some of the *dreck* available in today's housing market for as much as $145,000.

Northern Products Log Homes' *Somerset II* is a spacious 1,890 square foot two-storied, two-bath, three-bedroom home with flat interior log surfaces. The upstairs bedrooms—one 13'9" x 22'3" and the other 12'9" x 22'3"—are larger than some studio apartments in Manhattan. With its 13'9" x 26" living/dining area, and 35' front porch, this is a home that provides unusual space, comfort, and privacy for a fair-sized family. As with all of its designs, Northern Products Log Homes will provide a free design service for the purchaser who wishes to further modify this model. Cost is just over $25,000.

The Virginian, offered by **Boyne Falls Log Homes,** has one of the higher price tags of any log home kit listed in this book. But, at $42,032 for Model #2109, 1,456 square feet, it's actually a good value. First of all, Boyne Falls Log Homes uses top-quality materials: northern white cedar logs (cedar buildings once used by French fur trappers and Jesuit missionaries are still standing in parts of Canada and Upper Michigan after two centuries) and oak flooring throughout. Consistent with Boyne Falls' quality materials, all bark is hand-peeled from the logs, which produces surface patterns that add to both the *cachet* and resale value of the house. Unlike most log home companies, they offer three building methods: horizontal, vertical, or sill and post. In addition, as much as possible of each home is preassembled at their plant; this makes construction that much easier and faster. For example, homes built using the sill-and-post system are shipped with exterior walls 75 percent assembled.

A Boyne Falls kit comes with just about everything, including floor joists, floor insulation, subflooring, finish flooring, outside walls, partition walls, ceilings, ties, rafters, timber trusses, log purlins, roof plywood sheathing, roof insulation, roof shingles, interior doors (in the Virginian, these are handmade cedar-plank doors), wood double-glazed windows, screens, coated nails, door and window hardware, and exterior doors, and trim. The only building items not included are foundation, erection, wiring, plumbing, kitchen cabinets, heating, and air-conditioning system.

If you hire a builder to construct this house, you ought to budget between $68,000 to $70,000 without the cost of land. If you do it yourself, hiring out the necessary masonry work, you ought to be able to realize savings of between $10,000 to $12,000.

The Zion by **Alpine Log Homes, Inc.,** of Victor, Montana, is one of the largest and most expensive log homes we've seen. But if you long for a Teddy Roosevelt-size country retreat, consider this one . . . and save $25,000 to $30,000 off the price of a comparable preconstructed home.

For just under $35,000, Alpine Log Homes provides the logwork only: exterior walls, interior log partitions, ceiling beams, gables (if you want them), roof beams, and floor joists on the second floor. All logs used are dry when cut and are then hand-peeled. Logs average 8½″ thick.

The Zion has 1,764 square feet on its main floor, 308 square feet on its second floor, 132 square feet of exterior balconies, plus 264 square feet of porches. The two-car garage measures 21′4″ x 23′4″. This amazing house has four bedrooms, all rather small: downstairs bedrooms average 11½′ square; the upstairs master bedroom is 13′ x 13′6″ (there's a 6′ deck off the master bedroom). What it does have is quite a large living room (21′4″ x 16′8″) and a very nice library, 21′4″ x 12′6″. The connecting kitchen and dining room are, again, larger than many studio apartments. Despite its size, this looks like a very cozy house—a marvelous place to entertain both family and friends.

Home Kits Utilizing
Post-and-Beam Construction

Bow House, Inc., of Bolton, Massachusetts, offers some of the lovliest traditional Cape Cod style architectural packages on the market. Each comes with bent laminated roof beams, creating what is known as the ship's bottom roof line—an extremely appealing alternative to gambrels, dormers, and mansards.

Their *¾ Cape,* ranging in price from just under $20,000 to just under $22,000 (square footage can range between 1,790 square feet to 2,070 square feet), is just one of several models offered by them, and modified or redrawn to suit individual needs, site conditions, and budgets. (Least expensive is their *¼ Cape,* a small house with two bedrooms, 1,182 square feet, which retails for just under $14,500.)

A standard Bow House architectural package includes roof rafters, gable rake boards, attic ventilator, handmade exterior doors, Boston-style twelve-panes over-twelve-panes windows, front window shutters with hardware, white cedar roof shingles, exterior trim, cedar siding, pine interior trim, and 12″ or wider #2 pine floors. Also, stops and casings for surface hinges. Plus: stairs, including pine treads, skirts, risers, railings, banisters, newels; #2 pine fireplace mantel; fireplace crane and eyes; masonry for snow cap; edge-beaded base molding; copper rain diverters; exterior and interior door hardware;

window pins; Parsons cupboard door; interior stain in four shades; metal strapping; Scotch truss nails; and insect screening. A very remarkable package indeed. Optional items (well worth considering) include things like old-fashioned-cut flooring nails, georgeous hand-forged hardware, and ballast brick.

Shelter-Kit, Inc., of Tilton, New Hampshire, produces three of the least-expensive kit house choices. Since each kit is modularized, adding to the structure as time and money permit should present no major problems.

Unit One, measuring 12' x 12' and needing only a poured-concrete pier for each of its six posts, sells for less than $3,000. Since it has nonload bearing walls, expanding it is relatively easy. The Unit One with a deck and outdoor toilet is a nice solution for the artist or writer in your family—or for anyone requiring a very simple, wood stove-heated cabin in the woods. Unit One can be expanded into as much as a three-bedroom home (with inside toilet), and it costs less than $13,000 for a very complete kit, which even comes with its own tools. No access road is necessary to build this home; components are tied into hundred-pound loads in case they are to be walked into a deeply wooded site.

Shelter-Kit also produces two other models, the *Lofthouse,* a 16' x 16' one-bedroom home, which sells for less than $5,000, and *Lofthouse 20,* measuring 20' x 24', an excellent two-bedroom model retailing for less than $8,000. Lofthouse 20 can be constructed in about two weeks by two inexperienced builders.

All Shelter-Kit homes can be built to accommodate a roof-mounted solar connector for domestic hot water.

In northwest North Carolina, there's a progression I saw among young farm couples: When they were first married, the couple would move into a trailer home, which would be set on land they had inherited from their daddy or grandaddy. Then, as soon as they had saved a little money (to earn extra cash, the wives would work at Dr. Graybar's pipe factory or at the pants factory), relatives and neighbors would pitch in their labor, and work would begin on a solid, secure, well built home, which invariably looked more like a suburban tract house than a hill-country farm dwelling. Many of the house kit models available from **Miles Homes** of Minneapolis remind me of those comfortable Jefferson County homes.

Their *Spokane* model, for example, is a three-bedroom ranch home with two baths, small family/dining room, 14'9" x 11'6" living room (other models have larger living rooms), enclosed back porch, and attached two-car garage. The $30,500 price includes everything but plumbing, heating, wiring, and finished flooring. Even interior trim and kitchen cabinets are included in the price.

The *Sierra Madre,* a four-bedroom model, with 11'6" x 23'4" living room, more closely resembles the chalet-type homes mentioned in the log home section of this chapter; it's a very attractive home. About $32,300.

Miles Homes offers a financing plan, which is available from no other **kit** home manufacturer I've seen: In many cases, no down payment is necessary, and Miles will hold the mortgage (and their mortgages have *very* low monthly payments).

Sawmill River Post & Beam, Inc., sells some of the most attractive home-building packages on the market. Square footage ranges from 1,086 square feet to 2,496 square feet, and their prices range from just over $17,000 to just over $33,000. Their basic package price includes the complete timber frame and all frame fastenings; all wood to construct the exterior wall system; all wood to construct the roof system; 1½″ pine decking for floors; all windows and exterior doors. Most important, Sawmill River designs *feel* good; they're light inside, with white walls comfortably defined and broken by attractive interior wood framing and beams.

One of their most interesting models for the single person or young (or retired) couple, is their 1,086-square-foot *Series 1100*. This marvelous home, retailing for just over $17,000, has a 12′ x 20′ living room with cathedral ceiling and unusual high window bank, 8′ x 10′ dining room, kitchen, bath, and 10′ x 12′ bedroom. Upstairs is a 14′ x 20′ loft with skylight.

Timber Kit homes were designed by **Blue/Sun Ltd.,** a pioneer in the use of solar energy in the building design field. These attractive homes have a minimum of openings on the north to reduce the effect of winter winds, and a maximum of glass areas to pick up the winter sun's warmth on the southern exposure. Overhangs shade the south-facing windows from the higher summer sun. Prices seem reasonable. One of their homes is 1620 square feet and has three bedrooms, an upstairs den, two bathrooms, and a living/dining area. Kit price is under $22,000.

Barn conversions were never cheap, but with today's inflated prices, the cost of land, a barn, and restoration and winterizing costs, you'd have to be pretty affluent even to think about that spacious yet cozy life-style. But now **Yankee Barn Homes, Inc.,** of Grantham, New Hampshire, offers a chance to achieve the felicitous comfort and space of barn living for considerably less cash than you might have supposed.

Yankee Barn rescues original yellow pine beams from old New England mills and other sturdy but unused structures, treats them with wood preservative, and incorporates them into some of the most attractive four- and five-bedroom kit homes available.

To quote *Professional Builder* magazine, "The framework is constructed in the same manner as the old and original Yankee Barns. Nearly four-inch thick flooring is laid over a four-by-fourteen timber girt system and rough sanded before the framework erection. All the framework post and beams (6 x 6, 6 x 10) are precut, numbered and pre-stained. Besides using old timbers, Hanslin Associates [Yankee Barn Homes] go one step further and use old-time cut nails and spikes. Exterior panels are glued and machine fastened, sandwich panels fully insulated with the windows installed. The exterior faces are ⅝″ grooved, rough sawn plywood giving the old plank barn effect. The roof is constructed of four-foot by sixteen-foot interlocking panels, glued and machined in the plant."

Yankee Barn Homes range in price from about $40,000 completed do-it-yourself cost, to about $97,000.

Yankee Barns have been featured in magazines like *House & Garden* and *1001 Decorating Ideas*—and for good reason: They're *very* sturdy, comfortable, and a pleasure to look at.

Kits for Dome Homes, Round Homes, and Tipis

Cathedralite Domes of Aptos, California, markets several geodesic home kits, which range in sleeping capacity from one bedroom to five or six bedrooms. The geodesic dome is made by joining triangular space frames to create a circular building. All parts of the dome are straight, and no curved surfaces are used. Triangles are formed of ½″ plywood skin, glued and stapled to kiln-dried fir spars to form a space frame. Frames are prefabricated at their factory and shipped ready to bolt together. The average space frame weighs approximately 75 pounds.

The kit consists of thirty-eight to sixty preassembled wooden space frames and all necessary bolts, nuts, washers, canopies, and straps to fit the triangles together to form the shell of the structure.

All types of heating can be used, including solar panels. According to the manufacturer, the dome shape costs less to heat and cool. In the box-shaped house, they say, air tends to get caught in corners, whereas, in the dome, it is free to circulate. This results in less fuel consumption.

Erection time, using four to five workers, should take no more than two days.

The prices are as interesting as the structures: as low as well under $5,000 for the Rio, 426 square feet, plus loft area; around $20,000 for the 35′ Vista Dome with 1,745 square feet.

Options, at reasonable prices, include operable skylights, extensions, and riser walls.

If you are at all interested in living in one of Buckminster Fuller's dream houses, do send for the Cathedralite catalogue—you'll drool.

Earthworks of North Ferrisburg, Vermont, is run by a group of dedicated craftspeople, who produce a fine tipi kit for people with good sewing skills. The basic design is Sioux, with Cheyenne smoke flap extensions and a narrower doorway than usual to make it tighter and drier in a storm.

They use 100 percent cotton natural-color canvas, which is water-repellant, mildew-resistant, and preshrunk. Canvas comes in two weights, but they recommend the sturdier 12.63 ounces per square yard.

Tipi kits are available in 18', 20', and 22' sizes; this measurement refers to the diagonal height in the front and the approximate floor diameter. The 20' size is approximately 12' across at the 6' height.

Kits include precut and marked materials, thread, rope for tie loops, hemming tape, and instructions. A standard home sewing machine can be used for this project. Prices range from about $250 to $350 for the 12.63 oz. tipi kits, $50 to $75 less than preassembled prices.

Tipi liner kits are also available; liners are recommended as insulation against both cold and hot weather. Liner kits cost about $100 to $125, saving you another $25 to $30.

Geodesic Domes, Inc., of Davison, Michigan, markets handsome dome home kits constructed of prefabricated triangular sections. Their shell kits are very reasonably priced—less than $4,000 for the 26' Alpine model, under $9,000 for the 45' Omega model. Risers, extensions, dormers, and openings are available at extra cost. Commercial and church domes are available as well.

Geodesic Domes has an interesting discount plan: Because dome homes tend to generate a lot of local interest and press, if you're the first in your area to put up one of their dome homes, they'll give you a 5 percent discount—and an additional 5 percent of the selling price of any dome homes you can talk your neighbors into buying.

Meyer Round Structures sells prefabricated circular homes available in 30' diameters (733 square feet), as well as much larger sizes. They claim that the Meyer Round is the only completely circular design (prefab or kit) in existence, owing to the curved wall-door-windowsill and heater system.

There are one- to five-bedroom models, each designed around a central core, with rooms radiating out from the core.

The floor is a radial beam system with a precut wedged tongue-and-groove sub-floor. Exterior curved walls are sectionalized 4' x 8 wood-rib systems with a variety of exterior plywood finishes available. Gypsum-board interior is installed in the field. 3½" R11 factor insulation is installed in the field as well.

Interior curved walls are sectionalized wood systems with gypsum board on both sides.

Window frames are curved bronze or anodized aluminum with curved acrylic "glass," which can be tinted. The roof timber beams are radial and tapered; the taper creates a slope to the central core. A special snow-load roof is available.

These are extraordinary-looking homes, probably best suited for your property with a view.

Monterey Domes sells geodesic home shell kits, which come to you completely precut, predrilled, and color-coded. Prices seem quite good, with their Alpine Series, for example, going for less than $12,000 for the 45' model. All kinds of options are available at extra cost: dormer packages, skylight packages, opening extensions, base walls, Monterey Shake synthetic siding, foam insulation, and solar collectors.

When they opened their office in Allentown, Pennsylvania, they sent me an offer of $500 credit toward shipping. It might pay to get on their mailing list and see if they have any special offers in your region.

Nomadics of Bend, Oregon, is a low-key operation, which uses a design based on that described in *The Indian Tipi* by Reginald and Gladys Laubin, Sioux Indians. Their sew-it-yourself tipi kits come with canvas, all nylon for peg loops, Dacron thread, reinforcing pieces, and thirty pages of clear and precise instructions. Covers and liners are available in sizes from 14' to 26', and in 10-ounce or 13-ounce marine-finished canvas, with or without flame-resistant treatment. The 14' tipi kit costs $223; the preassembled prices is $248. The 26' tipi kit costs $555; the preassembled price would be $650. You'll want a liner for each as well. The 14' liner, 6' or 9' high, costs $90 in kit form, $100 preassembled. The 26' liner kit costs $298; $343 preassembled.

Polydome Inc., of El Cajon, California, offers a variation on the standard triangle-based dome home kits. The Polydome is a ready-to-assemble wood dome, which consists of twenty-four triangular-shaped space frame panels and three trapezoids bolted together.

In some dome designs, the framework is put together and the door openings cut out, and part of the structure removed. Polydome, however, has standard openings designed into the structure. You can put low-cost sliding glass/door/window combinations into any of the openings without wasting time or expense.

Solar Home Kits and
Companies Manufacturing Solar Panel Kits

Sadly, most home kit manufacturers have not developed plans and packages for the growing number of customers who want to stretch their budget by living in solar-powered homes. A few, like Shelter-Kit and Timber Kit, have from the start designed homes with passive solar systems in mind. It seems to me that some, like Beaver Log Homes, have designs that could be adapted for use with solar panels.

I hope that five years from now, the listing that follows will be laughably inadequate; right not, it's about all that's available.

Beaver Log Homes of Claremore, Oklahoma, has one model, the *Cascade,* which cries out for solar panels. Unfortunately, few of their customers seem to be interested in this modification. I did speak with the manufacturers, however, and it is possible.

Contemporary Structures, Inc., of Ludlow, Massachusetts, plans *all* of their handsome post-and-beam home kits to accommodate solar systems. That is, pipes and ducts are installed behind the Sheetrock, making future solar installation easy, clean, convenient and economical.

All of their designs make use of as much passive solar heating as practical. Passive solar systems use the house as storage, and windows and other glass elements as collectors.

They state in their literature that solar domestic hot-water heating systems are the most cost effective of the active solar systems. They can design into your structure closed-loop or drain-back solar heating systems for domestic hot water. Solar space heating can also be incorporated into their designs, with roof or ground-mount solar systems. These solar space heating systems can be air or hydronic with properly sized backup systems for energy efficiency.

Prices will depend upon the shape and size home you want. A rough guideline would be: $4.50 to $5.00 per square-foot floor area for the framing kit; $7 to $8 per square-foot floor area for the roof system; and $3.00 to $3.50 per square foot for the walls, including inside surface, 3 inches of insulation, and outside siding.

Heritage Log Homes of Gatlinburg, Tennessee, offers an exciting log home design ideal for passive solar energy components: the Foxfire model, retailing for less than $12,000. This two- to three-bedroom home has more than 1,000 square feet of living space; it combines the rusticity of log house living with energy self-sufficiency.

Monterey Domes, Inc., of Riverside, California, offers a system of solar collectors to complement their geodesic dome home designs. They use flat plate collectors, which will generate heat even from diffused light. The collectors are permanently located in the six triangles that form the highest hexagon in the dome. A glycol/water solution is used as the heat-transfer medium. A number of different types of heat storage and exchanger devices can be used in conjunction with the solar collectors to complete the system. Depending on local conditions, the solar collectors will provide most of the energy necessary to produce hot water and space heat for the dome home for which it is designed.

Shelter-Kit's modular house, Unit One, is "the perfect shape for solar heating. Virtually all introductory handbooks and courses on the subject use illustrations of buildings identical to Unit One to explain passive solar heating fundamentals." So reads the introductory paragraph of Shelter-Kit's informative flyer *Passive Solar Heating for Shelter-Kit Homes,* prepared by Engineered Systems, Inc., a solar engineering firm of Hampton, New Hampshire. You ought to send for a copy.

Clearly, Shelter-Kit is one of the leaders in the solar home kit field. Their new Lofthouse design can also accommodate the roof-mounted assemblies of solar-heated domestic hot-water systems.

The **Suntree Solar Company** manufactures two solar-collector kits. Their Suntree Solar Type "A" Domestic Collector Kit consists of an assembly drawing; one copper collector plate (34″ x 74″); one piece of fiberglass-reinforced glazing material (34″ x 76″); two precut side rails, predrilled for assembly, treated and painted black; one precut center glazing support; and ten wood screws to fasten the wooden frame rails together. Considerably less than $200 each.

Their Solar Type "B" Kit consists of all the items above, plus a tempered masonite back cover, a tube of GE1200 silicone, and an aluminum angle-trim set (¾″ x ¾″). The kit costs $65 more than the "A".

Do write to them for more information.

Timber Kit of Amherst, Massachusetts, specializes in post-and-beam ready-for-solar homes. Each Timber Kit is designed to accept an active solar system or any conventional heating system. Solar collectors can be installed either during construction or at a later date for space heating and/or domestic hot water.

Yellowstone Log Homes of Rigby, Idaho, has one model, the 900-square-foot Alpine, which clearly could be adapted for use with solar panels. For more information, write to them directly.

Greenhouses, Storage Sheds, Gazebos, and Other Kits for Your Home

Greenhouses

Four Seasons Solar Products Corp. has single-, double-, and triple-glazed lean-to and freestanding greenhouses, which you can install yourself (while qualifying for a solar-energy property tax credit, to boot). Their System I GE Lexan® double-glazed greenhouse needs no foundation, which facilitates installation by the home craftsperson; these are excellent for growing plants at 50 percent the cost of conventional greenhouses. If you'd like to add an extra room and use the greenhouse as a solar connector, they recommend their System II triple-glazed models with foundation. Prices range from around $1,000 for the smallest lean-to to around $5,000 for a solar health spa built to accommodate sauna and hot tub.

J. A. Nearing Co.'s *JANCO* greenhouses seem to be among the easiest to erect. Each aluminum part is precut to size, marked and identified to correspond with a set of blueprints for each model. Each lite of glass is precut to size and identified to correspond with the plans. Frankly, I'd be drawn to the JANCO models because one doesn't have to be a mechanical genius to erect them.

JANCO has a full range of lean-to and freestanding models. To me, however, the most interesting is their easily installed Window Garden greenhouse, a simple five-panel contraption that sits on the outside window ledge, turning a city co-op into a country garden. Cost: $190 to $235, depending upon the size of your window. A warning: Before ordering your window greenhouse, find out if your landlord or co-op will permit its installation.

Peter Reimuller greenhouses are constructed of acrylic panels and redwood. Only one model has the fancy curved lines of some other greenhouse companies, but neither do they have the prices. Of particular interest is his Sun Dome II model, a 15' diameter geodesic dome, which is exceptionally easy to construct. $1,100.

Texas Greenhouse Co., Inc. has some interesting, relatively inexpensive redwood-and-fiberglass or redwood-and-glass greenhouses. Since their range is too extensive to describe here, you may as well send for their attractive, lucid catalogue. You'll enjoy it. My own favorite of theirs is the Oasis model. It's not exactly pretty, but it's very strong and easily erected. Designed and tested by the Virginia Polytechnic Institute, it is constructed of 5 ounce opaque fiberglass, and it can stand up to strong winds and weather. It's pretty inexpensive, too: $625.

Turner Greenhouses has been in business almost twenty-five years, specializing in quality greenhouses at reasonable prices (about $900 to $2,500). Their greenhouses need no costly foundation and are relatively easy to erect. Interestingly, you can extend these greenhouses as your green thumb begins to dominate your life, as it may.

Outbuildings

Bow House, Inc., of Bolton, Massachusetts, the excellent producer of post-and-beam home kits, recently introduced a new gazebo-type building called the Belvedeary. This charming structure measures 10½' inside and has a plate height of 8'. The curved roof rafter adds a touch of nostalgia. There are at present five versions: divided light windows, screen, lattice, louvers, and open rail. All except the open rail have a solid lower panel. The screen and glass panels are interchangeable.

All materials required are supplied with the kit, with the exception of deck materials. All parts of the kit are precut, with the exception of the roofing boards. The kit is designed to "bolt" together with lag screws. Bow House estimates that the frame can be erected in two hours. The white cedar roof should take one person about two days. The glass version costs over $3,000; all other versions cost quite a bit less.

Jer Manufacturing, Inc., of Coopersville, Michigan, markets some attractive kits for small barns or storage sheds. They call them Kit Barns. They never did answer my inquiry, but I've heard good things about the company.

Sears, Roebuck & Co. has several attractive storage building kits you might consider if your lawn equipment and children's hobbies have forced your car out of the garage. Their 8' x 8' wood-storage building kit, for example, has a hot-dipped, galvanized steel frame with prenumbered and predrilled parts for easy assembly. The kit includes precut exterior grade, ⅜" plywood panels and pine trim boards. Complete hardware package. There's not even any need to paint the building; it's already been done (barn red, with white trim). The 8' x 8' kit retails at less than $500. It's just one of several fine storage building kits they carry.

Stairs

American General Products' Studio Stairs® are very sturdy spiral staircases of whatever dimensions and with whatever detailing you require. All of their spiral stairs are shipped knocked down and, with the exception of the all-wood design, are prefinished. Their Studio Stair S-360, with wrought-iron trim, looks pretty ugly to me, but their S-360 all-wood design is magnificent—totally constructed of oak.

The Iron Shop® produces the best-known spiral staircase kit; you've undoubtedly seen it advertised in the back of *House & Garden* and *House Beautiful* magazines. What you might *not* have known is that the stairs can be assembled either left-hand or right-hand up—a boon for lefties. Another thing you might not have known is that these kits are relatively inexpensive—from $375 to $575 per kit, a lot less than a preassembled staircase. The Iron Shop® also produces nonstandard-size kits.

Mylen Industries, Inc., manufactures spiral staircase kits starting at $295. As does the Iron Shop, Mylen designs their stairs for left-hand or right-hand rotation. They have all kinds of options: oak handrails, fancy wrought-iron detailing, safety diamond-plate tread. They'll also sell you kits for spiral fire escapes.

Mylen also produces kits for open-riser straight stairs—excellent for the *klutzes* in your family (like me) who invariably fall down spiral stairs.

Storm Windows, a Stove, a Weather Vane, and a Gaslight Conversion Kit

Bay Country Woodcrafts, Inc., sells an inexpensive (around $15), very dashing white pine Flying Duck Weather Vane kit to tell you which way the wind blows. You can install it atop a fence post or in any breezy location. There are two ways of finishing the kit: You can either stain it or paint it in mallardlike colors. Personally, I prefer the painted version.

Elgar Products, Inc., of Beachwood, Ohio, markets an interesting *do-it-yourself Therma Frame® Storm Window kit* through such hardware dealers as Ace Hardware, American (Servistar), True Value Hardware, Blue Grass Hardware, HWI Hardware, Our Own Hardware, United, and S & T Hardware. If your dealer doesn't carry it, he or she can order it for you by calling Elgar's toll-free order number: (800) 321-4970. Therma Frame, using all vinyl construction, is easy to cut, assemble, and install on either the outside or inside of your windows. The system uses standard acrylic or glass panels, and it can be painted or stained.

Fisher's Products, Inc., of Conifer, Colorado, will sell you, for less than $50, an upright *Glass Door Barrel Stove kit.* You supply the barrel and stovepipe; they supply a 64-square-inch Pyrex®-glass door assembly, four leg assemblies, templates, and parts to fit the steel drum of the capacity you choose. They also offer (for more money) a kit—the Fireball No. 78—that will produce a horizontal stove with very attractive glass and heavy cast-iron door. Options include firebrick. If you can't afford a Jôtul, you might try one of these.

In-Sider® Storm Windows by **Plaskolite** of Columbus, Ohio, fit *inside* your windows, further cutting heat loss, even if you already have outside storm windows. They claim, in fact, that In-Siders can save up to 21 percent on your heating bill. In-Siders are clear, rigid plastic, which fit almost any window, whether casement, slider, or double-hung. You can get them for patio doors, too, as well as mobile-home windows. In-Siders recently were being sold through Montgomery Ward, Sears, Ace Hardware, True Value, Ben Franklin, K-Mart, American Hardware, and other hardware stores. If you can't find these kits near where you live, write to Plaskolite, and they'll tell you where you can get them.

Tyzall®, of Glen Head, New York, sells *"weather window"* instant *screen* and *frame kits,* and clear vinyl *window insulator kits.* The inside storm-window strips can be used with vinyl sheet, polyethylene sheet, or other soft materials. The same channel frames can be used with tinted vinyl sheet or other soft materials to add extra protection against sun-induced fading and scorching and to cut down on air-conditioning bills. Naturally, your "weather window" kits are eligible for federal tax credit. These kits are sold through local hardware stores. They are certainly the easiest-to-assemble inside storm-window kits I've seen. If you can't locate them, contact the manufacturer.

The 1978 Energy Act imposed a ban on the burning of natural gas for outdoor lighting. Local gas companies are required to turn off all gaslights by January 1, 1982. But **Yardlighting Systems, Inc.,** of St. Paul, Minnesota, has developed an attractive and practical *gaslight conversion kit.* The kit comes with a decorative 115-volt 15- and 25-watt two-bulb fixture, which mounts directly onto the existing shaft of any double mantle gaslight. The *Re-lite kit,* as it's called, has been recommended to their customers by three Minnesota gas companies. Yardlighting Systems claims that your energy savings will pay for the installation within two years.

A note about hot tub and sauna kits: There are several hot tub and sauna units being advertised as kits. After speaking with dealers and with Marty Sylvester, who bought one of the hot tub kits to install in his house in East Hampton, New York, I have to say that these "kits" are more trouble for the do-it-yourselfer than any possible savings are worth. If you're a plumber or if you have installed several hot tubs, you may be in good shape buying one of these kits and doing your own installation; otherwise, I'd be very wary of them.

6

Toys

Dolls, Doll Clothing, and Stuffed Animals

Charing Cross Kits has terrific 17″ *boy and girl rag doll kits* that come with either brown or pink skin colors. Kitty, the girl doll, has a charming, smiling face, and comes complete with an exquisitely printed cotton dress, striped dungarees, printed peasant blouse, floral design knickers, and a little print pocketbook. The clothing will fit any other 17″ doll. The kit also includes washable, good-quality polyester filling, thread, binding, and tiny press studs. An incredible value at $13.50. You may be able to find a store-bought rag doll for about a dollar more, but these usually have neither the charm nor changes of clothing of the Charing Cross dolls.

Kit, the boy doll, comes with striped trousers, plaid shirt, a jaunty American Indian-looking vest, a hat, bookbag, and marvelous pajamas printed with stars and owls. Also $13.50. Most of the clothing can, of course, be worn by either the girl or boy doll.

Charing Cross has additional sets of *clothing kits* for 17″ dolls, one of which includes, for example, a very pretty sundress printed with apples, a skirt and sleeveless dress with strawberry design, a sun hat, shorts and shirt, a nightdress and kimono—all for $9.95. Another terrific value.

If your child would like bedding for his or her girl doll, Charing Cross has that too: A kit for a fabulous stuffed quilt, pillow, printed sheet, and very pretty nightgown sells for less than $13.

Cross Patch Quilting Center of Garrison, New York, has a very charming and funny 26" calico *Mother Goose kit* with white calico body, red calico beak and webbed feet, and blue calico bonnet. About $15. A similar hand-crafted toy would cost at least $10 more.

The Enchanted Doll House always has a few excellent doll or stuffed-toy kits in their catalogue. Since these change from year to year, check the current catalogue before ordering. At the time of this writing they have several *antique replica doll kits by Judy Mager and Linda Sharp.* Judy Mager's *Byelo* doll kits come with finished, assembled, hand-painted shoulder plate, swivel head, blue eyes, wig, shoes, stockings, and stuffing. Sizes range from 9" to 20", and prices range from under $25 to just under $35. Preassembled, the dolls cost about twice the price. Linda Sharp's antique replicas include a 14¼" Simon Halbig, in cream satin, under $35—very pretty indeed. The Enchanted Doll House also carries four doll kits from *Little Women,* including bisque head, arms, legs, and fabric and instructions for a 15" doll. A very good buy at about $10 each.

Eva Mae Doll Company has a very wide selection of *antique reproduction doll kits,* plus marvelous kits for their *original designs.* Reproduction kits include one for a Pouty doll, which is, to my mind, one of the most beautiful dolls ever made. The kit is available in 12" china for under $35 in kit form—hundreds of dollars less than the real antique and sure to make up into one of the nicest gifts you can give any little girl who loves dolls. Their kits include head, arms, legs, plus patterns and instructions for making the body and clothing.

Eva Mae Doll Company's best original kit is an exquisite 18" bisque doll, which represents a ninety-year-old friend of their family. A most unusual doll, surely a future collectible. The kit sells for $75—$70 less than the finished doll.

The **Mark Farmer Company** has *dozens of doll kits,* including First Lady doll kits and *bisque, porcelain, and china antique reproductions.* They offer some original kits as well. They have, in fact, so many beautiful doll kits that it's almost impossible to choose one or two to feature. Among the prettiest, I think, is their doll kit called Prudence. She is 15" tall and has a very pleasant, delicate china face, with green eyes and a red wig, which can be curled, braided, or anything else you'd like. Less than $70. Their Victoria, a 14" porcelain doll with elegant, rather snooty face, is perfect for mid-Victorian costumes, and she costs less than $40. Preassembled and dressed, this doll would cost you about $125. You might want to send for this catalogue even if you're not in the doll kit-making mood; most of these kits are available fully made up and costumed, and a few, like the Elizabeth I doll—less than $100 in kit form, about $650 made up—are among the most interesting contemporary dolls available.

Haan Crafts has terrific *stuffed Teddy Bear kits*. These range in size from a 7″ bear, about $4, to a *31″ panda,* a real beauty, for less than $20. If you've priced stuffed bears lately, you'll appreciate how low these prices are. (The last time I was in F.A.O. Schwarz on Fifth Avenue, in New York City they were charging $36 for a 10″ bear and $100 for a 20″ panda!)

Larry Houston Studio has a very wide variety of bisque and other *antique doll reproduction kits*. Some of my favorites (and sure to be yours, too): 22″ Pouty Boy, $125 for the kit, $155 made up; 14″ Laughing Jumeau, with glass eyes, wig, porcelain body, $50 for the kit, $70 made up; 21″ Rentille, $55 for the kit, $80 made up. Houston doll kit prices range from $8.98 to well over a hundred dollars. They carry a few historical character dolls, like Martha and George Washington and Abraham Lincoln. They have a few kits too for black dolls.

Marie Louise Originals has four very reasonably priced *cloth doll kits*. These kits come with body fabric, buttons for eyes, plastic inserts for arms and legs, cloth pattern, dowels, and iron-on face transfer. You supply yarn for hair, stuffing, and clothing material. All have charming, smiling faces, detailed fingers and toes, and nice plump bellies. Daisy and Timmy are their baby doll kits. Huck and Polly are toddler dolls. Well under $15 per kit. All are easy to construct. Wonderful dolls.

Mary Maxim always features a few stuffed animal kits, plus a few *rag doll kits*. The rag dolls are especially nice to knit from worsted Orlon yarn. All materials included. Each kit makes two dolls—one boy, one girl—approximately 18″ tall. Available as white or black dolls. About $10 for the kit. Another nice knitted toy kit is their Miss Piggy-type kit, very charming; about $7. Inexpensive kits, too, for knitted doll clothing and accessories.

Needlepunch has those wonderful *folk art stuffed animal kits* one used to see everyplace but which are now becoming rather hard to find. These, including two different cats, two different dogs, and a bunny rabbit, are replicas of stuffed toys in the nineteenth-century collection of the Museum of the City of New York. Hand-printed on cotton broadcloth. Very easy to construct. The 14″ Tabby Cat costs under $8. The little 4″ dog or cat costs about $4. Made up, these stuffed animals, when you can find them, cost at least 50 percent more.

Rainie Crawford's **Pattern Plus** produces some of the most amusing cloth doll kits available. These are great dolls, and they're *very* inexpensive. An an example, 16″ Timothy—with "button-on" short-pants suit in beige and white with blue trim, tan felt shoes, tan and blue felt hat, and matching blue stockings—has one of the sweetest, saddest, slightly self-conscious faces I've seen on a contemporary doll. He has red hair. Skipper, another boy doll in old-timey dress, also have a very funny, slightly surprised look, plus red hair. His old-fashioned sailor suit is navy and white stripes with navy trim and red tie. His funny big navy sailor hat is decorated with colorful embroidered flags. Each sells for less than $8.50, including postage and handling.

Ms. Crawford's little girl dolls have great character also. Dinah, a winsome blond doll, 15¾″ tall, wears a charming pinafore costume, a peculiar chef's hat, and holds a honking goose (included in the kit)! Marvelous. Less than $8.50, including postage.

Pattern Plus has several other interesting doll kits, all in very original costumes, all extraordinarily charming.

Children like their dolls to take naps, too. If you don't feel like spending a fortune for a preconstructed doll bed, you might consider the *reed doll cradle kit* from the **H. H. Perkins Co.** The cradle is made on a 7″ x 15″ x 11″ base, and it looks great lined with calico or gingham. Less than $8. A preconstructed doll cradle like this would sell for at least twice the price.

The Standard Doll Company of Long Island City has an unusually wide range of *china doll kits, porcelain bisque doll kits, apple-head doll* kits, plus other types as well. Their prices are very easy to figure out, which is more than one can say, for example, of the Eve Mae Company, source of some similar merchandise.

There are *many* interesting kits here. Among my favorites: Charles, 24″ tall, has a sweet, serious china face, with blue eyes, dark hair, black one-strap shoes, and a pattern for an early 1900s child's romper suit. Available with blond hair as well. Less than $25. Scarlet, 22″ tall, is clearly modeled after Vivien Leigh. A knockout at less than $25 for the kit. Abraham Lincoln, 18″ tall, costs less than $20. More spectacular is their 24″ Mabel doll kit. This is an American reproduction of a great-looking German doll with "satin flesh"-finished china head, arms, legs, and painted brown eyes. An open-fingered hand with slightly bent elbow gives this doll an unusual sense of movement. The dress is patterned after the old Schoenhut dolls. This kit sells for about $35, but you won't want to buy it without the old-fashioned wig, an additional $11.50.

Standard Doll has many stunning porcelain bisque antique reproductions, too. But most unusual are their Granny and Gramps apple-head doll kits. (In case you've never seen dolls like these, the heads are made from dehydrated and puckered whole apples. If you're not familiar with them, this may sound a little weird, but the shriveled apples really do begin to resemble the weather-beaten faces of old folks.) These are $7.50 each, two for $14.00—a little less than half the price of equivalent fully assembled apple-head dolls. Standard Doll also sells bunny and tabby cat folk art stuffed toys, almost identical to the ones described above under the Needlepunch entry; the difference is that these sell for about $5.50 for the 14″ kit.

Cardboard Houses, Buildings, and Villages

G. P. Putnam's Sons recently introduced a line of "Cut-and-Paste" books, which make up into marvelous replicas of famous buildings. *Build Your Own Empire State Building,* for example, makes up into an impressive 4' structure. *Build Your Own Chrysler Building* makes up into a 3' model. *Build Your Own Brooklyn Bridge* becomes a handsome 10' long model. Each costs $6.95 (plus $1.25 postage and handling); they are available from Brentano's.

Dover Publications has several cut-and-assemble cardboard towns. Each is HO scale, but these towns are not limited to use with model train layouts. Their *Cut and Assemble a Western Frontier Town* by Edmund V. Gillon, Jr., contains materials for ten authentically detailed buildings for a main business block, including Wells Fargo, a dance hall, hotel, sheriff's office, jail, and other places. All are printed in color on heavy card stock. An excellent buy at $3.50. Their *Cut and Assemble Victorian Houses* contains a minutely detailed, architecturally authentic group of four Victorian-style houses, an Italian-style villa, octagon house, and a Second Empire-style house. Also available is *Cut and Assemble an Early New England Village,* also $3.50, which contains twelve authentic buildings, including models of the Adams home in Quincy, Massachusetts, the Oliver Wright house in Sturbridge, Massachusetts, a Methodist church, blacksmith shop, and more.

The Gift Shop of the **Metropolitan Museum of Art** has two model villages. The *Chinese Village* contains more than fifty easy-to-assemble structures, representing a Chinese village of the Ming Dynasty. No scissors or glue needed. Includes river gates, road gates, boats and bridges, a teahouse, lantern shop, silk shop, grain market, bow and arrow shop, temple with two cypress trees, plus many other places. Assembled, the village measures approximately 2' in diameter. Also available is a *Medieval Village.* Each costs approximately $10.

Monte Models has a *huge and fascinating selection of paper/card models of fine American architecture,* plus a selection of buildings in England, Germany, Switzerland, Holland, and Denmark. Uniformly inexpensive, these models are wonderful for the child or adult interested in architecture, and they create a strangely appealing decorative accent.

Models of American buildings available, at a scale of 10' to the inch, include: the Robie House, Chicago; Boston State House, where the Declaration of Independence was first read; the Old Courthouse, Vicksburg, Mississippi; St. Michael's Cathedral, Sitka, Alaska; the Clock Tower, Ghirardelli Square, San Francisco; Rhode Island State House; Monticello; the Bolduc House, Ste. Genevieve, Missouri; Washington's Headquarters, Newburgh, New York; the United States Capitol, in Washington, D.C.

Models of foreign structures include the Chateau d'Hautefort; the Parthenon; Canterbury Cathedral; Castle of Culzean, that Scottish beauty; Ulm Cathedral, Germany; Iglesia de Andalucía, Spain; and many others.

Many of these models cost less than $3. The Parthenon, for example, costs less than $5. Even the most expensive, the U.S. Capitol, costs under $13.

Dollhouses and Dollhouse Furniture

The Artply Company of Brooklyn, New York, sells three most attractive *dollhouse kits*. All are made of Philippine mahogany plywood, with tab-slot construction, which requires no nails, screws, or specialized equipment for assembly. Recently I saw these at a trade show at the New York Coliseum; they're attractive basic kits, which will need some sanding, papering, and painting. The Franklin Model, #124, retailing for about $55, measures 30″ high x 31″ wide x 20″ deep. It's a three-story, nine-room house, with one straight staircase, one curved staircase, dormer windows, fireplace in one room, and wraparound porch. One second-floor room has French doors with a small balcony outside. Very nice gingerbread trim, as on all Artply dollhouse kits. The dollhouse looks rather Alpine/Country Victorian (if there is such a thing—there certainly is in dollhouses . . .). Their Rutherford model, about $50, measures 37″ high x 30″ wide x 16″ deep. Three stories high, with ten rooms (one is an attic/tower room). Small front porch, with an additional balcony off the second floor. Quite nice. Their Tennyson model, three stories high and a few dollars less, contains five large rooms, staircase, fireplace, a dormer window, and wraparound porch and balcony. This one is more urban Victorian. Preconstructed, similar dollhouses generally sell for as much as twice the price.

Bee Jay's Little World sells a number of classic *New England-style dollhouse kits*. My favorite is their New England saltbox, 26½″ high x 30″ wide x 23″ deep. It has three floors, eight rooms, lift-off front so you can get into the front rooms, and a handy hinged roof. Constructed of birch. This is an exquisite dollhouse that should pass from generation to generation. To assemble, you'll need glue, fine sandpaper, screwdriver, hammer, and ¾″ wire brads. Because it's such a fine dollhouse, you may want to add wallpaper, parquet flooring, and other fine details before assembling the house. (You can buy these finishing touches from **Favorites from the Past;** the address appears in the Appendix under "Sources of Dollhouses and Dollhouse Furniture.") This kit is not exactly cheap, about $170, but it's at least $100 less than you could pay for a comparable-quality dollhouse. It really is a beauty.

James Bliss & Co. has some interesting *Chippendale-style dollhouse furniture kits*. These range from a graceful Chippendale bench, about $5, to a kit for a Chippendale broken-bonnet highboy, a design dating from about

1725, for about $18. (This may sound expensive, but miniatures are getting so expensive you'd actually be getting a buy if you found something like it, preassembled, for even $25.) Many Chippendale chair kits. The only kit they carry that I would not recommend unless you plan to supply your own covering is their Chippendale wing chair. I excitedly received this one as a sample for my own dollhouse, and it was the most disappointing kit I came across in the process of researching this book. My problem was one of aesthetics. I like only pretty things in my dollhouse, things of a style and quality I can't really afford in my own apartment. This chair kit arrived with ugly green-and-white plastic "upholstery fabric," whereas I had expected a pretty calico or similar material. If you do order the chair kit, you may want to plan to use your own tiny-scale fabric, perhaps the type sold for use in patchwork quilts. (A good source is Cross Patch Quilting Center, listed in the Appendix under "Sources of Kits for Dolls, Doll Clothing, and Stuffed Animals.")

You may not be aware of it, but you can actually buy chandeliers for your dollhouse that light up! You'll need to install a 12-volt electrical system first, of course (for this, see the next entry below), but once you do, you can take your choice of *kits for at least four gaslight-era working chandeliers*. Available from **Chrysolite, Inc.,** these chandeliers range in price from about $16 to about $23. Frankly, I think they're worth the price. My own favorite is their Golden Era Chandelier kit, the least expensive model available directly from them. It looks like the old elaborate cast-iron fixtures with kerosene lamps I salvaged from my aunt's farm; the chandelier comes with two tiny "kerosene" lamps without shades—and it's just what you may need for your Victorian or American country-style dollhouse.

If you're looking for a simpler fixture, say for a country-style kitchen, they have a kit for that too. It's called the Zenith Hanging Lamp kit, and it sells for about $8.

And if you're too lazy to make your lighting fixtures from kits, **Favorites from the Past** (listed below) carries many made-up fixtures, for a little less than twice the price (sometimes more). A Chrysolite three-arm lamp that might cost less than $9 in kit form will set you back $20 preassembled; a library lamp that would cost about $8 in kit form would cost about $13 preassembled.

If the idea of *electrifying your dollhouse* excites you (it certainly does me . . .), you'll have heart palpitations over the **Cir-Kit Concepts** catalogue. Dollhouse electrification means that you can have beautiful brass chandeliers that actually light up, table lamps that work, fireplaces that flicker, and miniature Christmas trees with tiny working lights. Electrification changes the atmosphere of a static, pleasant-enough dollhouse, to a dynamic live little world. That's the good part. . . . The bad part is that dollhouse electrification, even using these kits, does not come cheap. There *is* a starter kit (#1000-1) that costs under $25, but the six-room deluxe kit goes for closer to $75. Of course, you may then want to spring for spotlight bulbs (85 cents each) candle-flame bulbs ($3.00 for four) plus a Christmas tree lighting kit ($13.95), a faceted parlor lamp ($4.50), a pair of brass wall sconces ($12.00), a glass ceiling shade kit ($5.98), a pair of mantle lamps ($10.00).... Maybe your little girl or boy doesn't need dollhouse electrification; big girls and boys probably will. If you're reluctant to work with electricity yourself, you may be able to get a professional electrician to do it for you for under $50; but you're probably better off finding a handy friend to help you. While I was researching this book I contacted several electricians, and my favorite lamp repair store, all of whom seemed to think I was out of my mind when I asked if they'd help me electrify my dollhouse. Even our local doll hospital was no help.

Constantine offers one relatively inexpensive mahogany plywood dollhouse kit at a scale of 1' to the inch. This is a *two-story country style house* with porch, four deep rooms (two with fireplaces), inside staircase, plus low attic room. Comes with windows, window templates, sandpaper, etc. Veneers, not included but appearing elsewhere in the Constantine catalogue, can be used to cover floors, roof, interiors. This is a pretty basic dollhouse, which would certainly benefit from imaginative finishing. About $30.

More interesting perhaps is Constantine's selection of wood furniture kits, everything from luxurious old-timey bathroom fixtures, $17 for the set, to a kitchen, nursery, and traditional library.

Country Stitching of Willow Grove, Pennsylvania, has extremely attractive *counted cross-stitch dollhouse rug kits*. Designs and sizes range from the 3½" x 4½" American country-looking Flower Basket design ($4.50), to a 6" x 9" Bukhara-influenced design called Red Afghan ($8.00). Other styles range from formal Chinese designs to Navaho-influenced area rugs.

Craft Products Miniatures has an extremely handsome and relatively inexpensive kit for an urban-style federal row house. Called the *Georgetown Doll House Kit,* it comes with a ready-molded Georgetown front. You color bricks, shutters, and shingles; hinge front to "box"; and glue in window. Kit contains front, cut-out birch parts, red marker, hardware, and windows. 30" high x 15¾" wide x 13⅞" deep. About $35. One of the best dollhouse kit values on the market.

Another dollhouse kit, their three-story *Town Doll House Kit,* has front-closing doors to keep tiny furniture dust-free. This house measures 39½" high x 20½" wide x 12½" deep and it contains five rooms (but no staircase). Pretty window boxes with flowers are included. About $50.

Craft Products has one other kit, a *Swiss Chalet Doll House,* completely cut of birch plywood, which needs very little sanding. 27½" high x 29" wide x 14" deep. Very elaborate trim. About $90.

They have many interesting kits for dollhouse furniture, including chandeliers, lamps, rugs, a potbelly stove, and a fabulous *working grandfather clock kit,* which contains an electric watch movement that will run for a year on its tiny battery.

The Enchanted Doll House has a magnificent kit for a *basic birch wood Federal house.* Designed by Joe and Pat Fromberger, this extremely handsome three-story house has six rooms, three central hallways with staircases, and measures 36″ wide x 15½″ deep x 31″ high. Comes with two 4½″ high chimneys, "brick" foundation, clapboard on three sides, working windows. The kit comes with assembled doorway and all precut pieces. About $350 for the basic kit. An electrical kit, with wiring, transformer, all lamps, outlets, chandelier, and two coach lamps, costs an additional $200. If the basic kit doesn't satisfy you, you can add an attractive addition for another $95, plus $53 more for the electrical kit for the "new wing." Preassembled, this house would cost more than $1,000.

If a great *Victorian dollhouse kit* is more to your liking, the Enchanted Doll House offers one that starts with a basic six-room house with porch, 20½″ deep x 20″ high x 33″ wide for $175. Add a second story to make a nine-room mansion with two doors, two porches, balcony. Another $114. Then (if you must—and can afford to), add a two-story left wing with wraparound porch—extends your bit of Victoriana to twelve rooms, 4′ long. $160 more. Need a 3′ high tower as well? It's available in kit form too; three more rooms with attic for $81. A right extension completes this phenomenal dollhouse, another $53—creating a 5′ long, two-story mansion with tower, fourteen rooms in all. That adds up to a hefty $583; a similar dollhouse, not built from a kit, would cost you at least $1,500. Remember, though, that this kit does not include electrification, wallpaper, furniture, rugs, etc.

The Enchanted Doll House has several other fine dollhouse kits; they're not all as expensive as the gems described above. They also carry an extensive selection of fine miniature furniture and dolls; their kits range from tiny needlepoint pillow kits by Jennifer Bennett ($4.00 each), to wonderful needlepoint rugs ($5.00 to $7.00), to unusual upholstered furniture kits (my favorite of these is a charming pink velour chaise, $7.00 for the kit), to X-Acto's® Chippendale looking-glass kit ($5.95), to a treadle sewing machine kit by Chrysnbon.

Mark Farmer Company has fascinating *dollhouse doll kits.* The dolls come with white china heads and limbs or porcelain bisque heads and extremities. Prices range from around $20 to $30 per kit; very beautiful faces.

Favorites from the Past of Kennesaw, Georgia, has three dollhouse kits, ranging in price from $110 to $130, and in style from Southern plantation to farmhouse Victorian. These kits do not include doors or windows, available separately from this dollhouse supply store.

Favorites from the Past has several furniture and accessory kits not very widely available. They have, for example, several *ceiling light fixture kits* you might want; my favorite here is a three-chain lamp with brass body, which looks a little like old Bohemian ceiling light fixtures. Their needlepoint *Colonial Eagle Rug kit,* 8″ x 10″, with deep red border, gold background, blue/tan design, is exquisite—great for a traditional interior; and worth the $12.95 they're charging. In addition, there are fabulous needlepoint rug kits by X-Acto®, Victorian furniture kits by Realife Miniatures, X-Acto® Chippendale kits, and polystyrene kits for a cook stove, china cabinet, wall clock, wall spice drawers, and organ, all by Chrysnbon.

Hill's Dollhouse Workshop hand-manufactures many fine dollhouse kits. Each is constructed of ⅜″, 5-ply, furniture-grade plywood. House sections and windows are dadoed for easy assembly. Room partitions and center floor slide out for painting or papering. Included in the kits are loose attic and bathroom partitions, stairs, railings, prehinged back roof section. My own favorite is their *Country Victorian Farmhouse,* a simple, clean-lined two-story house plus attic, seven rooms, with small front porch, bay windows, and relatively simple but elegant gingerbread trim. 27″ high x 30″ wide x 14″ deep. Less than $140 in kit form. Additions are available as the doll family grows and/or becomes more prosperous.

House of Miniatures carries *furniture kits* by X-Acto®. Among the most interesting: a fine-looking Chippendale canopy bed; a Chippendale corner chair; a lovely hooded baby cradle; a fine corner cupboard, styled after one dating from 1730–50; plus a wide and fascinating selection of the *X-Acto® Tidewater Series Oriental Rug kits.*

I can't praise these needlepoint oriental rug kits too highly. Designed by Katherine Callas Knowles, these 18-mesh, cotton mono canvas rug kits come with Persian wool, needle, plus design charted in the directions and stamped on the canvas. They make up in a few evenings and produce nicer rugs than you may have in your home. Available in ten different designs, Tabriz Hunt, Chinese Antique, Sarouk Saraband, Hertz, Bokhara, Johagan, and more. Their masterpiece is a 9″ x 12″ Savonnerie design. The two I made up were a 3″ x 5″ Chinese medallion, and a 5″ x 7″ Hamadan. *Fabulous.* Prices range from about $5 to about $17.50.

Illinois Hobbycraft has a nice range of furniture kits, but you'll probably find them most interesting if you're looking for working *dollhouse light kits,* especially wall lights, ranging in price from $6.50 to $9.50, some of which appear in no other catalogue I've seen.

Mildon, Inc., sells the fabulous *Fantasy Island dollhouse kit,* a tiny version of Mr. Rourke's house on that TV series. 36″ x 25″ deep x 20″ high. Constructed of ⅜″ particle board, masonite, basswood. The kit comes with prehung door, shingles, rabbeted joints. Five rooms, plus bell tower. The kit sells for about $100.

My Uncle, Inc. of Fryeburg, Maine, has a nice selection of dollhouse kits. Particularly charming is their smallish *Nantucket Cape Kit:* 25″ wide x 17″ deep x 22″ high. About $60. Three rooms, fireplace, eight windows, shutters all around, window boxes in front. Roof opens up and front opens out. The front door has a half-round doorstep. A marvelous small dollhouse. This is a nice starter house, especially nice if you plan it as part of a dollhouse "community." The perfect companion might be their fine *New England Saltbox kit,* about $250, an extraordinary house, 37″ wide x 27¼″ deep x 31½″ high.

Perfection Products Company has lovely *dollhouse furniture kits,* all of which are constructed of maple—a far cry from the ratty balsa-type wood used in too many dollhouse furniture kits. The Hepplewhite pieces are my favorites, especially the Hepplewhite dining table and side table. Also wonderful: a four-poster Sheraton bed. The Hepplewhite dining table costs about $6 in kit form, $9 assembled. The wonderful Sheraton double-bed kit sells for about $11 in kit form, about $20 assembled. Other kits represent similar savings.

Scientific Models, Inc., is one of the larger suppliers of *dollhouse furniture kits.* Many of these kits are for complete room settings. Among the most interesting is their Victorian series, with kits for a Victorian bathroom, bedroom, dining room, and parlor. These room setting kits retail for about $17—substantially less than preassembled pieces. Their Heritage series contains some nice pieces too, especially the music room kit, with grand piano, stool, music stand, and Chippendale sofa; again, I'd recommend using a different fabric as sofa covering. Their country kitchen kit is great too, with icebox, Hoosier cabinet, sink with pump, and wood stove.

Skil-Craft manufactures several fine dollhouse kits, several of which are available with all dollhouse furniture, in kit form, in the same package. These dollhouses are *very* good values, priced so that you can afford to buy and decorate them without sacrifice. Their *Colonial dollhouse kit* is very, very nice. It's constructed of ¼″ precut, notched mahogany plywood, with realistic-colored, formed-plastic exterior siding and shutters, interior wainscoting and fireplace, plus wood trim to finish. Each kit comes with two wood staircases, wood room partitions, and printed vinyl windowpanes. Two stories plus attic, six rooms. A fine dollhouse, 26″ x 24″ x 13″ deep, for about $35.

Their *Victorian dollhouse kit* is a fine dollhouse for a young child, too. Specifications are the same as for the colonial house described above, and it has the same very reasonable price. The difference, really, is in the style of door and window moldings, and the trim at the bottom and top of the roofline.

Slightly more expensive, but definitely worth the additional $15, is their extraordinary *Country Manor dollhouse kit.* This eight-room country Victorian home has a three-sided porch and ornately etched windows, and it measures 29″ high x 34½″ long x 20½″ wide. Architectural details include fish-scale-siding effect on the dormer, and printed latticework on the porch. Country clapboard exterior of formed plastic.

Skil-Craft has also recently introduced a roomier 37″ long x 14½″ wide x 28″ high *Federal dollhouse kit,* with two wings with sun porches, three classic dormers, and double chimneys. There are only five rooms, plus one hallway, but they're big enough for a substantial amount of furniture—and fantasizing. $37.50

Wicker furniture for your dollhouse can be *extremely* expensive (when you can find it), yet there are times one *must* have, for example, a wicker porch rocker. The inexpensive solution is paper quilling, a technique that requires a bit of patience (no more so than, say, needlepoint), but that produces wonderful wickerlike furniture and accessories. For just $3, **Quill Art, Inc.,** of St. Louis, Missouri, offers a kit that makes up into a fine-looking Victorian-influenced rocker, a chair-side "wicker" table, and planter and plant holder. If you were able to locate wicker miniatures like these you'd pay at least ten times the price. Other furniture kits make up into "wicker" tea carts, lamps, etc. Quilling is also an extremely handy technique for making little houseplants for your dollhouse.

Woodline Products has more than a dozen dollhouse kits. One of the nicest, around $100, is their *Prairie Manor dollhouse kit,* with six rooms, 11″ deep, with two adjustable walls, and a small attic on the third floor. The completed house measures 36″ wide x 24″ high x 2″ deep. A wonderful prairie house, with front porch and pine clapbord siding.

Grandma's House is another beautiful kit, also around $100. 22″ high x 36″ wide x 22″ deep. It resembles a Midwestern farmhouse of the early 1800s. Wraparound porch, five rooms, plus large attic with hinged roof.

Woodline has many other fine kits, including one for a two-story *general store* with upstairs apartment or doctor's office. It comes with an outside staircase leading to the second floor, plus front porch. It's made from pine and hardwood parts: $42.

Rocking Horses, Wooden Trains, Backgammon Boards, and Other Toy Kits

The American Museum of Natural History has at least three kits your young paleontologist will adore. Each contains a fossil reproduction "buried" in clean, rocklike material, plus the equipment needed to complete the dig. Available is Eohippus, ancestor of today's horse; Saber-tooth cat; and Invertebrates, consisting of six marine fossils. Less than $10; even less if you're a museum member.

You may recall **The Bartley Collection** from chapter 1; they generally manufacture fine antique-reproduction furniture kits. But also included in their product line is the finest *antique reproduction rocking horse kit* I've seen. This kit is modeled after one originally constructed by Woodbury Gerrish in Portsmouth, New Hampshire, in 1844. It had been commissioned by Charles J. Colcord for his son, Jay. The original of this reproduction can be seen in *Antiques of American Childhood* (Clarkson N. Potter, Inc., New York, NY 1970) by Katherine M. McClinton, and in *American Folk Sculpture* by Robert Bishop (E. P. Dutton and Co., New York, NY, 1975). The original now rests outside the toy shop in the Henry Ford Museum. This reproduction, reasonably priced at about $125, comes with hand-carved head and leather ears. Solid oak. Seat cushion included. The kit requires no specialized tools for assembly. It measures 22½" high x 47½" long. Preassembled, the kit costs more than twice the price.

The **Dick Blick Company** has some nice craft kits. They have, for example, the largest selection I've seen anywhere of *wooden dinosaur replica kits,* ranging from a Tyrannosaurus kit, 12¼" x 8¾" x 3¾", at less than $7, to a Plesiosaurus kit, 37½" x 13⅜" x 19¾", for about $45. Other interesting kits include inexpensive fabric-printing kits, which allow you to print with real leaves, ferns, feathers, etc. $5.95 each; Color-Me-Mugs,® which allow children to create inexpensive gifts, $17.40 for twelve; and marvelous silk-screen printing kits, excellent for classroom use, $25.00 and $35.00.

Educational Design, Inc., has an inexpensive *fingerprint kit* that seems to fascinate children. Everything necessary to bring out, preserve, and catalogue hidden fingerprints. About $5.

Stephen Ellis has marvelous *wooden toy kits* for a log truck and for a wooden steam train, which includes engine, coal car, log car, passenger car, and caboose. About $23.

Nick Lecakes has wonderful *clear-pine train kits* with moving parts. The locomotive costs a hefty $39.95 in kit form, but it's still $20.00 less than the assembled price. Kits for the other carts start at $26.95.

Nasco produces several fine craft kits, including loom kits and weaving pillow kits. Arts and crafts teachers may be interested in their wide range of *silk-screen printing kits* and *fabric-screen printing kits.*

The New York Botanical Garden Gift Shop carries relatively inexpensive *sun-print kits,* for making sun prints of leaves, ferns, flowers. Originally developed for the Lawrence Hall of Science of the University of California, the sun-print paper goes through a chemical change when exposed to light, making a photographic image without chemical processing. $6.50.

As an adolescent, I occasionally visited relatives staying near Truro, Massachusetts. It didn't take long before I equipped myself with graphite, rice paper, and masking tape, and began a systematic tour of local graveyards, in search of fine old grave carvings and memorial poetry. You may not live near these beautiful old graveyards, but there are undoubtedly carvings in your area, which your child would enjoy making rubbings off. **Oldstone Enterprises** has an excellent, inexpensive *child's rubbing kit,* which contains paper, no-smear wax, light cardboard for collages, scissors, and tape. $4.25 postpaid. If you'd like a starter set for yourself or for an older child, Oldstone also sells their *Original Oldstone Rubbing kit,* including five sheets of 24" x 36" hemp rubbing paper, two 2-ounce cakes of rubbing wax (one black, one brown), roll of tape, bristle brush, and a copy of *Oldstone's Guide to Creative Rubbings.* Materials arrive in leatherette carrying case. $11.50 postpaid.

The **Woodworkers Store®** of Rogers, Minnesota, has two gorgeous kits for *veneer checkerboards.* One kit, only about $7, makes up into an exquisite chessboard, with 2½" dark and light veneer squares to make a regulation-size chessboard. The kit comes with seventy squares, contact cement, veneer roller, glue brush, and veneer strips for the border and edges. Only $2 more, their multicolored chessboard kit is a real beauty, with light birch squares that contrast with an assortment of six exotic veneers. A good veneer chessboard like the latter sells for about three times the price of the kit.

If backgammon is your game, you'll probably be interested in looking at their two fabulous *backgammon kits.* The first, only $9, contains all the die-cut veneer pieces you'll need to make a very attractive board. Veneer only, and it does not include the board. On a grander scale, you'll probably want the Woodworkers Store®'s *Deluxe Backgammon Chessboard Kit.* The complete kit is 19¾" x 20" open. All machining and die cutting have been done. The corners of the solid walnut frame are mitered and ready to assemble. This kit includes light and dark squares for chessboard, prescored walnut, maple, cherry triangles, inlay bendings for the chessboard, additional cherry veneer for the backgammon board, solid walnut frame pieces, hardware, base materials, backgammon checkers, dice, dice cup, and instructions. About $35. Assembled, this board would go for at *least* $15 more.

They also carry a kit for a *wooden hobby horse.* The completed horse is 18″ high x 8″ wide x 20″ long. Requires simple nailing and gluing. All parts precut, needing no machining. Body, seat, head, are ¾″ pine. Cross-piece legs are 2 x 4's in fir. Kit includes unfinished lumber pieces, casters, felt for mane, carved wood trim for bridle, dowel handle. Less than $20.

Kites

Frostline Kits has several attractive kits for kites. All are constructed of high-quality, long-lasting nylon. They have a traditional *diamond kite,* a *manta kite* (shaped like a manta ray), and a *six-sided rainbow kite;* prices range from about $8 to $11. Most interesting is their *dragon kite kit.* This will, of course, last much longer than the more common plastic version. It comes with fiberglass support rod and two "face" options, either a dragon or a troll: about $12.

If you like kites, you undoubtedly know of or have been to **Go Fly a Kite,** the marvelous kite store on Manhattan's Upper East Side and in Southampton, New York. Frankly, it amazes me that Go Fly a Kite doesn't carry more kits than it does, but the Stratton kite kits it does carry are gorgeous. They're as nice for children's room decorations as they are to fly. There are five different styles, all modeled after antique aircraft, and each is a bargain, considering what a good preassembled kite can cost. The *Fokker Tri-Plane Kite,* 30″ x 48″, is colorful, and costs only (about) $12; preassembled, a kite like this would cost at least $20, possibly more. Their yellow and blue *Sopwith Camel bi-plane,* 30″ x 48″ is the same price, as is their F3F, 30″ x 48″. The wonderful *Wright Flyer,* 31″ x 58″, sells for $2 more. Assembled, each would go for almost twice the price. They also carry a *Ghost Clipper,* measuring 2′ wide x 4′ high x 5′ long, about $40.

Rafco has a *rotating airfoil kite kit* called Roll-o-Kite: 17″ wide x 7″ diameter. The unusual design of this rapidly spinning airfoil is reputed to cause strong lifting forces in the wind. The complete kit, $5 prepaid, includes fittings, instructions, 100 yards of string. Discounts available on orders of six or more.

Backyard Playground Equipment

Big Toys® are *cedar log component systems* that require no concrete for stability. Installation is relatively straightforward and requires no special tools. Five kits are available. BY-1 is an A-frame climbing structure. It includes a turning bar and a climbing tire. The structure size is 7′ x 8′ x 6½′ high. Well under $200. Good for your two- to six-year-olds. For four- to seven-year-olds, they have a 9½′ x 16′ structure, which includes two swings, a low platform for little kids, a turning bar, and much more. Swings are of safe rubber belt material. As many as five children can play on this at the same time. An excellent value at about $400. You could, of course, go beyond the second system described above, but to me it seems like overkill unless you're planning to run a nursery school in your backyard. These systems remind me very much of the play structures of the nursery school at Goddard College in Plainfield, Vermont; the little kids chased me off their equipment more than once.

Child Life Play Specialties kits can save you at least 20 percent of the cost of their preassembled backyard play equipment. They have many combinations of equipment. A simple three-ladder swing set with double bronco, trapeze bar, rings, and soft-seated swing would cost about $180 in kit form. Possible combinations are too extensive to detail here, so do send for their catalogue. All their equipment, by the way, comes with flush-fitting nuts (installed with an Allen wrench) to avoid injuries. Playhouse available too.

Model Ships

James Bliss & Company has many fine imported and domestic model ship kits. Imports include fine kits from Italy, Spain, and Denmark.

Among the Corel kits from Italy, my own favorite is *La Sirene,* a *French 30-Gun Frigate of 1775.* This kit is quite large, measuring 32½" long x 27¼" high. Scale is 1:75. Much detail. This man-of-war was designed for the French king. About $190. Preassembled, it would probably cost you at least twice the price for this model, and for almost all the models mentioned below.

Among the ancient ship models by Aeropiccola of Italy, my own choice would be the *Indiscret,* an *Algerian pirate vessel dating to 1750.* Overall dimensions: 100 x 74 x 18 centimeters. Approximately 40" x 30" x 7". About $140. Aeropiccola kits come with a seventy-one-page dictionary to translate words and phrases of Italian-language instructions. Plank on frame construction.

Of the Mantua ship models, I'd choose *L'Astrolabe,* a *French corvette* famous for the explorations made by Dumont D'Urville, 1815–50. This kit is 1:50 scale, 43" long, 32" high, 12½" wide beam. Excellent details. Under $200.

The *Billing Boat kits* from Denmark are terrific, too; there are several beauties here, but I'd choose their inexpensive 1:20 scale *Viking Ship.* This one measures 25½" long x 6" wide x 14" high. Lines taken from a Viking Ship raised in 1962 and presently on display in the Viking Ships Museum at Roskilde. About $30. Their *Bluenose* kit is wonderful too, as is their *Northsea Cutter "Mary Ann."*

Bliss has nice Art AMB Fusta kits from Spain, too. A favorite here: their

Ballenera Whale Boat. Approximately ninety individual pieces. 8½″ long. 1:34 scale. Under $25.

Bliss's American-made kits include a selection from Scientific Models, Model Shipways, Dumas, and Replica—described further on in this chapter. They also carry kits by the Marine Model Co., with choices ranging from a wonderful small whaleboat, to the U.S.S. *Gearing,* a destroyer used during World War II. If I were able to pick even two of these kits, I'd probably choose their *Victorine, a Hudson River Sloop,* 22″ x 24″ (about $40) and their *fishing schooner Pinky* (less than $30), designed for fishing on the Grand Banks.

Bluejacket Ship Crafters has several marvelous model ship kits requiring average shipbuilding skills. All kits include a machine-carved wooden hull, usually clear sugar pine, rigging cords and wire, materials for masts and spars, wood cut to size for superstructures, rails, etc. Scribed wood decking (except steel deck ships), plans, and brass and cast fittings of Britannia metal.

There are many fine ship kits here, so many it's difficult to single out two or three. My own favorites: *the Bluenose,* built in 1921 at Lunenburg, Nova Scotia, to work the rough waters of Newfoundland. This beautiful kit measures 22″ x 18″. Less than $60. Their *Robert E. Lee* steamboat, 31″ long x 11½″ high, is a standout for any model ship collection: less than $115. Their *Atlantic* auxiliary Schooner yacht, 1905, measures 29″ high x 21″ long. Less than $90.

Bluejacket Ship Crafters has several models for use with radio control systems. A particular favorite here: the 25½″ long x 12½″ high *Harbor Tug,* a model of a powerful steam tug still seen in New York Harbor. Less than $60 in ⅛ scale; ¼ scale about $160.

The Brookstone Company has *museum-quality showcase kits* for ship models. These are relatively difficult to find in kit form, and preassembled showcases are astronomically priced. Top and bottom frames, with platform, are completely assembled and drilled. You cut corner posts to desired length, apply finish, and install glass (not included). Frame is solid mahogany; platform is ¼″ mahogany plywood. Available in three sizes, 17″ long x 9″ wide x 37″ high, less than $20. Medium showcase, 24½″ long x 10¾″ wide x 37″ high, less than $25. A 38″ long x 15½″ wide x 37″ high size sells for well under $30. Preassembled, these cases would be at least twice the price.

The Dromedary of El Paso, Texas, has a wide selection of Aeropiccola, Art AMB Fusta, Billing, Carta, Corel, and Mantua imported kits. American-made kits as well. They also carry kits for model cases, which are generally more expensive than those offered by the Brookstone Company, but these come in larger sizes than Brookstone has.

Of the Movo kits from Italy, all utilizing plank-on-frame construction, I particularly like their *Cocca Veneta* kit, 27½″ long x 21½″ high. These small merchant ships were built around the fifteenth and sixteenth centuries expressly for service between Venice and the East. The ship has a high prow, very high stern, and relatively simple rigging. About $120.

Dumas Products has a fabulous line of radio-control boat kits; these range from sailboats, to cruisers, to hydroplane kits.

Among the most interesting: the American Enterprise, *a high-speed crew-boat* for taking crews to *offshore drilling rigs*. Precut plywood, with deck hardware included. 52″ long, 12″ beam. About $75.

Another fine kit: the 30″ *Star sailboat kit* (8″ beam). Mahogany plywood frames; planking and deck, 1/12″ mahogany. Built-up spruce mast 44″ high. About $55 without radio.

One of my other favorites is their *U.S. Coast Guard Lifeboat:* 33″ scale model. Kit includes all deck hardware. About $70.

A. J. Fisher, Inc., has many fine model-ship kits. Among the more interesting here is the *Brig Niagara kit,* a model of Perry's 1812 flagship. One-eighth inch to the foot, this model measures 20″ in length. Under $75. They also have a fine *U.S. Constitution* frigate kit, with detailed blueprints by H. W. Potter. Very elaborate rigging; a fine model. About $160.

Model Expo has a fine variety of model-ship kits. Since they generally have pre-Christmas sales offering substantial savings, you may want to wait for their sale brochure. One of their wonderful kits is of the H.M.S. *Bounty.* This handsome kit from Sergal of Italy features a walnut keel and ribs and double-planked hull of walnut and limewood strips. Brass guns, stern galleries, transoms, bow ornaments, cast bronze figurehead, plus hundreds of finely detailed fittings are included. It comes complete with sail and rigging. This kit is supposed to be okay for beginners or intermediate model builders. Usually, about $200; nearly $40 less during sales.

Model Shipways has a staggering variety of excellent model-ship kits. If you'd like a change from rigged sailing ships, you might consider their *steam canal barge kit,* the *City of Pekin* of Peoria, dating from 1911. The model measures 13½″ long x 3½″ wide, with ⅛″ equaling one foot. $16.50. This barge was originally built as the mule-drawn *City of Henry* in Chicago in 1875, but was converted to a twin-screw tow barge in 1911. It carried grain, lumber, coal, beef, etc., between LaSalle and Chicago.

Model Shipways also carries case kits for your models at fair prices.

Preston's catalogue lists more than fifty available ship models, from the clipper ship *Cutty Sark* to 10′ *radio-control models of ocean-racing sailboats.*

Some of Preston's models are sold fully assembled—if you want to confirm how much you're saving by putting these kits together yourself (usually, about $100 to $200). Preston's also carries a most interesting *ship-in-bottle kit* for well under $15 (less than half its preassembled price). This interesting kit is for the clipper *Flying Cloud.* Overall length of bottle is 12″, with 4¼″ model. It comes with a mahogany stand.

If you're looking for an easy-to-assemble model for a beginning model builder, you may be interested in their very inexpensive (about $13) model of the *Schooner Yacht Atlantic.* The kit contains a carved wood hull, preruled deck material, precision cast-metal fittings, simplified rigging, real cloth sails, colorful pennants, hardwood masts and yards, display stand, and metal nameplate.

If R/C (radio control) boats are more to your liking, you might want to investigate their handsome *tuna clipper,* a 37″ scale model of the 220 *Purse Seiner* built by Campbell Industries of San Diego. Plywood construction, with mahogany planking, 6½″ beam. About $50.

Replica Creations' models are constructed through a building technique that *closely duplicates modern ship-construction methods.* From laying the keel to making and rigging the sails, you follow the key steps employed in the actual construction of full-size boats built of ferrocement and fiberglass. Six quite inexpensive models are available (with prices ranging from around $18 to $26).

Scale-model kits (½″ equals one foot) are available for an 18′ Cape Cod catboat, about $18; a 25′ sloop, about $20; a 23′ sloop, $20; 25′ steam launch, $18; 26′ Elco cruiser, $22; and 35′ ketch, $26. Both the 26′ cruiser and the steam launch can be motorized. None of the kit parts is precut or premodeled. Marvelous kits.

Scientific Models must sell thousands of ship kits each year; their kits are found in just about every mail-order catalogue dealing with the subject and in most hobby shops. Many of these kits are real beauties.

Especially nice is their *Gloucester Schooner kit,* the *Sharpshooter.* 15½″ long. This schooner has a very sharp bow and is typical of the Gloucester schooners of the 1850s. Well under $15. Their 20″ long x 15″ high *Santa Maria kit* would be a wonderful school project and tool for teaching about early nautical exploration and shipbuilding history. Well under $25. Their *Baltimore Clipper kit* is a larger-scale kit for an intermediate or advanced ship-model builder. This pirate brig model measures 22½″ long x 16½″ high. Under $35.

You may also enjoy their very colorful *Golden Hind kit,* a model of the flagship of Sir Francis Drake, 20″ long x 15″ high. Painted to resemble a Spanish Galleon. (The *Hind* sailed from Plymouth, England, in 1577 to plunder the riches of the Spanish colonies of the New World.) Under $35.

South Street Seaport Museum Model Shop offers many wonderful services, including model-building classes and model restorations. They'll custom-build cases for your antique or modern ship models, and they carry already-constructed models at pretty reasonable prices. In fact, they'll custom-build almost any model ship in which you're interested.

All of their kits are from Model Shipways. (Model Shipways' *City of Pekin* kit is described on a previous page.) There are several fine kits for sale here, including one for the *1847 Coasting Schooner Eagle,* a bulk carrier employed in the Bath, Maine, to New York City packet trade. If you wish, you can copper the bottom of the *Eagle's* hull, using packets of copper sheathing available from the Museum Shop. About $50, without sheathing material.

If you're a regular ship modeler, you might consider joining the museum; individual membership is only $15 ($10 for students and people over sixty-five). As a member, you qualify for a 10 percent discount on purchases, and you receive several excellent publications.

Sterling Models has some marvelous R/C model-boat kits, including one that can definitely serve as an outlet for fantasy: the 40″ long x 10¼″ wide model of a *Chris Craft 63′ motor launch;* for most of us, this is the only 63′ Chris Craft we'll ever own. Also available are R/C models of an American Scout freighter, the battleship U.S.S. *Missouri,* a 42′ Chris Craft Corvette, and an amphibian Puddle Jumper. Nice operational sailboat models too.

Model Airplanes, including Kits for Radio-control Aircraft

Bridi Hobby Enterprises has a huge selection of *R/C airplanes and glider kits.* Their newest kit, the UFO, has a 64½″ wingspan, with a 692-square-inch area. Designed for a .60 pump and pipe with retracts. The UFO has an epoxy glass fuse and fin, foam wing and stabilizer, swept-back wing, and anhedral stabilizer. The kit includes fixed gear, engine mount, and building notes. About $150.

Fliteglas Models is owned by Ralph White, winner of more than a few sport scale events.

I particularly like his U.S.A.F. *El Bandito* kit, with 57″ wingspan. It's excellent for pattern flying, and it takes the new .40-size engines. Fuselage weight is only 15 ounces. Basic kit includes joined fiberglass fuselage with molded canopy, bulkhead, foam-wing cores, landing-gear wire, and blocks. About $70. Deluxe kit includes all necessary wood and hardware (except fuel tank, wheels, and engine mount). Less than $100.

Majestic Models has a very wide selection of *rubber-powered models* (models powered by heavy rubberbands) and *free-flight glider kits.* The gliders, by the way, are infinitely safer for your children than R/C airplanes; I wouldn't advise unsupervised play with the latter. Of the Keil Kraft gliders, I particularly like the *73" Span Aquarius.* It's a Nordic A-2, designed by Ed Baguley. All wood construction; no plastic. Optional plug-in or one-piece wing, auto rudder. About $30. Many of their kits, particularly the gliders, are much less expensive, averaging well under $10.

If you're not familiar with R/C airplane models (and even if you are), you'll flip when you see the sales material from **Bud Nosen Models.** Nosen produces *huge* R/C kits; they're both gorgeous and relatively inexpensive. My favorite (and I like lots of these; so will you) is his *1933 Gere Sport biplane.* Top span is 96¼". Bottom span is 90¼". 14.5 pounds flying weight. 2,790-square-inch area. This kit requires .60 engines. All wood construction. With its 12-ounce wing loading, it gets into the air in about 15 to 20 feet; flying speed seems to be in the 15 to 20 mph range. It's easy to land. This is a *terrific* biplane kit—and, I think, a bargain at about $130.

Rockford Model Aircraft has terrific plastic model kits of commercial and civilian aircraft. Particularly interesting is their *Boeing 747;* the largest commercial model plane on the market, it measures 28½" long x 25½" wingspan. Markings: United Airlines. This Boeing 747 has fine interior detailing, including skylounge, cockpit, and engines. It comes with a display stand. Less than $35. Another interesting kit: their *Concorde Supersonic Airliner.* This measures 23½" long x 10" wingspan. Markings: U.S. Air Force. About $16. A 17" long model, with Braniff markings is available for about $11.

Sig Manufacturing has a huge variety of R/C airplane kits at fair prices. Especially nice is their *Clipped Wing Cub kit,* a Reed clipped-wing conversion built up from a 1941 Piper J-3 cub. Wingspan: 56". 42" long. Utilizes .19 to .40 engines. Constructed of die-cut balsa and plywood, with stable design and one-piece wing. Aluminum engine mounts, formed landing gear, and molded engine cowling. About $50.

Sterling Models has many fine *R/C model plane kits.* They also carry *stick-model kits,* plus *peanut scale models.* One of their nicest stick-model kits is their reasonably priced *Fokker DR-1 Triplane,* with 23½" wingspan. A very easy to assemble model of the Red Baron's airplane.

Williams Brothers, Inc., has some unusual plastic scale-model airplane kits. Models are available for a *Boeing 247,* a forerunner of today's transports; a French *Cauldron,* winner of the 1933–35 Coupe Deutsch de la Meurthe races in Europe; *Curtiss C-46* transport plane; and the *Gee Bee Racer,* the Granville Brothers' R-1 racer. Other kits too. Kits average about $7

Model Railroad Kits

The real meat of this chapter appears in the Appendix of this book under Additional Sources of Model Railroad Kits. You'll find listed there thirty-five great sources of kits for model railroad buffs, including at least three places where you can buy your kits at *discount*.

What follows here is just a very tiny sampling of the scores of kits available.

Herkimer Tool and Model Works has all-metal HO gauge passenger-car kits. Models include coach, astrodome, observation car, sleeper, baggage/coach, baggage car, diner, postal/baggage, and dome/observation car. Available as 60' shortys or 80' scale. Easy-to-assemble kits with fully assembled trucks, predrilled floors, die-cast ends, sealed parts tube, N.M.R.A. couplers, and Talgo-type trucks. These are *very* attractive kits. The shortys range in price from around $9 to $11; the scale models cost barely a dollar more per car. Undercar detail and ventilators are a few cents extra. Comparable quality preassembled passenger cars would cost at least $5 or more each.

Little Engines Shop of Lomita, California, has some of the most incredible kits I saw in the course of researching this book. These are kits for steam-powered locomotives so big that they will dominate your backyard and attract every child in the neighborhood and most adults within a nine-block radius. Some of these engines are so powerful they can ferry you and a band of children around and around your yard.

You don't even need specialized equipment for most of these. Their *American type 1½" scale,* for example, requires some drilling, some tapping, and some filing—all of which can be done with hand tools. The track is secured to redwood ties and laid on the ground, with decomposed granite used for ballast. The engine measures 37" long, 19½" high, with 100 pounds of steam pressure. Fuel is coal or oil. Minimum track radius is 25 feet.

Many other styles are available as well. Be prepared to spend at least a couple of thousand dollars for a modest layout.

Quality Craft Models, Inc., has both metal and plastic railroad car kits. Of the metal kits, I think the most exciting is their *brass Pennsylvania N5C caboose kit.* Made of chemically milled brass. It can be constructed using Ambroid cement, or it can be soldered. An excellent value at about $20. Preassembled, a comparable quality caboose would set you back at least $8 more.

R & R Distributors offers several kits for *wall-mounted train cases*—a fine way to display and protect your rolling stock. All measure 32" long, and come in four-shelf, six-shelf, and nine-shelf versions. All wood has been mitered and dadoed. The kits come with hanging hardware and knobs for glass. Glass not included. Available in N gauge, or HO gauge. Six-shelf, N gauge: $28.95. $3.00 shipping charge for each. Nine-shelf, N gauge: $35.95. Four-shelf, HO gauge: $30.95. Six-shelf, HO gauge: $37.95. Do check for current prices before sending your check.

Walthers publishes catalogues for N-scale and HO-scale trains. These are *the* model railroaders' wish books, with a staggering variety of kits. Their Vourner building kits, for example, offer everything from a police headquarters to a fire station with tower, plus many old-time buildings, from old-time city railroad station to box-truss bridges. *Many* kits, too, for rolling stock.

7

Needlework

Some of the best bargains available are needlework kits, everything from knitted sweaters to needlepoint chair upholstery. Sweater kits can save you about two-thirds or more of preworked prices. Some of the patchwork and needlework kits (chair upholstery kits, particularly) can save you even more—*hundreds* of dollars, in fact.

And nothing communicates care and love as much as handcrafted needlework gifts. In your own home, they're a sign of warmth and a connection with the traditions and accomplishments of "women's work" of past centuries. I think that Judy Chicago's *The Dinner Party* has finally made people of both genders concede that needlework of all types (not just patchwork) can be and has been a form of "art" for some time; that is, of course, not exactly news to most of us.

Knitted Sweaters and Knitted and Crocheted Afghans

Alma's Original Alaska Patterns has kits for *jacket-type sweaters of bulky* 3-ply Orlon or 4-ply wool *yarns.* Sweaters are available in adult and children's sizes. These kits are similar in style to the wonderful jacket sweaters Mary Maxim has been selling for years. Each of Alma's kits has a large graphed motif on the back, in very unusual designs. You can order children's kits with designs representing a seal on an iceberg; a map of the state of Alaska; standing goat on rock; little red devil; Eskimo girl waving; and standing Big Horn sheep. Adult patterns in designs for: a bear with fish in mouth; charging bear; standing goat; sheep head; side-view sheep head; standing husky; large husky dog head; Eskimo girl with spear; clog team with driver; howling wolf with cache; roses; gold panner with pan; Eskimo in kayak; and several others. I particularly like the Alaskan totem pole design.

Prices are reasonable. Orlon kits in sizes 2 to 12 for children range from around $17 to around $23. Wool kits for children range between around $23 and about $32. Adult sweater kits cost between $32–$37 in Orlon, about $45–$51 for wool.

Kits for a beautiful *cabled raglan-sleeved jacket sweater* for women, of 90 percent Orlon, 10 percent wool yarn, costs about $30. A kit for a lovely *cabled vest* for women costs less than $8.

Alma has a few afghan kits, too, most well under $35.

American Handicrafts has several nice *afghan kits* to crochet. One of the nicest is their *Yellow Brick Road,* a crib-size afghan of washable synthetic yarn, which depicts Dorothy and Toto, the Tin Man, the Scarecrow, and a gentle lion. Finished size: 32″ x 42″. A marvelous gift at a bargain price: about $11. Some of their *crocheted-lace afghan kits* make up into real beauties; these measure 41″ x 62″ and 43″ x 64″. Synthetic yarn, and a bargain— about $12 each kit.

If you're a knitter, you'll probably enjoy their *Irish-patterned* washable afghan, synthetic yarn, 47″ x 56″. This one costs under $25. Frankly, if I were going to put that kind of work into an afghan, I'd want it to be knitted of wool, a richer fiber, which keeps its good looks longer. But you may be making the afghan for someone allergic to wool.

Annie's Attic of Big Sandy, Texas, has two very interesting crocheted-afghan kits taken from a classic patchwork design generally known as Sun Bonnet Baby. They call their versions *Sunbonnet Sue* and *Overall Sam.* Available in child's size, 41″ x 58″, about $30. Full-size kit, 41″ x 71″, about $40. Either kit available in the Sam design or the Sue design. Very nice for a little boy or girl.

Better Homes and Gardens Craft Kits has two exquisite and inexpensive kits for crocheted afghans, their *Paper Doily Afghan,* approximately 41″ x 51″, has the kind of lacy detail you may like in antique doilies. Acrylic sport yarn, less than $15. Their *Fisherman Filet Afghan,* also off-white, measures 48″ x 81″, and makes a fantastic gift. Just over $20. Store-bought handmade afghans like these would cost at least four to five times as much.

Sandwiched between the Belleek china and Waterford crystal, **Emerald Mail Order** has one of the best sweater kit bargains I've seen. It's a knitter's pack/kit of fine natural Irish wool, complete with needles, patterns, and buttons, if necessary for the sweater you choose. You'll really have to look through the catalogue to choose which style of *Aran fisherman knit sweater* you'd most like to own. Styles include crew-neck, turtleneck, collarless cardigan, and V-neck cardigan. All are stunning. Even more stunning is the kit price: around $20! As you're undoubtedly aware, Aran sweaters like these generally sell in this country for about $100 each.

Icemart, the mail order catalogue of Keflavik Airport, Iceland, has a wonderful kit for a *traditional Icelandic pullover sweater.* Instructions are in six languages. Available in four basic colors: white, gray, brown, black. About $25, plus $3.80 postage. That's still $40–$60 less than a store-bought Icelandic sweater. (In fact, it's considerably cheaper than the wholesale price my brother and I paid for ours.) Don't be afraid of this kit; the patternwork around the neck is not that difficult. Besides, it works up quickly.

Janknits has *Scandinavian design sweater kits* so beautiful they defy description. All are made from wool grown on the Cherry Creek Sheep Ranch, operated by the owners of Janknits kits. If you like knitting, or even if you just love hand-knit sweaters, you really should send for this catalogue.

Among the many Scandinavian design kits in this catalogue are several that very much resemble knitting patterns my mother brought back last year from Norway. In fact, one of the cardigan kits—an astoundingly inexpensive $34—very much resembles a hand-knit pullover my mother brought back, too; it cost over $90 in Norway (it would be even more here). A similar sweater kit for men costs well under $40. For children, less than $20.

Janknits has *many* other fine kits for knitters, including fabulous *Aran design 100 percent wool afghan kits,* from $40 to $55. A *man's Aran design pullover kit* is priced at just over $30.

If you like the look of *knitted-lace sweaters,* Janknits has those, too, all under $20! Plus *women's wool cabled vests,* well under $20. *Cabled wool mitten kits:* under $4. *Two-ply socks:* under $6.

There are kits combining *knitting and sheepskin,* too.

This is truly one of the most remarkable kit companies I've encountered. These sweater kits are *very* inexpensive; you'll never do better.

La Knitterie sells *relatively expensive silklike high-fashion sweaters.* Their varigated V-neck long-sleeve sweater kit with puffed set-in sleeves sells for about $85. Solid-color kit with V-neck or crew neck costs about $60, plus postage.

My mother has been making **Mary Maxim** sweater kits for well over a decade and a half. Their charted patterns are very easy to follow, and materials are always good quality. These sweaters, especially the wool sweater jackets, last for *years* and never seem to go out of style.

Mary Maxim is, of course, best known for their *jacket-style sweaters* with snowflake, Greek key, diamonds, and other designs on front and back. Even more distinctive are Mary Maxim's jacket sweaters with designs on the back of reindeer and pine trees, polar bears, geese, pheasants, horses, and (my favorite for the past several years—my mom made one for me, but we made it too big) a Hereford bull. Other designs include a CB radio, a trailer truck, an antique auto, cross-country skier, ice skates, roller skates, a football player, and dogs of all varieties. Some of these pictorial designs border on kitsch, but they're consistently amusing, sometimes beautiful, and heaven knows they're warm. Prices range from just over $20 in Orlon, size 32, to just over $50 for sizes 42–44 in wool.

Mary Maxim has *terrific jacket sweaters for children.* These come in Orlon only, and they average a little less than $15. I *love* their blue-and-white *Choo-Choo Charlie* locomotive design, their red, beige, and white *Carousel* (with carousel horse) design, and the *fire engine* (white body, red engine) and *Big Bird* (white-and-yellow) sweaters. Their new *Poochie Pup* (it sounds awful, but it's cute) is marvelous for a child who loves animals: beige body, brown, black, and white puppy design.

Mary Maxim has *lighter-weight sweater kits* too, including a beautiful hooded sweater in 6–12 month size, less than $5 and a fancy lacy-knit woman's jacket and scarf set, under $12 in sizes 36–38. There are many new *linen-look sweaters* to knit, too, in beautiful feminine styles, most well under $20. There's even a sweater kit for your dog, up to 15″ long, less than $4.

Every time I look at the Mary Maxim catalogue, there's something new, something interesting. There are dynamite afghans in this catalogue, too, as well as crocheted bedspreads and tablecloths sure to be heirlooms. Sales are held each spring, with even more savings possible.

David Morgan of Seattle, Washington, has a fine kit available for a *Guernsey turtleneck sweater,* a marvelous warm sweater worn by British sailors. This Guernsey comes in 8-ply Cleakheaton yarn (medium weight), or 12-ply (heavy weight). The medium weight, in size 38, would cost well under $25. In heavy weight, the kit costs barely $28. Nice colors available. This sweater, store-bought, would cost you *at least $75.*

Patternworks is a relatively new kit company with excellent chenille sweater kits ranging in price from $24 ro $40. Their easy-to-knit *roll-collar jacket sweater* is a classic design worked in rib stitch, with two patch pockets. Material is 100 percent natural cotton yarn loomed in North Carolina. Another fine kit is their *raglan pullover with cowl neck.* But the most interesting styling is their *Victorian jacket with broad shoulders* and tapered sleeves worked in seed stitch. One button at fitted waistline.

The Pirate's Cove in Babylon, New York, carries top-quality Irish yarn and fascinating Aran sweater patterns. At the moment they have only one kit, but it's for one of the most beautiful *Aran-patterned afghans* I've seen. Finished size is 40″ x 60″ without the fringe, and the afghan is knitted in one piece. Available in traditional off-white Aran wool, with the lanolin left in, or one of many exquisite colors. This is a gorgeous afghan; it's the kind of thing you'd love to give or receive as a gift. About $50, and well worth it.

The Scottish Lion in North Conway, New Hampshire, has a marvelous and reasonably priced kit for a woman or man's *fair isle sweater*. The kit comes with hand-knitted yoke, enough wool for a pullover or cardigan, small buttons for a pullover, and large buttons for a cardigan. Sizes 32–42. Colors are coral, brown, green, natural, or blue. About $30.

I've been to the shop at **Shannon International Airport** only once, on the way back from Istanbul; we were there for less than an hour, but it was fascinating . . . full of Irish hand-knits, Shetlands, cashmeres, and very expensive smoked salmon and other culinary treats. My peripatetic mother, a great knitter as well as a traveler, has stopped there many times, returning from each trip with at least a few Aran sweaters.

If you haven't seen the Shannon catalogue, you ought to send for it. It has almost as many treasures as the shop itself, at bargain prices. But an Aran hand-knit sweater, even ordered through this catalogue, costs at least $65. (The same-quality sweaters sell in this country for almost $100 each.) But now the Shannnon catalogue offers *Aran sweater kits* with 35 ounces of Bainin wool, buttons, and needles included for well under $25—an excellent buy. The kit makes into a pullover or cardigan for men or women. Excellent.

As you may already have determined, I'm crazy about Scandinavian patterned sweaters. Some of the very best *Scandinavian sweater kits* are available from **Snowflake Kit** of Nesøya, Norway. Each of these kits comes with excellent quality, soft Norwegian wool, knitting needles, pewter buttons or clasps, and instructions in well-written English. More than fifty different designs, some with embroidered borders, are available for men, women, and children, plus gloves, hats, and fabulous cross-country ski socks. Prices range, generally, from around $30 to a high of $45. Postage can add as much as $7 for one kit ($8 for two) for surface mail, $10 for airmail. In addition, foreign kits may be subject to a customs duty upon entering the United States; check with your local post office before ordering. But these kits are still a bargain; equivalent hand-knitted sweaters cost a bundle, even in Norway. These are extraordinary designs. My mother and I are always on the lookout for collections of Scandinavian sweater patterns, and I've never seen this kind of variety and quality of design in one book or catalogue.

Although **P. Straker, Ltd.,** doesn't refer to their sweaters as kits, technically they are; you simply can't buy any of their fine sweater patterns without the materials to make them. There are about fifty designs here, ranging from a *traditional Danish turtleneck* sweater of the type worn by *the Faroe Island's fishermen* to a *honeycomb stitch Aran pullover* to a soft *mohair cowl-neck sweater* with bloused cuffs. Some of these sweaters—like their simple cardigan Becky, knit of hand-spun wool—are excellent for beginning knitters. Some, like Penelope, a lightweight and very unusual Aran cardigan knit of Rygja yarn, will entertain even an experienced and somewhat jaded knitter. Many of these designs are more contemporary and fashionable than the patterns in most commercial pattern books of the past couple of years. They also have several attractive packages for hats and scarves. Prices are extremely good, ranging from around $25 for the Faroe Island kit, in size 36, to around $50. A few of the sweaters in larger sizes cost more.

Needlepoint Decorative Accessories and Other Needlepoint Kits

Several years ago there was in this country an enormous revival of interest in needlepoint. Everywhere you looked there were magazine articles on needlepoint, fancy new books on needlepoint, needlepoint supply stores, and well-dressed young and middle-aged women carrying designer handbags and hand-painted canvases with Persian wools. But during the past two years or so, the needlepoint market has stabilized, leaving, I think, a very strong and still populous hard core of needlewomen and men who will now accept and buy only the best and most unusual designs available. The section that follows is for those people.

The American Museum of Natural History Museum Shop catalogue usually contains one or two needlepoint kits designed to tie in with their exhibits. A recent catalogue featured, for example, a *Pompeiian design pillow of marine animals* derived from a mosaic of the first century, B.C. The 16″ pillow kit (still available at this writing) tied in with their Pompeii 79 exhibit. A unique decorative accent for just under $40.

Bay Country Woodcrafts has recently begun to offer one or two needlepoint *pillow kits with wildfowl designs.* Their most recent catalogue contained an interesting loon design hand-painted on #14 canvas. A nice accent for a beach house or for a sporting man's or woman's home. Under $50. Measures 12″ x 12½″. This kit is available only from Bay Country Woodcrafts.

Better Homes and Gardens Kits has just a few needlepoint designs. But three pillow kits are so exquisite—and inexpensive—that you'll want to consider them. One is called *Ardebil Mosque pillow,* an extremely rich and elaborate mosaic design in browns, beige, and navy. Very beautiful. Printed on 14-mesh canvas, 14" x 14"; comes with Persian yarn. About $20. Two other beauties are their *Pegasus* and *Arabic Designs pillows.* Each kit measures 15" x 15" and comes with 14-mesh painted canvas. Richly entwined medieval colors (primarily browns and blues, with some gold metallic yarn). Pegasus is the winged horse of Greek mythology; the other is an Arabic cross with elaborate geometric patterns. These are very beautiful pillows, about $20 each.

The **Boston Museum of Fine Arts Shop** always includes a few fascinating needlepoint kits in its catalogues, particularly around Christmastime. All come with designs hand-painted in oil on imported white mono canvas, and come with Paternayan yarns. Recent designs have included *a clutch bag based on a nineteenth-century Japanese woodblock print by Hiroshige* (relatively inexpensive at around $35); an eyeglass case based on an illustration from D. M. Dewey's *Nurseryman's Pocket Book of Specimen Fruit and Flowers,* about $16; a small owl on 10½" square background, from the Egyptian hieroglyph for the letter *J* from the Bersheh coffin, Middle Kingdom, Twelfth Dynasty, 1991–1786 B.C., under $15; and a bird on a peony branch pillow, a detail taken from an Iranian painting on silk of the Timurid period, 1410–20. About $50.

I found a tiny ad for **Canvas Creations'** kits in a sailing magazine—and, appropriately, they have terrific *nautical map kits of waterways* from the Bahama Islands to Biscayne Bay to Nantucket Island. My mom made one up for me this past winter of Eastern Long Island, with Southampton, Sag Harbor, and Montauk Point spelled out in contrasting color. These pillows are white, pale blue, and pale yellow, about $35; they're terrific for a beach house or for a friend whose heart is not on dry land. My mother did have to rework the Southampton legend twice; the letters were a little too small for comfort. Other waterways kits: Sandy Hook, New Jersey; Tampa Bay, Florida; Hilton Head, South Carolina; Mackinac Island, Michigan; West and South Rivers, Maryland; Cape Cod; Annapolis; Essex-Old Lyme, Connecticut—and many more.

If you have a downhill skier or golfer in the family, Canvas Creations' ski boot and golfing shoe needlepoint pillow kits may interest you, too; about $25. Very attractive.

Despite a lifelong interest in needlework and crafts, I never was particularly interested in doing needlepoint myself—not until last spring when I received **Everlume Corporation**'s catalogue and saw their *Bi-Plane Error stamp pillow kit.* Having grown up in a stamp-collecting household, I found the design appealing, and I haven't stopped needlepointing since. The bi-plane kit really is a stunner; I worked on it two summers ago in Westhampton, and people kept sitting down next to me to tell me about their stamp collections, past and present. Since it's a design to which men particularly respond this and Everlume's *Graf Zeppelin stamp kit* would make great gifts for your male friends who used to or still collect stamps. Everlume has many other postage stamp needlepoint kits, too, including the pharmacy commemorative, the Grandma Moses commemorative, the nursing commemorative, and others. Kit prices average about $17, an excellent value. Very interesting kits to work on.

The Freer Gallery of Art of the Smithsonian Institution usually includes a few fascinating and complex needlepoint kits in its catalogue. Recent offerings have included an 18″ x 15″ *Lotus Pond* design from a Ming Dynasty ceramic jardinière decorated in cloisonné style, about $50; *Parrots,* 16″ x 16″, a design from a polychrome tile from Turkey, Ottoman period, early seventeenth century, about $50; and a 14″ diameter round pillow, about $30, a flying goose design from a T'ang Dynasty Chinese pottery dish.

The Horchow Collection, that pioneering luxury goods catalogue, almost always contains a couple of tasteful and unusual needlepoint kits. The latest catalogue (at the time of this writing) offers one of the handsomest needlepoint *jewelry cases* I've seen, complete with UltraSuede interior, two zip pockets, and a storage bar for rings. $30.

The Krick Kit Company has many fine needlepoint pillow kits, including several *American country designs* such as a primitive fruit basket design (about $40), a traditional stencil-type pineapple design (around $20), a very charming sandpiper (about $25), and *British blockade runner,* after the painting by William York, now hanging in the downstairs sitting room of the Edmund-Alston House in Charleston (around $50).

They also carry kits for a needlepoint duck doorstop, available in pintail, wood duck, mallard, or widgeon, about $22. Nice belt kits, too.

But, perhaps most interesting, Krick Kit will *create a needlepoint portrait of your home.* This can be used as a picture, a pillow, or a doorstop. You send them a color photograph, and any special instructions, and they hand-paint your house on #18 white canvas. About $75.

My Krick Kit brochure arrived with a $5 discount certificate, good for the first order from them.

If you've done much needlepoint, you probably know the **Elaine Magnin** catalogue. There are *many* excellent designs here. Especially nice is her needlepoint *Oriental Picture Frame* kit, 14″ x 16″, to accommodate an 8″ x 10″ picture, and her many fine *needlepoint purse* kits. Of these, my favorite is the 2-ply colorful elephant design—a marvelous evening clutch, about $65.

The Metropolitan Museum of Art's terrific mail-order catalogue always includes a few embroidery and needlepoint kits. These have been designed exclusively for the Metropolitan and for the Royal School of Needlework, London. My favorite this year is a 14″ diameter round pillow, featuring a charming squirrel and hazelnut leaf design adapted from the *Hunt of the Unicorn*. About $40. 18-mesh canvas. One of several beautiful kits.

The Met By Mail, the opera lover's catalogue operated by the Metropolitan Opera Guild, has three fascinating kits. The *Boris Godunov* kit evokes the architecture and splendor of old Russia. The *Otello* kit is based upon Franco Zeffirelli's Lion of Venice. Each kit measures 15″ x 15″ and costs under $40. The new *Don Carlo Needlepoint kit* is Erica Wilson's transformation of David Reppa's luxe curtain for *Don Carlo*. Printed on 18-mesh, 12″ x 16″ canvas. About $50. The latter is a very complicated kit for a neophyte; either the Otello or Godunov kits would be better for someone of medium skills.

The Mystic Seaport Museum Store has wonderful needlepoint pillow kits for the sailors in your life. Particularly nice are their *sloop, ketch, Hobie cat,* and *Sunfish pillow kits*. The sloop and ketch pillow measures 14″ x 14″ and costs well under $30. The other two measure 12″ x 14″ and sell for around $25.

Needlepoint Portraits will convert your color or black-and-white photograph into a surprisingly good-looking needlepoint portrait kit measuring 12″ x 12″. $40 for a monochromatic kit; $70 for full color. They use a TV camera connected to a computer to form the coded graph.

Papillon has a very interesting gift catalogue with many needlepoint kits. Recent catalogues have featured some unusual needlepoint items, including *floral jewelry roll* with pansy design (about $40), needlepoint *wood covers* for a favorite golfer ($68), needlepoint *scissor case* ($19), and terrific *eyeglass cases*. A recent catalogue also features a custom-designed pillow kit ($30), which can be made up from your child's drawing.

Mrs. Kitty Parfet of Invergrove Heights, Minnesota, will create needlepoint canvases to match a favorite fabric or china design, or she'll create a design based on a favorite activity or hobby. Her specialty is handbags. Kits, without yarn, generally range from $30 to $100.

Eva Rosenstand Corporation has some perfectly riveting *Danish needlepoint pillow and chair seat and back sets*. The needlepoint pillows are subtly colored in earth tones, with very beautiful and unusual patterns; prices are fairly high, from about $40 to $75.

The *needlepoint upholstery covers* are among the most beautiful I've seen *anywhere*. These are, I think, fairly priced; the needlepoint design I'd like to make, Danish pastoral scenes framed by a dogwood border, runs about $220 per set. A few covers are cheaper, but I think this one would be beyond my ability to buy if I were to find something as nice preworked. These are *fabulous* chair cover sets.

Sandeen's Scandinavian Gift Shop of Saint Paul, Minnesota, is one of the few places in America one can find kits for authentic klostersøm and diamondsøm needlwork. *Klostersøm* translates as "block stitch" and resembles the satin stitch; it is a mosaic effect of blocks of each color formed by clusters of stitches the same length. *Diamondsøm,* the diamond stitch, is a double cross stitch. These klostersøm kits have most unusual patterns, strongly reminiscent of Norwegian hand-knit sweaters. These can be worked in two colors for a stark dramatic room accent or in multiple colors. Well worth looking into; many of these kits are very beautiful and *very* inexpensive. The multicolor klostersøm pillow kit that most interests me costs well under $15.

The School of Needlepoint, Great Neck, New York, has the best selection of kits for *needlepoint tennis racquet covers.* Designs range from a funny turtle hitting a shot to a more sedate beige-and-brown abstract design with three tennis balls. These kits average about $30. There are magnificent *needlepoint vest kits* here, too, totally premounted, available in two dramatic Oriental designs, and one floral design. Very fairly priced, I think, at $64.

The school has some fine *needlepoint handbag kits,* ranging in price from $65 to $88. Also pillows and wall hangings, of course. Some of their designs look like the work of the painter Vasarely. If a needlepointed Chagall or Picasso or Gauguin painting is what pleases you, they have those, too.

Sign of the Peacock has some very unusual needlepoint pillow kits. Perhaps more interesting are the hand-painted reproductions of the *American Primitive artist Clementine Hunter's memories of plantation life in Louisiana.* Scenes of washday, going fishing, Saturday night, a wedding, pecan harvest, picking cotton, and a Nativity scene. Kit with yarn costs just over $45.

Of their bird kits, I very much like (and plan to make) their *Sandpiper kit.* About $35. Most unusual are their *needlepoint compacts.* Available in dogwood or moutain cabin design. Under $10.

The Stitchery of Wellesley, Massachusetts, has an enormous selection of needlepoint kits, everything from *Christmas tree ornaments* to *belts* to *eyeglass cases* (I made one of these with a wild duck design—marvelous), to *pillows* and *wall hangings.* Each catalogue contains much completely new merchandise; I've yet to see a catalogue of theirs from which I didn't want to order at least one item. If there's a new baby in your family or if one is expected soon, you may be particularly interested in their charming *rainbow mobile,* a colorful rainbow from which are suspended a smiling sun, a hot-air balloon, a butterfly, and a little person in a helicopter, about $16. Designs range, generally, from the traditional to the cute.

Stitchin' Time of Rochester, New York, handles the complete catalogues of several manufacturers, including Spinnerin and the Elsa Williams Collection. Elsa Williams has some stunning *needlepoint pillow kits in designs from ancient Egypt;* their Reeds of Thebes design, reasonably priced at $24, is one of the most attractive needlepoint pillows I've seen. Their *pinecones* pillow design, 12″ x 8″, under $20, is another wonderful kit, a nice accent for a country home. Their needlepoint rug kits are beyond belief.

I think **Jane Whitmire** designs some of the most beautiful and amusing needlepoint kits available in this country. Her design training includes a B.A. from the Chicago Art Institute and an M.A. in Art Education from Columbia University—and it shows. Right now I'm working on her *Primitive Pussy* pillow. An adaptation of an early American painting, it has tweeded background and very defined and beautiful lines; this kit appeals to my love both of Americana and of cats. 14″ x 18″, about $45.

There are many other terrific and unusual designs from this designer. If you like Coptic art, or even if you'd like an unusual "angel" as a Christmas accent, you'll adore her *Coptic Cupid* pillow kit. The Copts were, of course, early Egyptian Christians who often mixed Christian and pagan symbolism in their art—so this cupid *does* look like an angel. Adapted from a seventeenth-century tapestry. 13″ x 15″. About $40.

Other marvelous designs include a *Scythian horse,* adapted from the Pazyryk Carpet in the Hermitage Museum, Moscow; a fine *American eagle,* a faithful adaptation from an early American woven coverlet; *Shakespeare* and *Beethoven;* a *lute player,* adapted from a tenth-century Islamic plate; several adaptations of *American patchwork* patterns; and a very amusing 9″ x 9″ *griffin,* straight from medieval heraldry.

World Arts will inexpensively create a needlepoint portrait of your home. You send them a color photograph, and they adapt the design onto a 12″ x 16″ mono canvas. No wool included. About $22. They'll also create needlepoint canvases of your coat of arms, boat, car, or a favorite landscape. They'll make up needlepoint portraits of loved ones, too; these latter look a little grotesque to me.

Patchwork and Appliqué

Barbara Allen Quilts of Oak Ridge, Tennessee, has fabulous full-size and crib *quilt kits* available in patterns ranging from Oak Leaf and cherries to star and crescent to Dutch girl. There are more than fifty different kits available. A standard-size quilt kit for a double bed seems to average about $50. This catalogue is a bit difficult to read, but what you ought to do is look through it for ideas, then write to them for more information.

Annie's Attic has several charming kits in crochet and in patchwork. Of the patchwork kits, the most interesting is their *Patch by Number® Lattice Quilt,* completely reversible, the same on both sides. Construction is not that complicated, since it really is put together by following the numbers. Crib quilt costs about $20; twin size, about $60; double, about $80. The latter is about $300 less than you'd have to pay for a comparable quilt.

Judy Bean Crafts has several unusual patchwork pillow kits at extremely reasonable prices. Their *horse weather vane pillow kit,* for example, less than $10, is a design based on the kind of old weather vanes I remember seeing as a child on top of barns in Pennsylvania. 18½ " x 14½ ". They also have a very charming patchwork tote bag kit, only $12, of a funny black, yellow, and white school bus. The tote measures 13 " x 18 ".

Better Homes and Gardens Kits has several quilts in its catalogue. Most interesting are their crib quilt called *Barnyard Friends* and a large quilt called *Aunt Mary's Flower Quilt.* Barnyard Friends measures 40 " x 50 ", and it combines appliqué and embroidery with sewing. This exclusive Better Homes and Gardens® design depicts a cat, a dog, a hen, a cow, a pig, and a goat in calico. About $25. Matching pillow, train of piglets, plus quilt sell for under $30 as a package.

The *Aunt Mary's Flower Quilt* measures 81 " x 81 ", and it is a beauty in shades of pink, green, and white. Adapted for hand or machine appliqué. Kit has precut pieces with borders in a cotton/polyester washable broadcloth; ninety-nine pieces in all. The quilting itself is quite elaborate. A bargain at about $40—at least $160 less than a comparable presewn contemporary quilt. The batting costs about $9 more.

Cher's Kit and Kaboodle has some charming appliqué and quilt kits. My favorites include a *child's reversible denim apron* with colorful appliqués of glue, scissors, and paintbrushes poking out of the large front pocket, about $9; a *clown nap mat,* with iron-on clown quilted to double-batted cotton/polyester mat, about $16; and a fabulous machine-appliquéd and quilted *busy barnyard* wall-hanging with Velcro-attached cow, sheep, pig, and ducks. Approximately 35 " x 21 "; under $22.

Since Cher's Kit and Kaboodle periodically has sales, you can sometimes get these reasonably priced kits for even less than the prices quoted above.

Cross Patch Quilting Center has a terrific crib for beginners. It's their version of the traditional *Rocking Horse,* designed for them by Susie Weldon. Includes cotton fabric for top and backing, polyester batting, patterns, quilting diagrams and designs. Sample fabrics on request. An excellent quilt kit, at less than $25.

Ginger Snap Station of Atlanta, Georgia, has an extraordinary collection of patchwork kits for quilts, pillows, hats, tennis racquet covers, stuffed toys, and other novelty items. One of the most charming **crib quilt** kits is for a *Bonnet Baby* quilt top, in a delicately colored gingham, calico, and denim—less than $20. Preassembled, it would cost at least $60 more. A Bonnet Baby pillow kit costs under $10.

They have an excellent *Rolling Star quilt kit* in 84" x 101" queen/double size, in pink or tan, for about $50. This quilt can be assembled by traditional techniques or put together via a quick-quilt technique, which requires no hand quilting and no quilt frame. Hundreds of dollars less than a preassembled quilt like it.

Their *Dresden plate* quilt kit is exquisite, too, with all precut pieces of calico. Finished size approximately 84" x 99½". About $50. A gorgeous *Dresden plate pillow kit* sells for under $15.

Also available: Mexican Star quilt top kit, fine calico house pillow kits (only $11), a fabulous country cathedral-window pillow kit, plus totes, patchwork hats, golf club covers, and marvelous patchwork tennis racquet covers, about $10.

Hearthside Mail Order has some of the most extraordinary quilt kits I've seen. Their *Small Fry Quilt* is a combination of Bonnet Baby designs with flowers and butterflies on a heavily quilted muslin background. Simple and beautiful. Top only, about $20. Complete kit about $30.

Their *log cabin quilt* is a real beauty. Comes totally precut. Finished quilt measures 81" x 96" (about $65) or 90" x 108" (under $90).

Their *Dresden plate* is one of the nicest kit versions of this classic design. All pieces for the plate and diamonds that edge it have been precut. This pattern uses twenty different small prints. Piecework and appliqué. Available edged in red or navy blue. 77" x 95" top only, under $50; complete kit, about $65. 90" x 108" top only, about $65; complete kit, under $90.

Mary Maxim always features a few quilt kits in each catalogue. Most interesting recently was their *Dresden plate quilt kit*—not as sophisticated as the one offered by Hearthside Mail Order, detailed above, but nice enough. Double size, 84" x 99" costs just over $50.

Less work but just as pretty is their *Garland of Flowers* quilt, a center circle of appliquéd roses, along the edges and in corners. Quite a bit of quilting. Less than $30.

Newstalgia® Designs has a very amusing 43" x 60" quilt kit that's good as a quilt, play mat, or wall hanging. Called *Son of the Newstalgia Choo-Choo,* this quilt is great for young model-railroad buffs, incorporating colorful designs of a water tower, train station, locomotive and tender, freight car, loading dock, passenger car, caboose, and various railside signals. About $30.

Patch-It has interesting, inexpensive patchwork kits for patchwork ties, pillows, and other novelty patchwork kits. Traditional design pillows, like their *pinwheel star* or *crescent star pillow kits,* average well under $10, including postage.

Quilts and Other Comforts is the quilt kit catalogue published by the owners of the *Quilters Newsletter,* the fascinating magazine for quilt makers. Most of these quilt patterns are not available from any other quilt kit company. You'll probably gasp when you see their *Martha's Mountain Medallion* kit—one of the finest buys available, at less than $30. This kit is utterly fabulous. Their *Summer Star* is magnificent, too, at about the same price, including 800 die-cut diamonds and full-size quilting patterns.

Saddle Valley Stitchery has several attractive patchwork-quilt kits in designs ranging from Tumbling Blocks to Log Cabin to Rolling Star. Perhaps most interesting is their new 83″ square *Broken Star* kit, available in eight color schemes. Kits include precut diamonds. You add the background of your choice. This very beautiful Broken Star kit sells for under $20.

Salter Path has excellent quilted-*pillow kits* featuring *hand-screened English Audubon prints.* These sell for just over $10, and they're very lovely. They also have botanical prints, as well as other bird prints, suitable for trapunto work. Most of these kits sell for under $13. Comparable quality presewn pillows would start at at least $25. (I've seen them go for up to $40.) Very good buys.

The Stitchery has a fabulous *white-on-white pineapple-motif quilt top,* which would make a fabulous wedding gift. The quilt top is stitched in squares, using a basic running stitch, so this is a portable project. The squares are joined by hand using a blind stitch. Twin size costs about $40. Double (70″ x 98″) size costs about $50. The queen size (84″ x 98″) goes for about $10 more.

Some of **Thompson and Thompson's** designs are a bit extravagant for my taste, but two are quite nice: *Addie,* a variation on the Bonnet Baby calico child, and *Butterflies,* colorful Oriental butterflies with reverse appliqué print and bamboo quilting design. The latter kit contains precut pieces of 100 percent cotton. Crib quilt top kit sells for just over $20; twin costs under $50. King size costs under $70.

Cross–Stitch Samplers, Crewel, and Other Embroidery Kits

American Handicrafts has a very extensive selection of cross-stitch embroidery kits for table and bed linens, samplers, and quilts with cross-stitch designs. Their *Daisy Spray tablecloth kit* is a very nice daisy-and-other-flower-cluster design on machine-washable polyester-and-cotton permanent-press fabric in sizes from 60" x 80" to 60" x 104" oblong, and 70" round. A 60" x 90" oblong cloth costs under $20. DMC thread kit extra. Napkins are well under $2.

Their prestamped pillowcases come in several attractive designs on cotton/polyester cloth. Two cases per package. Prices average about $6 per pair. (Frankly, I'd prefer 100 percent cotton pillowcases.)

Their *samplers* are quite nice, with reassuring homey sayings, such as "Be it ever so humble there's no place like home" and "Wherever you wander, wherever you roam, be happy and healthy, and glad to come home." On the lighter side, they have a sampler kit that reads "Those who indulge bulge." Prices range from around $5 to up to $12.

American Handicrafts' *cross-stitch quilts* are *very* nice indeed. My own favorite is their *Song Birds Quilt* with twelve different birds stamped on 100 percent cotton percale. The quilt top sells for about $20 in king size, and the DMC thread kit runs just under $30. Their *American Sampler* cross-stitch quilt is very nice, too, for a traditional home or for a home featuring country Americana. King size is about $20, with the thread kit doubling purchase price.

If a baby is about to come into your life or the life of a friend, you may be interested in their marvelous *alphabet percale quilt top* in 40" x 60" size. Well under $20, including thread kit. They have very nice *embroidered bibs,* too, about $5 for a set of two.

Another nice baby gift: a *crewel ABC pillow* combining letters and pictures in a block format. About $10. A *crewel comforter kit* to match sells for well under $20.

The American Needlewoman has an excellent selection of cross-stitch kits, including samplers, baby quilts, and bedspreads for quilting.

Cross-stitch samplers include a very colorful and charming pictorial "Home Sweet Home" (about $6); a sampler you can personalize, which reads "When two fond hearts as one unite, the yoke is easy and the burden light," about $8; and a fabulous reproduction of an antique sampler dated 1773, from the Cooper-Hewitt Museum collection, on imported linen, about $16.

Among the *cross-stitch quilt kits,* the *Wildflowers* quilt, on 100 percent cotton percale, is a delicate beauty. The double-bed size costs well under $20; DMC thread kit adds about $10 to the cost.

Other interesting kits include charming *counted cross-stitch dolls,* 11" tall, about $8, and a *Hebrew-inscribed Challah cover,* $6.

Better Homes and Gardens Kits has many fine cross-stitch and crewel embroidery kits. Most interesting among the cross-stitch kits are a beautiful sampler with a bright house design, which reads "Joy is for living, Life is for loving, Love is for giving," about $12; tiny *heart-shaped sachets* (with blended sachet included), three for about $7; a very unusual 13″ x 23″ sampler that reads *"Home Sweet Apartment";* and a fabulous *Peter Rabbit crib quilt* created by Erica Wilson, based on Beatrix Potter's designs, about $30.

Crewel kits include a marvelous Erica Wilson 16″ x 16″ picture or pillow called "All Things Bright and Beautiful"—kittens, an owl, a bird, and flowers. Another interesting crewel kit: an *After-Hours Caftan,* less than $20, with yoke you embroider with flowers—beautiful comfort.

Boycan's Craft Supplies has a few interesting cross-stitch samplers. My favorite here is one that measures 7″ x 19″, costs less than $5, and reads "Housework is a Bummer."

The **Counting House** of Pawleys Island, South Carolina, specializes in marvelous *embroidery kits, many imported from Denmark.* Among the nicest here, embroidered wildfowl pillows, just over $10 each; a "weeds of the garden" pillow, under $20; and a beautiful wall hanging, an elaborate portrait of a farm, with a legend reading "I will build myself a farm," 11⅛″ x 17½″, under $30.

Mary Maxim always carries a few attractive quilt and table linen kits. Most of these you'll find in other major catalogues. One that I haven't seen and that I like very much is their *Ming Tree cross-stitch tablecloth kit,* in Oriental blue-and-white chinoiserie design, to go with your Willoware collection. The 50″ x 70″ size costs well under $15, plus about $3 for the thread kit. A 68″ round cloth available, plus sizes up to 60″ x 104″.

The **Old Sturbridge Village Museum Gift Shop** has very nice *reproductions of fine antique cross-stitch samplers.* Particularly nice is their Richardson House sampler, 11″ x 14″, about $10. It includes an alphabet and two views of the Richardson House, plus pine trees.

Eva Rosenstand Corporation's Clara Weaver kits are *utterly fantastic counted-thread embroidery designs imported from Norway.* The birds and small animals here, on pillows, bell pulls, table linens, and eyeglass cases, are the best I've seen. There are *many* floral designs as well. If you love embroidery, do send for this catalogue. You may not care for some of their pictorials, but the 150 or so other fine kits more than make up for their occasional lapses. Pillow kits range in price from well under $20 up to $30. Place mats average less than $9. Eyeglass cases average under $6. Tablecloths range in price from about $35 up to $140 (most are less).

Saddle Valley Stitchery has some extraordinary cross-stitch quilt kits. One of the most unusual is their *New Amsterdam cross-stitch quilt* on fine cotton percale. This quilt has dense areas of monocolor floral tulip and leaf designs, and it looks, at first (at least, from a distance), like appliqué. Double quilt top costs about $20; the thread kit adds about $25 to the price.

There are many interesting *cross-stitch samplers* in this catalogue, including a very pretty floral and bird design that reads "To love and be loved is the greatest joy on earth." Other samplers include a very pretty 9″ x 22″ "Home Sweet Home" motif and an equally charming "God Bless Our Home," both stamped on 100 percent linen, about $8 each, including thread.

Jane Snead Samplers has the *largest selection of cross-stitch samplers* you'll probably ever find in one place. Legends range from "Houses are made of brick and stone/Homes are made of love alone" to "I know I'm efficient/Tell me I'm beautiful" to an elegant "Give us this Day our Daily Bread." There are more than 250 fine choices in this catalogue. Some are funny, some are sentimental, and a few are religious. All are printed on imported pure linen, and they're *very* inexpensive, rarely exceeding $7.

The Stitchery usually carries a fine assortment of *crewel pillow kits, embroidered napkins* and *place mats,* wonderful crewel pictures, and *cross-stitch samplers.*

Their most recent catalogue contained a fabulous Tree of Life crewel panel adapted from an embroidered picture in the collection of the Museum of Fine Arts, Boston. Finished size, 20″ x 21″; heirloom-quality needlework, about $25.

Stitchin' Time carries many fabulous *crewel embroidery kits by the Elsa Williams staff*—Kathy Robertson, Michael LeClair, and Nancy King. These are some of the finest crewel kits currently being designed and produced in this country. *Crewel kits range from pillows to clutch purses to pincushions and clock faces.* The *crewel purses* are *excellent* buys, rarely more than $20 each; a preembroidered store-bought purse like them would cost about $100. Pillow kits in Jacobean-influenced designs generally seem to sell for under $30. If you like crewel, you'll love this catalogue.

Jane Whitmire, one of my favorite needlepoint designers, also does some *outstanding crewel pillow kits.* Her best-known design is the 16″ x 20″ *William the Conqueror's Boat,* adapted from the Bayeux Tapestry, the ancient crewel depiction of the Norman Conquest. There are several other fine designs as well, including a charming 12″ x 14″ *Plantain,* about $15.

The World in Stitches, the mail-order division of The Needlework Shop of Nashua, New Hampshire, offers very beautiful *hardanger embroidery pillow kits from Norway and Denmark.* These fine and inexpensive kits even include contrasting lining material to put under the finished embroidery. Sizes are all 13″ x 13″, and prices are well under $20 each.

In addition, the World in Stitches carries *very* beautiful 100 percent linen *Dutch samplers*. These are generally large and complex, up to size 17″ x 31½″, for under $60. One of them has sixty-one motifs, five alphabets, and a very attractive border. It is a copy of a 1730 sampler and takes about three hundred hours to complete.

8

Transportation

Boats

Whether you're building a snipe or a 29′ ketch from a kit, you can generally expect to save about 50 percent (sometimes 60 percent) of the cost of a prebuilt boat. Naturally, the larger the boat, the more you save.

I suggest that you read catalogues from several manufacturers before deciding upon the right kit for you. Some boats are more difficult to build than others. Some kits come with just preassembled frames; some arrive with just about everything you'll need. In any case, many of the fine boat kits that follow can help make your fantasies come true—within your price range.

Kayaks and Canoes

Clark Craft of Tonawanda, New York, has one of the largest selections of boat kits of all types; in fact, they were, they claim, the first manufacturer to offer a "do-it-yourself" boat kit. Most of their kits are available in three different packages. The *frame kit* includes the difficult parts that require power tools and factory jigging; these come precut and preassembled. With each frame-pac kit, you also receive building plans slanted toward the amateur builder, plus patterns of all deck framing, seats, and, on larger boats, cabin sides, bunks, and many other parts. Their *hull kits* come with precut parts, all frames, transom, stem, etc. After you assemble the hull, you can then purchase the rest of the kit, if you wish, such as deck and/or cabin.

Their *complete custom boat kit* includes all frame kit parts plus all material parts necessary to completely assemble the boat, minus the hardware and optional accessories. This kit includes all fastenings.

Among Clark Craft's many interesting kayak and canoe kits:

The Victory #CC-1 Prelaminated Sectional Fiberglass Canoe Kit. Available in 14' or 16' lengths; the difference in price for the larger model is about $10. This excellent canoe measures (in the smaller size) 14' long, 36" wide, 15" deep, with a 17" bow height. Weight is 63 pounds, with 725-pound load capacity. The Victory #CC-1 kit features all fiberglass hand-laid uphull, including maintenance-free fiberglass gunwales, decks, bulkheads. Extra roving fiberglass cloth adds to rigidity. The canoe has good stability, load capacity, deep hull, and good width. The design handles well in a variety of water conditions. With the color molded into the fiberglass, this boat never needs painting. A square stern is available at $20 extra. A very good buy, the Victory Deluxe #CC-1 costs *well under* $250. The least expensive preconstructed fiberglass 16' canoe I've been able to locate sold last year for $350—so you should save at least $100 by making your own from one of these kits.

*The Niagara #CC-4 all wood **V**-bottom canoe.* Available in 13'6", 15'6", and 17'6" lengths. The 17'6" version measures 39" wide, 19" bow height, 13" deep, weighs 90 pounds, and has a load capacity of 900 pounds. The kit costs about $175; it is available with square stern for about the same price. The frames are made of ⅜" Philippine mahogany. Covering skin is ¼" marine-glued plywood. An alternative covering could also be fiberglass cloth laid over plywood for additional strength.

The **V**-bottom of this canoe eliminates the tippy feeling of most canoes. It can be rigged for sailing, if you wish. Floats on just a few inches of water. A good family canoe.

Their *#CPBK 56 Blandford Kayak kit,* designed by the New Zealander Richard Hartley, features a plywood hull over timber frame. This boat is assembled upside down on a building jig. It has a roomy cockpit trimmed with a breakwater, and one or two seats can be added. The size and shape of the cockpit can be altered to suit your requirements. This model is a very easy kayak to build. The finished boat is stable and seaworthy, especially suited, they say, for hard use and leaving afloat. Plans include details for making a sail rig, rudder, paddle, and trolley for ease in transporting it. 11' long, 27" beam, 48" cockpit, and weighs 62 pounds. The full kit costs under $150.

If a *racing kayak* is more what you have in mind, you may be interested in Clark Craft's new *#CC-6 Spitfire Sectional fiberglass kayak in kit form.* This is an extremely fast kayak. It's a single-seater sectional fiberglass kayak good for sport or touring. Very stable, and it turns well. Ample storage fore and aft. The cockpit is very roomy, so you can have your choice of several knee positions. A form-fitting contour seat is included, along with a multiposition adjustable foot brace. The hull is built from layers of fiberglass cloth, resin, and gel coat. An inside keel provides extra strength. The kit comes in two pieces: a hull and a deck. The only seam is fastened with fiberglass resin or epoxy.

Specifications: 14″ long, 24″ wide, 13″ deep, 39″ x 19″ cockpit, weighs 39 pounds, and costs well under $250.

You'll probably recognize **Country Ways** of Minnetonka, Minnesota, from chapter 3. In addition to a fine variety of sporting goods kits, Country Ways has an excellent selection of kits for canoes, kayaks, skate sails, and smaller sailboats.

Their 15′ *Canadien canoe kit* has a slight **V**-bottom for directional stability and tracking. Seats are laced with their own snowshoe lacing, and varnished, providing comfortable seating for day-long trips. The center thwart is positioned for traditional "paddle" portaging, and you can add their portage yoke if you wish.

The Canadien is built of mahogany plywood, measures 15′8″ x 3′5″, and weighs only 46 pounds. It's light, tough, and fast. About $350. (Two larger canoe kits are available as well, each with flatter bottoms.)

Country Ways also has six kayak kits available. Designed by Ken Littledyke, a pioneer of the stitch-and-glue method, these are lightweight yet strong and durable. Because these kayaks are made of wood, they'll float even when fully swamped, and foam or air-bag flotation can be added if you wish. All their kayak kits come with molded seats and adjustable footrests; the curved coaming members are already laminated and pressure-molded to shape.

Their *touring single kayak kit* is an extremely popular kit. Measures 14′6″ x 2′; only 31 pounds. This is a fast kayak, with excellent directional stability. Good for a beginner or a more advanced kayak enthusiast. About $250.

Other kayak kits from Country Ways include a touring double; a Scandinavian double, for the wilderness paddler; a "one-holer" double for touring with children. Other kayak kits will be available, too, within the next few years.

If you're looking for a *canoe or kayak paddle kit,* Country Ways has those, too, each kit under $25. Other handy kits: *a car rack kit; a sprayskirt kit; seat and yoke kits;* plus two fine kits for *rowing prams.* Upcoming kits from Country Ways: a *training model rowing shell* (with sculls), and an exercise model rowing shell with lower center of gravity and more stability.

Folbot Corporation has marvelous *modified kayak-type boat kits* with very heavy-duty hulls, which can stand up to use in white water. Decks are covered, with ample space between cross-frames for storage that stays dry. Sectional shelves are built under side decks as well, which makes these boats very handy for camping trips. One of the best features (to me anyway) is that the person in this boat sits below the waterline *with her or his body in a normal sitting position*—cushion underneath and foam pad as backrest; this is an extremely comfortable way to travel, and it feels very secure. Apparently, this boat is just about unsinkable; air bladders are inserted, out of the way, into ends and tips of the Folbot and can be quickly inflated by mouth. These are not a supporting structure of the boat.

Folbots come in a nice selection of sizes, from a 10′ Junior single-seater for children to a 16′ two-to-three seaters. Boats are constructed of wood with fiberglass covering or of all fiberglass. Some fold for storage in your car trunk or for airplane travel.

Prices are quite low, ranging from under $175 for the Junior single to well under $350 for the larger two-to-three seaters.

A note: Folbot insists these boats are not kayaks, although they certainly do *look* like kayaks, but with a more comfortable seating and padding setup. The Folbot catalogue states: *"NOT* a 'kayak'—but the completely functional CRAFT for distance cruiser, surfer, diver, guide, explorer, ocean voy-·ager, and fishing or hunting sportsmen." So be it. Do take a look at this catalogue. I wound up with a strong desire for their 15′ single-seater.

Riverside Fiberglass Canoe Company has fiberglass canoe kits in two different styles: the Challenger 15½′ model and the Cruiser 15′ and 17′ models. The *Challenger* has an all-fiberglass hull, including all-fiberglass gunwales and fiberglass decks. No maintenance needed. Very good load stability and load capacity, with extra-wide hulls. Sleek fast lines.

The *Cruiser* has classic old-time canoe looks, fiberglass hull, with natural-wood gunwales and decks. Easy handling, with high ride, low-weight streamlined hull. The Cruiser kits, requiring just a few hours of assembly time, sell for under $175. The Challenger kits go for well under $225.

Power and Pontoon Boats

Clark Craft Boat Company has kits for several fabulous powerboats. The following will probably whet your appetite.

Trailerable Crown Express Cruiser. It comes in 24′ or 26′ models. Each will accommodate inboard motors, single or dual outboard motors, or stern drive units. The 26′ model has an 8′ beam, 12″ draft, 45″ freeboard forward, 34″ freeboard aft, 6′8″ x 11′ cockpit, 6′6″ x 12′ cabin, 6′ berths, and 6′ headroom. It sleeps four. The boat weighs 2,000 pounds. The cabin is divided, with bunk area forward, and galley and head in the aft section of the cabin.

Side planking is ⅜″ 5-ply boat-hull plywood. Bottom planking: ⅜″ 5-ply plywood. Optional ¼″ double-bottom or fiberglass kit available, and recommended for use with high-horsepower engines. Deck is ⅜″ plywood. Cabin sides: ¾″ plywood and ¾″ solid mahogany. Windshield and side windows are 3/16″ Plexiglas. Assembly time is estimated at between 225 and 260 hours. The basic complete boat kit costs under $3,000.

20′ Mariner Cruiser or Fish & Ski Boat. The Mariner hull can take a great deal of offshore pounding because of its deep **V**-shaped heavily flared bow section forward and its modified **V**-shaped stern. It has adequate storage space under the front deck for anchors, life preservers, and other gear. There is additional storage along the gunnels, especially if side panels are installed. The center console supplied with the kit is placed in a suggested position and can be moved either forward, aft, or from side to side. An additional console can also be installed so that there will be two, side by side. Complete boat kit for the Fish & Ski version costs about $1,500; the Cruiser version costs about $2,000.

16' Hurricane Runabout and Sportsman. Designed for offshore use on lake, bay, or ocean. Features include an exceptionally wide beam for soft riding, plus high, flared sides for a dry ride. Crowned forward deck. Fast and extremely maneuverable. Takes motors from 7½ to 45 horsepower with speeds ranging from 17 mph to more than 40 mph. Specifications are 16' long, 74" beam, 72" forward deck, 42" maximum hull depth, 31" depth forward, 28" depth amidship, 21" transom, 59" top-transom width, 54" waterline-transom width, 39" aft deck length, 440 pounds weight, plus motors to 75 horsepower. ⅜" plywood bottom planking, ½" side plywood planking, ¾" plywood transom, ¾" mahogany frames. The complete kit sells for under $700.

Other Clark Craft powerboat kits are available for a 22' cruiser with flying bridge, 18'4" Barracuda offshore fishing boat, 18' and 14' runabouts, a fast 17' dragster ski boat, and a wonderful bass boat kit.

Glen-L Marine Designs has been in business for more than twenty-five years; it produces excellent frame kits and plans for sailboats, paddleboards, runabouts, and ski cruisers. Their plans alone cover houseboats, a fantastic 36' double-cabin cruiser, and many other cruising yachts and workboats.

They have a huge selection of frame kits for powerboats. The two that follow represent a tiny part of their range.

Stiletto, 16' Ski Boat. This outboard runabout is styled like the popular inboard ski boats. The hull is designed for high-powered motors. Sides flare out to provide additional buoyancy at the transom as well as acting as safety antitrip chines in faster turns. 6'6" beam, 2'2" hull depth, 440 pounds. Four passengers. The frame kit costs under $175.

Lazy Daze, 23' Sedan Cruiser. The deckhouse of this cabin cruiser features full headroom and berths that are a generous 6'6" in length. The head is fully enclosed, and there's a roomy hanging locker. The galley offers provisions for self-containment. Large widows make the cabin area feel light and spacious.

The Lazy Daze is designed for outboard motors, but you can use a compact inboard. The Lazy Daze can be transported by trailer. Sleeps two to four. The frame kit goes for just over $300. That's just the start of your expenses, of course.

Jamar Industries has two *boat ramp kits* for boats under 1,800 pounds, and for heavy inboard-outboard boats 1,800 pounds and over. The upper and lower section kit with rollers, for boats under 1,800 pounds will cost just over $350. The kit for heavier boats will cost about $500. Upper and lower sections are available separately, if that's what you need.

Rickborn Industries has several different one-piece *fiberglass flying bridges* that will fit a flat deck or any athwartship cabin top curve. Requires no cutting. Fairly easy installation. Available with or without controls or accessories. Prices vary widely. Bare bridges for single-engine boats range from $525 to $1,095. Complete units in the Econoline range from $1,499 to $2,615. The deluxe kit for a twin-engine boat can cost as much as $5,100 for the kit.

Rotocast Flotation Products has a fascinating, easy-to-assemble *pontoon-boat kit.* The basis of their boat is the modular pontoon sections, which bolt to a galvanized frame to provide the flotation base or hull. These pontoon sections are rotationally molded from high-density polyethylene plastic and are filled with closed-cell urethane foam. Since the polyethylene outer skin of the pontoon is resistant to abrasion and impact, your boat will look newer longer. The fact that the pontoon sections are filled with closed-cell urethane foam means that the unit will retain buoyancy even if punctured or ruptured.

Their smallest boat (17′) will hold about 1,500 pounds. Twelve to sixteen hours completion time. Requires no special skills or equipment for assembly, except for a small pop-rivet gun to fasten the deck trim in place. All kit components are of galvanized steel or marine-grade aluminum. Available in 17′, 20′, and 24′ lengths.

If you're thinking of building one of these pontoon boats, keep in mind that a low-horsepower motor, say for the 17′ pontoon boat, will cost you an additional $300–$400 secondhand or up to $2,000 new. The kit itself, in the smallest size, costs well under $1,500. (It's a lot of fun for the money.)

Sailboats

Mr. Anders Ansar of Stockholm, Sweden, sells a fascinating device for *skate sailing.* Called the Ice-Wing, this sail is shaped like a standing aircraft wing; the sailor stands inside with skates on his or her feet, holds onto a small front bar, and moves along the ice at up to 50 mph in an 18-knot breeze.

The leading edge of the wing is stiff; it is made from a sheet of transparent plastic. The remainder is made up from fabric held taut by an internal rigging of aluminum tubing. When folded together for transport or storage (the process takes only a few minutes), the fabric and aluminum tubing fold up against the leading edge to a size approximately 8′ x 1′ x 1′.

They recommend that while sailing at high speeds, you use ski boots fitted with a fairly long skate, wear a helmet, and carry an ice ax.

The kit costs approximately $300.

Clark Craft Boat Company has an excellent variety of complete sailboat kits for smaller sailboats, from an 8′ rowing pram, up. Once you move into the 20′-and-over category, they have a fine selection of frame sets, for a 26′ sloop, for example. Obviously, a beginning sailboat maker would start with one of the smaller boats from a complete kit, then move on to a frame-set package. If a 28′ plywood cruising trimaran is more to your taste, Clark Craft has complete plans and patterns available, as well as for a 43′ ketch or cutter, a 70′ cruising yacht, and other fine high-performance boats.

Among their most popular complete sailboat kits is *the Snipe,* the world's most popular one-design sailboat, designed in 1931 by William F. Crosby. Supposed to be the best all-around small racing craft.

The Snipe International Racing Association (SIRA) regulations permit the use of wood (¾″ solid planking), ⅜″ plywood or molded fiberglass. Apparently, most Snipes these days are built of plywood, and this relatively easy-to-build kit should be able to compete with the finest factory-made Snipe.

Total sail area: 116 square feet. 6″ draft, with dagger board up; 3′3″ draft with dagger board down. The complete boat kit, $100 or thereabouts, comes with plans, instructions, precut wood parts, semifinished mast and boom, aluminum dagger board, fastenings and glue. Sails, running deck, hardware, shrouds, and halyards not included. The snipe sails, Dacron, with battens and kit bag, plus the hardware rigging kit, will add a little over $300 to the price.

Another fine one-design, *the Windmill,* is fine for young or older sailors. Properly assembled, this sailboat can be registered and compete in one-design Windmill class regattas. This Windmill is built over removable frames, which are furnished with the kit. All solid wood is mahogany, with planking of ¼″ AB grade marine-glued plywood. Mast and boom are Sitka spruce, and sail grooves are accurately machined, laminated, glued, and require only hand finishing. Kit purchase price includes registration number, measurement certificate, and windmill class specifications. Just over $1,200, including hardware rigging kit, sail kit, and fiberglass covering kit.

Country Ways, Inc., has a terrific *skate-sail kit.* This is not as aerodynamically sophisticated as the Swedish skate-sail kit described above, but it works and it's fun. It does everything an iceboat can, upwind and down, tacking and jibing. The kit contains the nylon sail fabric, window material, hardware, and directions that tell you how to make the four wooden spars out of available wood. Three different sizes. Very inexpensive (less than $30 for the child size; well under $40 for the largest adult size).

Country Ways has also been carrying some wonderful sailboat kits; at the time of this writing, they're not on the new projected price list—so you might want to check with them to see if they'll be carrying any more.

Glen-L Marine's selection of frame kits for sailboats is pretty extensive; the couple described below represent just a tiny sampling of what's available. For more sophisticated builders and sailors, Glen-L has plans only for a wonderful 26′ fiberglass sloop you can transport by trailer, a 25′ cabin sloop, twin-cabin sloops, and an incredible 30′ cruising auxiliary sloop that sleeps four adults, two children, and has a cozy heated cabin.

Their *Glen-L 12′ Sloop* is relatively easy to build. The boat is stable and roomy enough for two adults and two children. The sloop rig has a generous sail area, and there's a good-sized jib. The frame kit includes preassembled frames, all deck beams, fully framed transom, stem, breast hook, daggerboard trunk, daggerboard, rudder, and plans. About $125. Also available for this fine small sailboat are Glen-L hardware kits, rigging kits, a spar kit, and sails. An *excellent* value.

Their *LaChatte 16′ Catamaran frame kit* is for sailors who like the speed and feel of twin-hull sailing. Lightweight in design, with high initial stability. The Chatte is roomy, with extra performance of a jib sail. Built using thin plywood sheet in a continuous piece between keels to sheer so that a lightweight, strong structure develops. Features a "knockdown" carrying system. The cockpit tray of the boat rests on a car-top rack, or carrier, and the two hulls sit on the tray. Daggerboards and rudders are carried in this tray, too. No launching ramps needed; no boat trailers either. The frame kit costs just over $250. A 12′ Catamaran is available as well, for just a few dollars difference.

The **Houlton Boat Company** has a *ply Tornado kit* using the stressed-ply method of construction. This method involves the joining of large panels of okoume gaboon ply together and cutting out hull sides that are joined at the keel and folded into a deck jig to ensure the correct shape. The complete kit, including rudder system, mast and boom, all blocks, line, wire rigging with adjusters, and trampoline system sells for just over $3,500. I spoke with one young man, Gary Phifer, who was in the process of building this kit in his parents' basement, and I heard little but praise for the kit. I might add that Gary has been working on his project, part-time, for over a year.

Luger Industries' *sailboat kits* can be ordered in packages that will include everything right up to interior finish—at prices that should save you about half of what you might expect to pay.

One of their most fabulous kits is for their *Voyager 30,* sloop or ketch that's comfortable enough to live aboard. Designed by Edwin Monk & Associates, in cooperation with Luger and Eric White (designer of the Morgan Out Island series of cruising sailboats), the Voyager qualifies for M.O.R.C. racing and also for documentation. This exceptional boat has 6′4″ headroom, shoal draft that measures only 3′ with centerboard up, optional inboard mounted auxiliary outboard motor plus 8′ trailerable beam.

The standard Voyager layout sleeps six, but, with slight modification, you can fit seven or more. The forward cabin sleeps two, the convertible dinette makes up into a double berth, and the settee and quarterbench each make up into a berth for one. All interior wood is mahogany. Headroom in the head area is 6'6". A hatch in the cabin roof provides ventilation.

This boat kit has a beautiful, exceptionally tasteful interior. Lots of storage space. Adequate workspace. Sensible arrangement of navigation.

No special skills are required to assemble this boat. When the kit is delivered, the hull and superstructure are joined by stainless-steel bolts at 4' intervals. You seal the hull and superstructure permanently with fiberglass bonding material, supplied with kit. All bonding is done inside the boat, where it is concealed.

You complete the cabin interior using the supplied precut, preformed, and subassembled component parts. After installation of the retractable centerboard, deck hardware, mast and boom, you're ready to sail.

And because fiberglass is immune to weather, you can work on this kit right out in your backyard. This is a *fabulous* kit, with self-tending helm, large, uncluttered foredeck, nonskid surfaces, as stiff and resistant to heeling as many boats with broader beams and more ballast. Also, the Voyager is self-righting, with mainsail equipped with reef points for jiffy reefing of the mainsail. The kit price for the ketch version runs about $13,000.

Other kits from Luger include a 26' sloop or ketch, 21' compact cruiser or racer, and a wonderful 16' fiberglass sloop (about $2,000), which can be towed by a subcompact car.

Tri-Star Trimarans has frame kits available for 18' to 65' trimarans.

Their *Tri-Star 18* can be used for ocean day cruising or summer lake cruising. Lightweight and hingeable beams make this easy to transport by trailer. The Tri-Star 18 has 7' long trampolines on which, if you wish, you can set up a boom tent for weekend trips. Sail plans are either sloop- or ketch-rigged. Kits are available for the frame, hardware, mast, and sails. About four hundred hours to build. About $1,200 for the cost of materials.

Many larger models are available as well. Their *Tri-Star 27-9* is a full-size family cruiser-racer, built of unitized flush-deck construction that strengthens and simplifies building, while providing a low streamlined silhouette. 6' headroom. Sleeps five. About nine hundred fifty hours building time. About $6,500 for cost of materials.

Yacht Constructors, Inc., has fiberglass sailing yacht kits with as much work done by them as you wish. If all you want them to do, for example, is complete the fiberglass hull, they'll do that and then sell you the rest of the materials you'll need to complete your dream yawl. You needn't buy all the materials right away either; if you wish, you can make this a project that will continue over several years, when you have the cash for it.

Sizes of these kits range from 27′ to 42′; the latter size is available in standard or cruising hull shapes.

Classic Automobile Reproduction Kits, Plus Kits for Supermodern Sports Cars

Kit car enthusiasts may find the listings that follow pretty "old hat." But, for most of us, this information is new—and exciting enough to whet our appetites for a reproduction "1937" Jaguar SS-100 or a car that looks very like the #246 Dino Ferrari.

The best news is that most of these kits are infinitely less expensive than the "real thing," and they can save you at least 60 percent of the purchase price of preassembled kit cars.

Although there are several British manufacturers of kit cars, you'll find only a few listed in the Appendix under some Additional Sources of Classic Automobile Reproduction Kits, plus kits for Supermodern Sports Cars. Frankly, if you're a beginning car kit builder, you'll probably want easy telephone access to the manufacturer, just in case of any problem. My own feeling is that imported kits for something this involved and expensive are for more experienced automobile kit builders.

If, even after sending for the brochures listed in the Appendix, you want to investigate the kit car market further before buying the car of your fantasies, I suggest that you contact Auto Logic Publications, Inc., P.O. Box 2073, Wilmington, Delaware 19899, (302) 478-3825. They publish a car kit magazine and an annual called *The Complete Guide to Kit Cars/Auto Parts and Accessories,* a fabulous oversized paperback that thoroughly details the kit-car market both here and abroad.

Antique and Classic Automotive, Inc., of Buffalo, New York, has replicas (they call them "replicars") of several classic automobiles, including the 1937 Jaguar SS-100, the 1934 Frazer Nash, the 1931 Alfa Romeo, the 1927 Bugatti, and a Phaeton inspired by the 1930 Bentley.

Their most popular is the *1937 Jaguar SS-100.* (Approximately 75 to 80 percent of their orders during the past year were for this model.) In the past, this fiberglass-bodied kit has used the standard Volkswagen "bug" chassis, but this past summer A & CA introduced a new Jaguar kit mounted on a specially fabricated frame (supplied by A & CA), which uses stock Ford Pinto or Bobcat running gear.

I can well understand why the Jaguar SS-100 kit is so popular; the original car is, of course, one of the rarest sports cars built (only 309 were produced). It is the classic forerunner of today's Jaguars. And this reproduction looks superb: Authentic details have been preserved from the stylized SS-cast in each windshield knob to the famous leaping-Jaguar radiator ornament. Appointments also include huge, deep headlamps custom-reproduced from the 12″ Lucas lamps right down to the distinctive stainless-mesh stone guards. A bright chrome badge-bar supports lamps and fenders. An exact reproduction of the windscreen gleams in bright chrome with fold-down brackets. Sliding bucket seats are comfortable and fully adjustable. Ample luggage space is hidden under the hood. And all-weather comfort is ensured with a tailor-made convertible top and matching side curtains.

Their replicar *1934 Frazer Nash* is a reproduction of the car created by Archie Frazer-Nash, which took the Mountain Class F record at Brooklands Track in 1935. Only seventy-six of these cars were ever built.

This reproduction is *fabulous.* A full-length windscreen folds flat across the long tapered hood. Uniquely contoured wings minimize road splash. Luggage space is underneath the front hood. A tailored convertible top and matching side curtains make this an all-weather car.

These kits come to you ready for assembly, with all parts marked and ready to fit. Steel structures and extension components are all precision-fabricated, predrilled, and jig-welded.

Basic kit prices are around $2,000. Deluxe kit prices are about $4,500. A completed auto would go for around $10,000.

Classic Motor Carriages, Inc., has two stunning car kits for you to assemble: the Gazelle, a replica of the 1929 Mercedes SSK, and their Bugatti 1927 35B kit.

The *Gazelle (replica 1929 Mercedes SSK)* is one of the most impressive four-seater cars you could ever drive. The kit is designed to be built with Ford Pinto or VW components. Since it uses the full-size pan, there's no lengthening, shortening, or welding involved. Assembly is designed for the person of average mechanical skills, using ordinary tools.

The basic kit features oversized chrome lights, chrome steel grill, leather strap for hood, watertight windshield and top seal, vinyl upholstery (leather is optional), full-width trunk-storage area, marine-quality chrome hardware, chrome bumpers, etc. You'll probably want the optional stainless-steel exhaust stacks, custom dash with classic instruments, running board, custom chrome wire basket wheels, and trumpet horns, too.

The standard kit sells for under $3,000. Deluxe kit goes for around $4,000. (Their custom-built Gazelle, for people who don't want to invest their own time and effort, goes for about $20,000.)

Their *reproduction 1927 Bugatti 35B* is another beauty. A few months ago I saw this kit, assembled, and it's one of the most fabulous kits I saw in the process of researching this book.

The Bugatti kit is installed on a VW chassis. The resulting car is much lighter than a VW and has a lower center of gravity; it handles like a sports car rather than the VW it was.

Cost is about $3,000 for the deluxe kit.

Daytona Automotive Fiberglass, Inc., has a fine kit available for a reproduction *MG-TD;* they call it the MIGI.

Their kit comes premarked for accuracy. The average builder should be able to assemble this kit in about a hundred hours. Chassis modifications are minimal. It requires no shortening or narrowing of the VW floor plan. The only required modifications are relocation of the shifter and pedals and lengthening of the brake push-rod and steering shaft.

The fiberglass body is reinforced with steel tubing placed at stress points, providing sports-car handling with structural soundness. The gel coat finish will not rust, and it requires no painting or waxing.

Purchase price for the unassembled kit ranges between $2,500 and $4,500, depending upon the accessories you choose. (A completed car is available for just over $9,000.)

Fiberfab, Inc., carries kits for a reproduction of the *1952 MG-TD* and for a futuristic sports car, the *Aztec 7.*

The steel-reinforced fiberglass body of the Aztec 7 comprises three main pieces. The gull-wing doors, which are part of the main section, are prehung at the factory and incorporate tilt-out, tempered, side glass windows and standard automotive latches and locks. The doors lift with the aid of mechanical assists. Also, part of the main section is a special safety-glass windshield (Department of Transportation-approved) with a monoarm wiper system. The nosepiece features manually operated popup (quad-rectangular) headlights and a gas-tank mounting pod with a removable access cover. The front bumper is reinforced fiberglass and is replaceable. Behind the main body is a large louvered tail-section, which is hinged and tilts rearward for easy engine access. Should more power be desired, there is ample space to convert to Corvair, Porsche V4/V6, rotary, or small block V8.

Construction time for this kit is a bit longer than for some of the antique reproduction kits mentioned above, but the results—if you have the time and patience—are worth it.

The deluxe kit price is around $6,000.

If you can't afford a Ferrari automobile (but you'd like one), you may be interested in **Kelmark Engineering's** *Kelmark GT.* This kit is *based upon the #246 Dino Ferrari,* and it's beautiful . . . not as outré as the Aztec 7 mentioned above but equally as impressive. Perhaps, best of all (if you're in a hurry for results), this kit is offered in a mostly preassembled version; all parts have been installed—from windows to instruments to doors—and all you have to do is bolt the body to a VW chassis, install the carpeting and seats, and connect the wiring, fuel system, and steering. The preassembled kit sells for well under $7,000. (If you'd like a completely assembled car, they have that, too, for just under $10,000, not including a sunroof, air-conditioner, or AM-FM tape player.)

Lindberg Engineering has several interesting kit versions of vintage cars.

I'm crazy about Mr. Lindberg's *F-11,* a kit *based on Henry Ford's 1911 "C" cab.* Lindberg took the basic design, added rather Walt Disneyish accents, and wound up with a showy, functional, fun small truck that would be a great (and, I suspect, tax deductible) promotional device for almost any business. It's cheap, too. The basic kit costs about $2,000. The complete kit costs well under $2,500. Even with a bunch of accessories like bulb horn, headlights, spare-tire mounts, wood graining, interior cabin lamp, etc., the completed vehicle should run well under $5,000.

The Lindberg *M-32* is pretty attention-provoking, too, a scaled-down interpretation of the *1932 Mercedes* 500. Since it uses the same bolting pattern that the VW used, you don't have to figure or cut or remake the perimeter of the pan to fit the new body contour. In addition, all major parts come predrilled to match, so this is largely a bolt-together operation. Well under $4,000 for the fiberglass-body kit, crating, and a 104-piece accessory kit.

The Lindberg *A-36* is a scaled-down interpretation of the *1963 Auburn Boat Tail Speedster.* This is another beautiful kit car with "bolt-on" assembly. About $4,000 for the fiberglass body and full accessory kit.

Total Performance, Inc., has several fascinating kits, including a *1930 Ford Model "A"* built on a chassis available from TP. The deluxe kit can cost you almost $7,000, but it's a fine car. Other kits include a Ford Roadster, plus a fiberglass hot-rod kit.

Kits for Tractors, R-Vs, a Steam-Powered Bicycle, and More

If you live on a farm or have a good-sized piece of land to maintain, you'll probably appreciate **Dahl Tractor's** *rubber tread crawler tractor kit.* With it, you can excavate around a home, pool, lake, ditch. Great for moving snow. Handles moving gravel or any grading job well with its front-mounted, hydraulically controlled blade. Available with **V**-snowplow attachment and buckets, too. With both attachments, the kit runs $6,200. Without the **V**-snowplow, $5,880. It fits into a pickup, so when your brother wants to borrow it, you or he can get it there easily.

There seem to be limitless uses for this tractor. Equipped with a crane hoist, it can hoist and drag logs. When hitched up to a standard trailer, it can quickly move bulky loads. Excellent for cultivating or to break up clods after plowing (you get aeration and a finer soil without compaction because of the even weight dispersal through the wide rubber trace). Handy for dry land loading of field trash. And the kit can be assembled in a weekend!

Glen-L Marine Designs, the boat kit company, also produces *kits for van conversions and R-Vs.* For example, you can buy an aluminum-skin kit, which will convert an ordinary pickup into an R-V, for a fraction of what a factory-built unit would cost. You wouldn't stop, of course, with the leak-proof aluminum-skin kit. There are kits for windows, doors, roof vent, sink/plumbing/lavatory, water systems, running lights, LPG systems, tubs/showers, stabilizers, and more.

Carl Heald, Inc., has kits for a *10-horsepower trail bike,* an *11-horsepower "Super Tryke,"* a *5-horsepower Trail Bronc, hauler wagons,* and a *snow blower."*

Their new *5-horsepower Trail Bronc,* powered by a 197-cc 4-cycle engine, has automatic torque-sensing transmission, wide flotation tires, and front and rear shocks. It has two simple controls, a hand-operated brake-lever, and safe-spring-return twist-grip throttle. A stop button is also mounted on the chrome-plated handlebars. The handlebars telescope down for easier transport and storage. A front ski kit is available, so the motorcycle can be used year round. Although they do have kits for more powerful bikes, I like this one. It's the kind of machine you can ride without frightening yourself to death. Under $400.

Sarlin Steam Works has a semikit for converting your bicycle to steam power.

This steam bicycle power unit may be attached to any bicycle with a 27″ wheel diameter in three minutes. No modifications to the bicycle are required. The front-wheel mounting allows the rider to view the pulsating engine and check the water level in the boiler. Sarlin Steam Works can provide a folder, which includes a history of steam-powered bicycles, an article on the Vesuvius power plant, and complete construction drawings for all the components for $15. The kit includes only the rough castings, which require access to a machine shop to finish. However, many of the small valves and fittings may be purchased from a supplier of such parts. Estimated contruction time is three hundred hours. Sarlin Steam Works also sells completed units, but be prepared to pay $3,200 if you're anxious to get steaming right away.

The **Struck Corporation** has two different *tractor kits,* the Mini-Dozer and the more powerful Magnatrac. Each takes about one weekend to assemble.

The Mini-Dozer is a crawler-type tractor not unlike the Dahlco kit described previously (even the colors of the brochures from these two companies are the same). It comes in your choice of 7- or 16-horsepower kits, with a very large selection of optional attachments to do the specialized jobs you need done. Cleats of the full Mini-Dozer track take snow or mud in stride—a smooth, continuous operation almost impossible to stall. Track cleats form natural open-and-close movement as they go around each sprocket and give the entire track a self-cleaning action. This machine is fine for almost any job you have around your property. Optional attachments include snow blower, blade, electric-lift mechanism, trailer, roller, disk harrow, drag harrow, scarifier, cultivator, plow, and planter-fertilizer.

The Magnatrac is a good investment if you intend to use it to earn some extra money, like snow-blowing driveways up and down the road where you live and on into town. Magnatrac is designed for jobs requiring continuous, nonstop power, on steep inclines and under slippery conditions. More than thirty attachments available.

The price for the 7-horsepower Mini-Dozer kit is just over $1,100, but extra attachments will undoubtedly bring the price up. The Magnatrac 16-horsepower kit starts at just under $2,700. They're both bargains.

Kits for Airplanes, Helicopters, and Gliders

From what I've been able to determine, several thousand Americans have built their own aircraft using plans or complete kits available from one of the following manufacturers. If flying around in a home-built airplane is your idea of fun, more power to you. Keep in mind that the Federal Aviation Agency classifies these as experimental aircraft, and although they need no special license for the first fifty hours of flight, if you fly within a 25-mile radius, your local FAA inspector has to inspect your airplane twice—the first time before you cover it and the second time before you fly it. As I understand the process, once the inspector okays the aircraft and after you receive your experimental aircraft license, if you install a radio, you can land anywhere.

Bensen Aircraft Corporation sells Gyrocopter kits the likes of which you may remember from the James Bond movie *You Only Live Twice*. Their Bensen B-80 is a new type of rotorcraft, which combines features of a helicopter and an autogyro. It has a 21' two-blade rotor that is free-wheeling, thus eliminating the need for gearboxes, shafts, and the torque effect. It needs no tail rotor.

This machine is supposed to be as easy to fly as it is to ride a bicycle. Controls consist of the main control stick, rudder pedals, and the throttle. Average learning time is three to five hours for beginners and two to three hours for licensed pilots.

Normal lifting capacity is 250 pounds, range is 120 miles, and it holds 6 gallons (two hours' worth) of fuel. Although it will not hover in calm air, it can maintain level flights at 19 mph, and it can get in and out of a strip some 40 by 300 feet. Float gear and ship are available.

The kit, without motor, costs about $2,000.

Bryan Aircraft has a kit for a *15-meter class sailplane,* the HP18. They say they have made very effort to reduce drag and weight to produce a superior competition machine with gentle flight characteristics.

Water ballast is carried inside the wing-box spars. Cross-country efficiency is improved by the use of a low-profile fuselage, better gap seals, new wing tips, and better streamlining. Flaps and ailerons are coupled together to increase speed. Ninety-degree flaps permit steeper approaches and slower, safer landing speeds. Direct rudder cable connections to the tail wheel give positive steering control on the ground at all speeds. Winglets have been added to increase glide ratio and improved aileron control.

Construction time is about seven hundred hours. The builder needs only hand tools, rivet gun, electric drill, and air compressor. You may, however, need help in the beginning from a local aircraft sheet-metal worker. Complete kit sells for well under $7,000.

The **BW Rotor Company** has a kit available for a *Giro Kopter, a rotary-blade aircraft.*

The BW Giro Kopter kit features a heavy-duty gimbal control head for flight stability. It is equipped with a new type overhead-stick control with a joystick also available as optional equipment. Gimbal control, seat frame, and nose-wheel fork are factory-finished for easy installation. The rotor blades are preglued, and the leading edge is cut to proper airfoil shape.

The only equipment needed to constuct the BW Giro Kopter is a hand drill and a few ordinary shop tools. The Giro costs nothing to operate and is small enough to store in the garage. No pilot license is required to fly this machine.

The airframe may be converted to a powered craft. Some engines that have been used on the BW-5 Kopter are Volkswagen, motorcycle, 72-horsepower McCulloch, and snowmobile. It takes a minimum of 40 horsepower to power the Kopter.

The kit costs about $500.

Eipper-Formance, Inc., has a kit for a *motorized glider,* the Quicksilver M.

Ground handling the Quicksilver M is relatively simple. Prop wash over the rudder in combination with the lightly loaded nose wheel make rudder inputs very effective upon directional control. At rotation speed (16–20 mph) the pilot pushes his weight back to lift the nose wheel and start the climb. All pitch control is accomplished through pilot weight-shift. This eliminates, they say, the weight and balance problems otherwise associated with the pilot being over half the gross weight of the system. Lateral control is achieved by shifting your weight in the direction you wish to go. The pilot's harness is connected through control lines to the rudder. A weight shift to the left turns the rudder left, yawing and rolling the aircraft into a left turn. The Quicksilver's generous wing dihedral makes the roll light and quick, and also provides high roll and spiral stability. The main wing is rectangular and single-surface, keeping the wing as light and simple as possible. Wing-tip washout, in combintion with the taperless form, makes the stall extremely gentle with no tendency to drop a wing and/or spin.

In flight, the engine may be shut down for climbing in lift and restarted in flight with two or three pulls of the starter cord. For landing, the power is cut back and the approach speed adjusted to 20–25 mph. With a 10–12 mph head wind, touch-down speed is little more than walking speed, which enables the pilot to land in incredibly small areas.

This kit requires twenty to thirty hours construction time. The kit includes assembly instructions, all materials needed to build, and supine pilot harness. It also includes all tube cutting, drilling, anodizing, tube bending where necessary, cable swaging, and completely finished wing-and-tail surface covers, ready to install. Engine is complete and ready for installation. Includes fuel tank, propeller, and all necessary hardware. About $3,000.

GLA, Inc., has a kit for a *sailplane,* called the Minibat. The Minibat is, they say, a unique concept in sailplane design. It was created to resolve several of the basic problems that have limited the growth of soaring in the United States.

First, it provides safety and performance equal to or better than the most popular sailplane in the world, at only 25 percent of the cost, by taking full advantage of current composite-construction technology and recent revisions to FAA regulations concerning home-built aircraft-construction requirements. Second, it requires only forty to sixty hours to make the aircraft, which is anywhere from one-tenth to one-fiftieth of the usual time associated with home-built aircraft. Third, its small size and compact configuration provide for an inherent "Learn-to-Fly" capability, which in turn, provides the owner/builder the opportunity to learn to fly *safely* and obtain an FAA pilot's license for less than $100. And, finally, the basic design is expandable to provide for up to 50 percent increase in performance without major modifications.

This interesting "tailless" aircraft has a span of 25′, 9.33′ length, and height of only 5′. It can be launched by aerotow, winch, bungee, or auto tow. Contrary to the popular opinion regarding tailless aircraft, this plane is inherently stable. I think it looks like fun.

About $3,500, with the 3-horsepower sustainer engine or wing-extension panels.

Mitchell Aircraft Corporation has two fine kits for *sailplanes.*

Their *B-10 foot-launch hang glider* is a cross between a hang glider and go-cart, powered by a 125-cubic-centimeter go-cart engine. Most people use the motor for taking off and gaining altitude. Wingspan measures 34′, wing chord 5′ to 2′. Wing area is 136 square feet. Top speed is 55 mph, with a stall speed of under 25 mph. This is, apparently, the only rigid-wing-powered hang-glider kit on the market. Cost is under $3,000.

Mitchell Aircraft also has a kit for a glider airplane using a 10-horse-power engine—the *Mitchell Super Wing U-2.* The U-2 uses one gallon of fuel per hour, needs no ground crew, has a pilot enclosure, spoilers, retractable landing gear, and air restart capabilities. The ribs are standard truss type and take about one hour each to build. The spars are precut along with most all other materials. One-millimeter aircraft birch plywood is used to give the leading edges a good smooth contour.

You should allow about a hundred hours to build all the main assemblies. Individual desires, detail, and finish work will vary from builder to builder.

The area over the ribs and control surfaces is covered with 2.7 ounces of Dacron fabric, after the wing has received several clear coats of dope. The fabric is stuck down with coats of dope over the contact area. Then enough dope is brushed on to seal the pores of the fabric, usually three coats, then the color or colors of your choice.

Mitchell states that "Ultralight flying is fun, but all pilots are warned that these ultralight airplanes bounce around in gusty conditions that seem normal in heavy aircraft. So, we recommend all your flying be done in smooth air, gradually increasing into more turbulent air.

"Total control at all times is a must, as every pilot knows. The engines we use are two cycle, and are not approved aircraft engines, so caution is recommended. Never place your total safety dependence on the engine's reliability. Leave another way out.

"In reference to the above warning, if you feel the risks involved in ultralight flying are unjustified, then you probably should not pursue the sport. The choice is yours. A confident and respectful attitude is essential for this type of flying.

"Before making any commitments toward building and flying ultralights, we recommend that you seriously evaluate your mental compatibility with the potential risks. Let this be the basis for your decision."

Mooney Mite Aircraft Corporation has a kit for an *airplane built along the lines of the famous British "mosquito" bomber.* The cabin is heated, soundproofed, and lined with a plastic-covered insulating blanket. Powered by the Lycoming 65-horsepower engine, known for economy and dependability and equipped with a 14-gallon tank, the Mooney Mite has a cruising range of 450 miles, and it flies, they say, at an average cost of 1.3 cents per mile. Discounting indirect costs and timesaving en route, this compares with 3.6 cents per mile for the average car on the ground.

It lands easily at main airports or out-of-the-way strips. It's easy for one person to move about on the ground, unaided. It flies beautifully at 10,000 feet and can go to 21,000 feet with ease.

The kit contains all the materials necessary to construct the basic airframe as defined in the plans, except the dope and fabric. Included are wheels and tires, airspeed indicator, altimeter, all nuts, bolts, Cotter pins, etc. Also included is all wood, plywood, glue, steel tubing, and sheet aluminum. A complete canopy is also included, along with certain extruded aluminum channels that are necessary to construct the canopy frame. The bubble is preblown and complete.

You will be expected to cut, fit, shape, weld, and otherwise fabricate the materials into finished parts. A requirement of the FAA is that an Experimental-Amateur Built aircraft is built over 50 percent by the individual. All their kits meet this requirement.

The M-18-X has limited aerobatic capabilities at a reduced gross weight of 740 pounds. At this weight it meets the strength requirements for the Utility Category (4.4 g maximum), and you may perform chandelles, lazy eights, and steep turns. Spins are prohibited.

For the most part, simple hand tools are all that are necessary for construction.

Complete kit price, including fuselage structure, wing structure, horizontal and vertical stabilizer, elevators, rudder, ailerons, flaps, controls and control systems, landing gear, retraction system, gear warning system and nose-wheel system, plans, specifications, and assembly manual costs well under $7,000.

Barney Oldfield Aircraft Company has component kits for a small, *single-place open-cockpit biplane,* the Baby "Lakes," which can be flown year round with the addition of a canopy. The materials kit costs about $5,000. It is fully aerobatic with no restrictions and stressed to 9 g's positive and negative at its maximum gross weight of 850 pounds. The design is well debugged, having been in existence for more than twenty years. The Baby "Lakes" can hold pilots weighing from 120 to 220 pounds. Instructions are included to customize the cockpit area to take pilots of different sizes, too.

The plane is well engineered and designed to cam part .03 (FAA design-criteria applying to biplanes). Drawings are complete and detailed, many templates are full size, construction manuals are clear, readable, and easily understood. Standard aircraft materials and hardware used. NASAD rating: Class 1 Rating.

Conventional aircraft construction techniques are used throughout. Fuselage, tail group, landing gear are welded tubing; wings are made of spruce spars and built-up ribs. A rib jig of one size is used to make all the ribs.

Performance varies considerably with engines used. Sixty to 70-horsepower engines give 110 to 115 cruise and 1,200–1,500 FPM climb. Seventy-five to 100-horsepower engines permit 1,500 to 2,000 FPM climbs and a cruise of 118 mph. The Super Baby "Lakes," a more powerful version of this kit, uses 108 to 115 horsepower and climbs over 2500 FPM; cruises at 138. Range for all is 250 miles and stall is 55 mph power off. VW engines of 1800 and 2100 cc's may be used and performance is similar to that of the 60- to 70-horsepower range.

C. Y. Parker has a kit for an *all-aluminum small airplane* called the Teenie Two. The model, powered by a Volkswagen engine, was featured in *Popular Mechanics* in May 1971. No bending brake is needed, nor is any metal or riveting experience required. Complete kit, including new VW engine costs $2,800 at this writing; but check the price, since materials costs keep rising.

One size aluminum sheet and angle is used for most of the construction. Push and pull tubes are used on all controls to eliminate high cost of cable and fittings. Detachable wing outer panels. Wing-spar channels are clamped between 2 x 4 studs and flanges bent with plastic-tipped hammer. Ribs are drilled, notched, and bent over one rib form for all.

Fuselage is also aluminum skin. Three-piece bulkheads are made the same way as ribs. And skin is wrapped around and riveted.

The dorsal fin is used to eliminate another bulkhead, by connecting leading edge of vertical stabilizer into center bulkhead to take care of front and back forces. Stabilizer spar takes care of rudder and stabilizer side loads.

Landing gear uses rubber hose as shock absorber and is supported by coil springs in tubing.

The kit includes aluminum to build the whole airplane, and all chromoloy steel tubing and sheet kit for landing gear and controls.

After the article ran in *Popular Mechanics,* they sold 3,000 sets of plans for this plane and 7,000 sets of plans for its companion model, Jeannie's Teenie—so there must be a *lot* of these in the air.

Pazmany Aircraft Corporation manufactures kits for two very *sophisticated and handsome airplanes,* the Pazmany PL-2 and the PL-4A. Each is sold through distributors, but you can write directly to Pazmany in San Diego for their information packages, plans, and a list of kit distributors.

According to their description, the basic configuration of the PL-2 incorporates two-place, side-by-side seating, low wing of rectangular plan form, and tricycle landing gear. The overall layout is compact and light compared with some other contemporary aircraft in the same category. The structure is stressed to +6 g's limit for safety and aerobatics. Aluminum 2024-T3 is the basic material. Landing gear and engine mount are made from 4130 steel tubes and plates. There are no double curvature skins in the whole airplane. Very few form blocks are necessary, considering that the wing and horizontal tail have constant chord.

The wing has a 15 percent thickness laminar airfoil, with the single spar located at the maximum thickness. The wing is assembled as a unit to the fuselage and can be removed in approximately two hours. The wing-fuselage connection is provided by two bolts at the main spar and two bolts at the rear spar. The seats form an integral structure with the wing. Also, the control sticks and flap-control lever are directly attached to the wing structure. The elevator trim is located in a center box between the sets. Aileron and flaps are piano-hinged to the bottom skin. Ailerons are mass-balanced and push-pull controlled, having differential displacement. The flaps run through the fuselage and have three positions.

The horizontal tail is all movable (flying tail) with an antiservo tab. This arrangement permits a reduction of approximately 30 percent on the tail area compared with a conventional tail. The antiservo tab provides adequate stick forces and is also used for trimming the airplane. The horizontal tail is mass-balanced and has a push-pull tube control. The sweep-back of the vertical tail has, mainly, eye-appealing justification but also provides a greater tail volume. The rudder is cable-controlled.

The PL-2 was designed to be powered by a Lycoming 0-235-C2C engine, rated at 108 horsepower for maximum continuous operation. It will also accommodate the Lycoming 0-290-G, 0-290-D2B, 0-320-A2B, and the 0-320-B2B. The basic advantages of using the more powerful engines on the PL-2 are better climb and ceiling. It should be noted, they say, that the PL-1, the predecessor of the PL-2, with a Continental C-90-12F engine (90 horsepower) has an initial rate-of-climb of 1,000 FPM, fully loaded. The prototype PL-2, powered by the Lyc-0-290-G (ground power unit), has a sea level rate-of-climb of 1,500 FPM, which is far better than most commercially produced light airplanes. Maximum speed and cruise speed will be slightly affected by horsepower. Therefore, it is advisable not to use heavier, more expensive, and more fuel-consuming, larger engines.

Pterodactyl Ltd. has a Pterodactyl Fledgling kit, an *ultralight glider based on the Manta Fledge II B hang glider.* It is fully collapsible for transport or storage. At this time, no license or registration is required, but it is possible that a student pilot's license will be required sometime in the future. Registration may also be required. This kit has been designed to comply with the FAA's "51 percent amateur-built" requirement for experimental aircraft registration.

The landing gear uses shock-cord suspension, 20″ motocross bicycle main wheels and a high-flotation nose wheel. This allows takeoffs and landings on unimproved fields. The power plant uses a 336-cc Sachs snowmobile engine with a direct driven 36″ prop. The price, about $3,300, includes seat, shoulder harness, sail bag, rib bag, and a shipping and storage tube. If you're comparing costs with other aircraft, they say you should remember the portability of the Pterodactyl Fledgling means no trailer or hanger is needed.

They estimate kit completion time as between forty and fifty hours of work.

Rand Robinson Engineering, Inc., has kits for two *two-place side-by-side low-wing monoplanes.* The KR-2 has removable wings, retractable main gear, and steerable tail wheels. It is designed for minimum outside dimensions but still leaves enough room inside for over 6-footers. Effective wing area is 80 square feet for the KR-2 and 62 square feet for the KR-1. The airfoil used is the RAF 48. This airfoil has a gentle stall characteristic and provides a comfortable spread between cruise and landing speeds. These airplanes are designed to use Volkswagen engines from 1600 cc to 2200 cc.

KR-2's with stock 1600-cc engines have cruise speeds of 140 mph and with the 2100-cc engine, 180 mph at 3200 rpm. The prototype KR-2 with a turbocharged 2100, cruises at over 200 mph above 14,000 feet. Climb rate is over 1200 FPM at 850 pounds, and over 800 FPM at 20,000 feet. Normal takeoff run is 350 feet. Design stress loading is plus and minus 7 g's for the KR-2 and plus and minus 9 g's for the KR-1.

For simplicity of construction, the airplane is designed in such a way that no machining or welding is required in building the airframe. All parts can be made and assembled with ordinary hand tools and small power tools.

Construction of the KR-2 fuselage is not unlike that used in making flying model airplanes, just scaled up a bit. The gluing technique is very similar, even to the use of waxed paper to prevent parts from sticking to the jig board. Rigid foam is very easy to work with. It can be sawed, carved, cut, and sanded easily and rapidly into straight, curved, and complicated shapes: such as leading edges, wing tips, fillets, and cowlings. If you get below contour, they say, just glue on some more foam. When the glue is dry, sand it down again. The Dynel fabric weave is open enough to adjust to almost any contour, and penetration by the resin is rapid. Air pockets are easily seen and worked out before the resin hardens.

Elaborate jigs and holding fixtures are not required. Kit components come to well under $2,000.

Schweitzer Aircraft Corporation has very sophisticated *sailplane kits.* Their 2-33 AK model for one is available in kit form.

It's unexcelled, they say, for training and two-place pleasure soaring. Ideal for individual or group ownership. Light wing loading, small turning radius, and low sinking speed permit soaring under light conditions. All-metal wing, Ceconite-covered steel tube fuselage and tail surfaces. Lined cockpit for pilot and passenger comfort. Easy operating dive brakes.

The 2-33AK is not a basic kit in the usual sense. It was developed for school and club construction. All of the welding is done, and the wings, which require large precision fixtures, are completed. The work left to be done includes installing the controls and seats, fairing the fuselge, assembling the canopy, and doping and painting it.

The construction of any basic kit of theirs usually requires two or more years to complete.

About $16,000 for the kit.

Stolp Starduster has two *duster-type airplane kits for aerobatic flyers.*

According to the manufacturer, the Acroduster I SA 700 is designed for unlimited aerobtic competition. It is also a nice sport plane when powered by a 125–160-horsepower engine.

Even though the Acroduster I is as easy to fly as a Cessna 140, it is one of the best-designed competition machines available. It has the advantages over its closest competitor, they claim, of a higher rate of roll, a higher rate of climb, more vertical ability, and a higher top and cruise speed. All this is an airplane that, at the same time, is very docile on the landing roll.

Unlike other aircraft, this airplane stalls more slowly inverted than upright. This is due to the flat bottom of the fuselage imparting part of the lift when inverted. The Acroduster I actually performs better inverted.

Increased performance is the result of its aerodynamic design. The elliptical wings help give a quicker roll. Greater Gap ratio, aluminum spring gear and flat fuselage sides add up to less drag. The higher vertical fin and rudder produce better directional control on landing roll and quicker spin recovery.

The kit is complete in every respect except for prop, engine, and some plumbing forward of the firewall.

9

Other Useful Kits

Down and Synthetic-fill Comforters and Pillows

Recently, several manufacturers of sporting clothing kits (down parkas, booties, etc.) have begun to offer kits for down and synthetic-fill comforters. Apparently, sales are booming. It does make sense, after all: Comforters are easy to sew, and bought in kit form, they cost half the price of what you would pay for a presewn comforter. The following manufacturers will help you keep your thermostats lower at night.

Altra Inc., has *50 percent down/50 percent feather combination-fill* comforters in twin, double, queen, and king sizes. The twin size costs about $80; king size is less than $125. All-down comforters sell for about $50 to $60 more. Easy to sew; all the fabric stays on the left of your machine.

Country Ways has a kit for a *PolarGuard-filled comforter* that you can put together in one evening. The "kit," in this case, is simply the Polar-Guard and directions. You choose the fabric covering. The comforter will be 1½″ thick. Twin, double, and queen/king sizes. Around $30 for the king size.

Frostline Kits has *comforter kits with prime down fill or a 50/50 mix of down and small feathers.* They include instructions for six different ways to quilt it, and you have a choice of taffeta cover or polyester/cotton/nylon-blend cover. A twin-size down comforter with taffeta cover costs less than $100.

If you have a baby at home, you may be interested in Frostline's *crib-comforter kit*. About $20, this kit is filled with nonallergenic Hollofil II, and it is covered in soft nylon taffeta. It's washable, of course.

Frostline also has *pillow kits*. For a firmer pillow, they suggest a down/feathers combination. Under $35. The down version, standard size, sells for around $45. Not cheap, but less than Bloomingdale's.

SunDown has *down comforter kits* in crib, twin, double, queen, and king sizes. Most interesting to couples, one person of which is always too warm and the other too cold at night (sound familiar?), they have a *"his and hers" two-temperature comforter,* with more goose down in half the comforter. I think it's a great idea. Kits for the double-deluxe "his and hers" comforter sell for well under $150.

SunDown has *pillow kits,* too, for about the same prices as Frostline.

Food-related Kits: Coffee Mills, a Cider Press, Beer- and Wine-making Kits, and More

Bacchanalia has a *master brewer's equipment kit,* which you can use to make four-to-five gallons of various beers. For about $20, you get a 7½-gallon fermenter with lid, a Red Top bubbler airlock, syphon tubing, beer hydrometer, "knock-on" capper, and handbook. *Ingredients kits* for Irish stout, or bitter ale, or four other types of beer are additional, under $10 each. Bottles not included.

They have a *home winery kit,* too, for about $60; it includes everything you need (except bottles) for your first 5 gallons (25 bottles) of wine.

Country Ways has two *maple-sugaring kits.* Each starter kit has a spile to set into the tree and a collecting bag, usable year after year. Should make a quart or two. The Family kit has six spiles and bags. The Starter kit costs about $10; the Family kit costs under $30.

Excalibur Products has a *kit for a modern stone-grinder grain mill* so that you can, ·f you wish, make breads from flour you've ground yourself. Great if you ha·e a large family for which you bake; a bushel of wheat, for example, sells for around $4.00 or $4.50. That'll bake up into a lot of bread. The kit sells for under $175.

Foothills Distributors, Inc., carries several stone-mill-related kits. First, they have an *adapter kit that will help you motorize the hand mill you now own;* it uses any old household motor, such as a washing machine or dryer motor. About $40. If you prefer a *pedal-driven stone mill,* they have a kit for that, too; you remove the rear wheel from your bicycle and pedal your grain into flour. Under $45. There's a do-it-yourself electric mill kit, too, plus a food dehydrator kit, about $80.

Garden Way has an *electric grain-mill kit,* too, with ¾ " birch veneer cabinet; front-mounted speed control, adjustable from extra-fine to coarse to cracking cereal grain; and gravity-fed hopper, tray, and auxiliary crank. Under $175—a savings of $50 to $100 on a comparable quality mill.

They have *beer- and wine-making kits,* too. The basic beer kit at under $25; a 5-gallon wine kit, under $15.

Best of all (to my mind) is their inexpensive *sausage-making kit.* Each kit includes a plastic stuffing horn, freshly cured and salted hog casings, seasonings, plus instructions—everything you need to make 10 pounds of sausage (everything except the ground meat). Available for country sausages, Italian sausages, or Polish sausages. About $6. The companion sausage making book costs about $4 more.

If you'd like your own *wooden cider press,* they have that, too. One to two evenings to assemble. Usually about $150 for the kit, but they occasionally have sales, when it sells for about $15 less. Save $40 to $50 by not buying the preassembled version.

Harvest Home Products, Inc., manufactures *food-dehydrator kits* for you to buy with or without the cabinet and/or trays. An eight-tray kit costs about $80 without cabinet, but if you're truly handy, you can buy a basic do-it-yourself kit for less than half the price.

Kittredge Bow Hut has *sausage-making kits* for making your own *venison sausage* at home (no more tough venison steaks!). All kits contain natural or fibrous casings, depending on the kit, soy protein concentrate, curing powder, spices, and liquid smoke, plus a 227-page book. Kits cost about $30 and are available for venison salami, Polish sausage, mild or hot breakfast sausage, pepperoni, Mexican chorizo, and other items. Makes up to 50 pounds.

The Woodworkers' Store has a very attractive *coffee-mill kit.* Simple gluing is all that's necessary for assembly. Base has molded edge, drawer front is shaped and lipped, and all other parts rabbeted where necessary. Includes heavy-duty mechanism. Maple is about $23; cherry about $25.

Birdhouses, a Doghouse, a Dog Run, and a Beekeeping Kit

Audubon Workshop has two birdhouse kits. Their *wren-house kit* has undereaves vents, screw-held swingout side, and 1" opening. Precut, rough-sawn lumber, plus hardware and instructions. About $5. Their *bluebird-house kit,* under $6, conforms to accepted standards with 3¾ ″ high x 3¾ ″ wide x 9¼ ″ deep nest cavity, and 1½ ″ entrance. Swing-out front. These are attractive, plain, serviceable birdhouses. Cheaper if you buy in sets of three.

Constantine offers plain and fancy *birdhouse kits,* as well as *an* inexpensive bird-feeder kit. Their fanciful Swiss Inn for bluebirds is made of durable marine mahogany plywood and requires no gluing or nailing: 11″ x 9″ x 11″. Under $5. The Lodge, for wrens, looks like a little chalet. Measures 8″ x 9½″ x 9″. About $3. There's also a simpler birdhouse kit for small birds, under $2. Their bird-feeder kits come plain and fancy; about $5 for the fancy Alpine chalets; about $2 for the simple but serviceable model.

Glen-Bel's Old-fashioned Country Store has a *beekeeping kit* that comes with ten sheets of Duracomb foundation, beehive, bee veil, hive tool, smoker, gloves, feeder, instructions, and a book called *First Lessons in Bee- keeping.* Additional equipment necessary as the colony grows. You supply the bees. Four weeks after bees are installed, you'll need a supplemental su- pering kit containing 2 honey supers, 20 frames, 20 sheets of bulk-comb honey foundation, plus one queen excluder. About $110 for the two units.

Glen-Bel also offers two birdhouse kits. Their *pinecone bluebird-swallow kit* is constructed of pine and can be stained or painted; 8½ ″ high, 5½ ″ wide, 5″ deep. Nails furnished with kit. About $3. Their *pinecone wren-house kit* costs a few cents less and measures 5½ ″ high, 7″ wide, 6″ deep.

Nasco has a very charming *wren-house kit* that looks like a little cabin. Roof boards cut from exterior plywood. Boards come cut to size with holes drilled. Nails included. Under $2.

They have nice *bird-feeder kits,* too, but these are available only by the dozen. *Extremely* cheap at under $10 for the dozen. Even cheaper if you buy them by the gross (perhaps for school or Scout use).

Your dog needs a home of his/her own, too. *Dog house kits* are available from **Shettel-Way Innovations** of Twin Falls, Idaho. Called Doggy Dens, the kits come in sizes for large or medium dogs as well as for small dogs. The kit is built from seven basic exterior-grade plywood panels, which incorporate suitable chases and cleat reinforcements to promote self-alignment during assembly. A rear-wall vent and plug permits cross-ventilation. Stain is included to seal exposed surfaces. Skid supports space the floor from the ground, and the understructure is Penta-treated to resist decay and dry rot. Floor pad, tether chain, and nameplate options are offered to furnish each unit completely. For very damp climates, the shingle-roof option provides increased protection. With mobile-home hardware, the kit is finished with attachments that permit quick assembly and disassembly for use, transport, or storage.

Optional accessories include cedar-shingle roof, asphalt-shingle roof, and mobile-home hardware. Floor pads are available, too. The small dog kit costs about $50; for large dogs about $10 more.

Sporty's Tool Shop offers a complete *dog run kit,* which allows your big dog 400 square feet of controlled movement. Vinyl-coated aircraft cable eliminates harmful vibrations that may cause your dog to bark. 40-foot cable is flexible but won't knot. Comes with spring-loaded shock absorber to protect your dog. Heavy-duty 7-foot leash and friction-free nylon pulley. Easy to install. Well under $20.

Wild Bird Supplies has a large selection of *birdhouse and bird-feeder kits.* Particularly interesting is their Log Cabin Feeder Kit—great if you're one of those lucky people who live in a log cabin and want your bird feeders to match. Pine construction. 10″ long 7″ deep x 6″ high. Well under $6. They have several less expensive houses and feeders, too, most under $4.50.

Luggage

If you're a person who sews (and even if you're not), it's probably occurred to you that prices of the new soft-sided luggage are stupidly high. Who in their right mind, for example, would want to pay up to $80 for a nylon garment bag? But people do. I've traveled with this kind of luggage for well over two years, and it's great: It's very light to carry, easily expandable, so you *can* fit in that extra pair of shoes, and it's rugged enough. I don't think any of us fool ourselves about soft luggage having the life expectancy of those hard-and-heavy-as-a-rock Samsonite pieces we schlepped through college, but lightweight-nylon luggage is the current trend, and here's how you can save 50 percent or more on the cost of the best-made examples of it.

Altra, the sporting goods kit company known for its high-quality gear, has an excellent line of *tough, nylon-coated Cordura nylon luggage kits.* All have hand and shoulder straps (the latter is *very* important), strong zippers, accent stripes (if you want them—I'd leave them off), and they're washable. My own favorite here is their garment traveler, which zips into a very handsome suitcase; its perfect for a weekend in the Hamptons or roomy enough for cross-country air travel. It has a hanging compartment with closet hook, separate zippered suitcase section, and two inside zip pockets. The shoulder strap is detachable. Available in bright blue, tan, or medium brown. About $40—half of what you'd have to fork out for a similarly constructed bag. Other luggage from Altra: large and small duffle-type carryalls, a splendid tote/overnight bag, and a "kangaroo bag," which resembles a backpack-without-shoulder-straps and will fit under airline seats.

If you're a new parent, or know someone who is, you'll undoubtedly welcome **Frostline**'s recently introduced *baby carrier kit*. The outside is made of warm corduroy or cooler-but-sturdy polyester/cotton twill; it has adjustable foam support for head and neck, storage pockets, and comfortable leg openings. The inside has an adjustable flannel pouch for infants, detachable bib, and zippered access for nursing. You can carry it on your back or around the front of you. Padded shoulder straps, large safety buckles, supporting waistband. Corduroy costs under $30. The twill version costs about $4.50 less. A *great* kit . . . and *much* cheaper than presewn baby carriers.

Frostline also has excellent Cordura nylon *duffle-bag kits* with shoulder straps; these are very inexpensive. (The large duffle, 28½" x 12" deep, costs under $20.) They have *garment-carrier kits,* too, a very sturdy *tote-bag* kit, and a nice *nylon pack-cloth wallet kit,* about $7—nicer than most of the French Le Sportsac accessories I've seen.

If you don't feel like plunking down $30 or more for a tennis bag, **Haan Crafts** has the solution—at about $13. Their 13½" x 13" x 3" *tennis bag kit* is made of 7.5-ounce waterproof urethane-coated nylon pack cloth, with outside racquet case with an attached three-ball pouch held closed by Velcro. The main body of the bag has a zipper closure and a separate wetproof compartment. Adjustable carrying strap. The piping serves as a stiffener.

Haan Crafts has several other colorful and sturdy kits for *gym bags, duffles* for traveling, and a handy *diaper bag.*

SunDown has very nice *Cordura travel bags* and *sports bag kits.* I particularly like their rectangular-shaped travel bags, in 16" x 12" x 6" and 21" x 15" x 8" sizes. Each has a large pleated pocket on one side with Velcro closing flap. The opposite side has two pockets for carrying magazines, etc. The main compartment has a covered, double-slider coil zipper, which opens on three sides for easy access. The smaller bag will fit under an airline seat. These bags are an excellent buy. The larger size sells for well under $20. Available only in medium blue.

Clothing and Accessory Kits for Men, Women, and Children, including Down Coats and Bathrobes, and a Sheepskin Jacket

Charing Cross Kits of Meredith, New Hampshire, has some of the most extraordinary kits I saw in the course of researching this book. *Their specialty is hand-printed fabrics in charming "folk" designs, which make up into unique and distinctive clothing for children and adults.* There are kits here for slacks, blouses, jumpers, dresses, vests, and aprons for little girls and boys. Most of the kits are imported from England, but somehow they're nicer than one might expect from the British; there's a French influence to most of the children's clothing. They publish at least two catalogues a year, and if you have a little girl or boy, do get on their mailing list. Their selection is (I think) better than the children's clothing departments at B. Altman & Co. or Bloomingdale's—and their prices are *much* lower than you'd ordinarily pay for children's clothing with any style at all. And if you're a mother-to-be, you'll probably be interested in their jumpers for women; most of these could be worn through the eighth month, and they're certainly prettier than most of what's available through even the better maternity clothing stores. These are *great* kits.

Family Circle Kits has four terrific and extremely inexpensive kits for beautiful *"Victorian" lace blouses.* Each can be stitched by hand or by machine, and they're just as pretty as presewn blouses for which you'd pay three or four times as much. Each blouse is put together from differently patterned strips of lace. Styles include an Ascot blouse, a blouse with boat neck and ruffled sleeves, an open-neck blouse, and one with puffy sleeves and classic Victorian high collar. Great party blouses. Total cost, including $2 postage and handling, is $18 each.

Nothing is as warm as a *down robe* or a *down coat.* **Frostline** has kits for both.

Their down robe kit has a polyester/cotton/nylon shell with down fill. It comes in ankle length with or without shawl collar and with or without long roll-up sleeves. It wraps kimono-style, and it's machine-washable. Pale blue or pale pink. *Great news for the larger woman; this robe comes in a size that will fit sizes 16–20.* Less than $60.

Frostline's down coats come in lightweight or warmer versions. Each is midcalf length and has horizontal channels. Their Down About model comes with cotton poplin or nylon/cotton/polyester blend shell (the latter is washable). Storm-covered two-way nylon zipper, wind-shielding collar, turn-back cuffs, and insulated stash pockets. The blend shell version sells for about $80—and it's worth almost twice the price. Royal blue or beige. The cotton poplin version costs about $120 for the kit. Royal blue, raspberry, or beige.

Frostline has a pretty patchwork hostess skirt, too, well under $25. Great for Christmas/New Year entertaining; good all year round, too.

Plain Brown Wrapper, Inc., has a *prime goose-down mid-calf-length down coat kit* with interesting box quilting. Double front pockets, interlined collar, pocket flaps, shirt cuffs, and placket. The cuffs and front close with nickel snaps. Pocket flaps close with hook and loop. Outer fabric is 60 percent Dacron polyester, 40 percent nylon Antron. Average loft is ¾". This kit has to be *the least expensive down coat available:* about $40 for the kit. Blue or tan.

SunDown has an extremely good-looking *down coat kit,* which can either be dry-cleaned or washed. Available with 60/40 cloth shell (navy only) or Klimate version (rust only)—sells for about $160. It's worth it; last year I paid more than $200 at half-price for the only other waterproof down coat I've seen.

Tandy Leather Company has an awful lot of garish tooled-leather wallet and handbag kits that children put together at crafts programs and then give to you as heartfelt but unusable gifts. But particularly now that Western wear is so popular, you may find a few items in this catalogue that will go well with your cowboy boots and hat. Their *tooled-leather belts* with Old West designs would look great with your American Indian-made belt buckles, and they're priced well under $10. There are other Western-influenced items here, too, that you might like, including leather handbags with horsehead designs (well under $30), a Western yoke bag that can be used with denim or suede fabric (an excellent buy at around $11), and some nice, inexpensive calfskin credit card/business card cases (under $3). They also have terrific moccasin kits for babies, $3 each—probably the "hippest" gift you could give an infant.

For the past few years **Allen J. Valero** has been building up the only kit company with *sherling vest, coat,* and *jacket kits.* Apparently response has been very good; every few months he and his wife Senja seem to add even more beautiful items to their line.

If the idea of sewing shearling sounds to you like instant broken fingers, send for their brochure. It comes with needle, thread, a piece of creamy soft shearling on which you can practice. I did it; my fingers are okay.

Valero's kits can save you a fortune—probably about half of what you'd pay for similar-quality shearling garments. I'm especially enthusiastic about the Valero Hugger shearling carcoat-style jacket with natural-wood toggles and choice of shawl or hooded collar. Each is available, by the way, in larger-than-average sizes for larger-than-average men and women. The jacket comes in four different colors: taupe scarface, stoney cinnamon, ranch chocolate, or, my favorite, Arctic white. The taupe kit, with shawl collar, goes for just over $200. (Add about $20 to each for the hooded style.) Arctic white with shawl collar costs about $300.

Some Useful Kits for Your Home, including a Hearth Brush, Chimney-cleaning Kits, a Negative-Ion Generator, and a Log Splitter

Black Magic Chimney Sweeps has a *chimney-cleaning kit* for woodburners that should save you $40 to $50 per year and prevent chimney fires. The kit comes with a stiff spring-steel wire brush, seven 3″ flexible fiberglass rods (enough for most two-story homes), couplings to screw the sections together, and a 27-page instruction manual. Prices depend upon your flue size and range between about $50 and $65.

Dick Blick sells a *rubber-stamp kit* that allows you to make over a hundred rubber stamps. The kit contains one hundred eight type characters, extra type rods, two stamp handles, stamp pad. Under $20. Perhaps more useful for an office than for a home.

Country Ways has the only *hearth-brush kit* I've seen. Constructed of nautical manila rope and twine. Makes a 12″ brush. A nice and affordable gift for the children to make. About $3.

Garden Way Research has an extraordinary *wheelbarrow garden-cart kit* with big bicycle wheels and huge load capacity. Very stable. Comes in three sizes. Price ranges from about $50 to under $120.

Gilliom Manufacturing has kits for the power-tool set. You can, in fact, build a *circular saw,* a *sander,* and a *bandsaw,* all for less than $170.

Golden Enterprises, Inc., has perhaps the only kit on the market for a negative-ion generator. Their Golden Air kit produces negative ions without producing ozone or radiation. The kit sells for about $150—$80 less than the assembled model. A surplus of negative ions are supposed to improve your sense of well-being, help your sex life, and prevent suicide.

If you heat your home with wood, you're probably yearning for your own *motorized log splitter.* Now there's a kit available that should save you about $100 on this handy device. Uses a 5-horsepower engine. You'll save a *lot* of backbreaking effort over the years with this kit, as well as saving on the cost of buying presplit wood. About $500, from **J-D Hydrolic Sales,** Warsaw, Indiana.

Mother Earth News has an *alcohol-fuel kit* to help you build your own still, turn corn into alcohol fuel, and beat the high price of gas and oil. The kit comes with a set of plans for your own still, *Brown's Alcohol Motor Fuel Cookbook,* a quart of diazyme L-100 liquid and two pounds of takatherm L-70 liquid, a fermentation lock, and a hydrometer. About $45.

Neff's Nifty Chimney-Cleaner Kit allows you to *clean your chimney from outside the house without getting filthy.* The mechanism is permanently installed within your chimney; it comes in 26″ and 36″ heights, in 8″ x 8″ width and 8″ x 12″ width flue sizes. Prices range between $100 and $150.

Kits for Craftspeople: Loom Kits, Potter's Wheel Kits, a Bookbinding Kit, Home Tanning and Taxidermy Kits, and Others

A-1 Kiln Kits has *kits for gas and electrical kilns.* The electric kilns are portable, top-loading, sectional models, made of separate rings stacked one upon the other. The kiln lid and bottom are separate units and can be used reversibly for double wear. The gas kilns are updraft, portable kilns, with three burners each to allow the kiln to heat evenly from floor tile to top of firing chamber. Will fire to Cone 10 with either natural gas or bottled gas. Electric kiln kits range in price from $150 for an 11¼" x 13½" firing chamber to $400 for a 23⅜" x 22" firing chamber. Gas kilns range in price from about $400 for 4-cubic-foot capacity to about $700 for 11.84-cubic-foot capacity.

Armour Products sells a kit that enables you to *etch glass.* You can use it on mirrors, glasses, jars, fireplace doors, stained glass, and more. If you don't want to do it free-form, you can use one of the forty-five patterns that come with the kit. $10.95.

If you love and/or collect books, you'll probably find the **Basic Crafts Company** catalogue fascinating. Included are several unusual kits for lovers of the written word. One is a *paper-making kit.* This kit comes with hardwood mold with special mesh, deckle (frame), two press boards, ½-pound pulp, twenty reusable couching (drying) cloths, plus detailed instructions. About $18. They sell additional pulp, of course, at pretty low prices.

If you'd like to make your own book or if you know some bright youngster who would like to make her/his own book, Basic Crafts has a *book-making kit,* about $13. It comes with all material necessary to make one complete book and to cover another 8" x 10" one or two 5" x 8" paperbacks. Contains everything needed, from metal-edge rules to imprinted endpapers.

There's been a resurgence of interest lately in marbelized papers. It is a fascinating craft, with beautiful results. If you're a newcomer to the craft and would like to buy all necessary materials at one time, **Basic Crafts** has a *marbling kit* that might interest you. Includes a wide selection of colors, a graining comb, a marbling comb, and directions—everything except the paper. About $50.

Country Ways has two loom kits. Their *floor loom kit* is a hardwood frame that permits work up to 36" wide. It folds away when you're not using it. Four harness, jerk action-rising shed, with 600 flat steel heddles, and one reed (choice of 8, 10, or 12 dent). About $325. Their *frame loom kit* is a version of the Beka SG-20 recommended for "first" and intermediate projects. Comes with two shuttles, a pickup stick, heddle blocks, etc. Takes work up to 20 inches wide and 5 yards long. Warp is 10 threads per inch. The kit costs about $30—$10 less than the completed loom.

One of the best (if strangest) gifts I've ever received was a pheasant a friend of mine shot and mounted himself. If there's a hunter or fisherman/woman in your family or if you'd like to preserve a small animal or bird you found by the side of a road, **Mould-N-Mount** has a *taxidermy kit* that may interest you. The process takes places over four days and it's messy, but you'll save a fortune; I recently saw mounted pheasants in one of my mail-order catalogues, prices at over $300 each. The kit sells for under $20.

Oak Hill Industries of Davenport, Iowa, sell several different *Kick Wheel Kits,* at least three of which are electric-powered. Their Mark IV-E Electric-Powered Kick-Wheel Kit has motor power transmitted to the **V**-belt to the flywheel shaft through an automatic clutch, which locks when the motor starts, quickly bringing the throwing head up to centering speed of 195 rpm. The basic kit costs under $400. For complete details, write to them at the address listed in the Appendix.

Pacifica Crafts of Ferndale, Washington, has another *electric potter's wheel kit.* Supposedly, it's the quickest wheel available. The kit costs about $300.

Still another kit for an *electric potter's wheel* . . . they furnish the "guts," and you supply the frame or table of your own design. If you're considering a wheel from a kit, you ought to look at their information, too. Available from **Pottery Equipment, Inc.,** of Silt, Colorado.

Weavers will enjoy the **School Products Company** catalogue with its huge variety of looms, including Swedish imports. Among their kits, they offer two *rigid heddle-loom kits,* one with 3½ " heddle, the other with 9 " heddle. This is a very simple loom kit for beginning weavers, an adaptation of the backstrip loom. School Products also has a *card-weaving kit* that's great for Scout or school use. The kit serves twelve students, about two projects each, and costs well under $20.

But, best of all, is their *Finnish spinning-wheel kit.* It's a reproduction of a traditional Saxony style and is very beautiful. Unfinished, well-dried birch wood, with pine wheel. Measures 38 " high, 22 " wheel diameter. Well under $200.

Sievers Looms sells three loom kits. Their 15 " table-loom kit is a 4-harness type on which you can weave anything up to 15 " wide. Not a toy. About $150. Their *folding floor looms* come in 22 " and 36 " widths. The kit comes with everything down to the brass paper fasteners used to hold the heddle bars in place. Under $350 each.

Van Dyke Supply Company of Woonsocket, South Dakota, has been supplying their clientele with taxidermy-related merchandise for more than thirty years. They have an excellent selection of *taxidermy kits* for mounting ducks, squirrels, fish, and pheasants. They also carry kits for horn mounting and home tanning. Wait till you see their full color pages of glass eyes.

Wallis Designs has very inexpensive *kick-wheel kits*. Kit parts include sealed self-aligning bearings, 1″ solid shaft, 10″ cast aluminum throwing head (reversible for use with bats), flywheel reinforcements, and directions. You supply the wood. Kit with 10″ throwing head, about $60. 12″ head, approximately $5 more.

An Easter Egg Kit

According to **Surma,** a small kit company located in the heart of New York's Ukrainian population, "Among Ukrainians there is a belief that the fate of the world depends upon *pysanky*. As long as egg decorating continues, the world will exist. Should the custom cease, evil, in the guise of an ancient, vicious monster chained to a huge cliff, will encompass the world and destroy it. Each year the monster's servants encircle the globe, keeping a record of the number of *pysanky* made. When there are few, the monster's chains loosen, and evil flows through the world. When there are many, the monster's chains hold taut, allowing love to conquer evil." Even if you don't accept the legend, you have to admit that Ukrainian Easter eggs are among the most beautiful. Now you can make your own with *Surma's Ukrainian Easter* egg decorating kit. Under $9.

A Passover Kit

As you'll determine from the next entry (Chanukah Kits), there are very few kits designed for Jewish needleworkers looking for holiday or holy-day-related items. Here is one Passover kit I found.

The **Jewish Museum Shop** on New York City's Fifth Avenue has a very beautiful *matzoh-cover crewel kit,* adapted by Erica Wilson from a textile made in Galatia about 1850. The kit measures 14″ in diameter, comes with Persian wool, needles, stamped design on linen, and instructions. It costs $15.95, plus $2.25 for shipping charges.

Chanukah Kits

Considering the number of Jewish people in this country who celebrate Chanukah in traditional ways and who also do fine needlework of all types, it's amazing how few Chanukah kits there are. In fact, there are just two.*

* Just as this book was about to go to the printer I discovered another source of Chanukah kits. You'll find the address listed in the Appendix under An Additional Source of Chanukah kits.

One, a cross-stitch Challah cover from **American Needlewoman** is listed in the cross-stitch sampler section of chapter 7. Here's the other one.

Studio 35 of Brooklyn, New York, has a terrific *needlepoint Chanukah dreidel kit.* A driedel is, of course, the four-sided top children love to play with during this festive holiday. The kit contains 4-ply acrylic yarn, gold metallic yarn, a dowel, and #10 plastic canvas. Finished cube size is 4¼". 6" overall. $5.25, plus 50 cents shipping.

Merry Christmas Kits

If you're the kind of person who buys every woman's magazine at Christmastime because of all the holiday decorations and crafts inside (I've been doing that for years), you'll be interested in this section. I think the companies that follow have some of the very best Christmas decoration and ornament kits available. If I've missed your favorite kit though or if you sell a wonderful Christmas kit that's not included here or in the Appendix, please write to me (enclosing the kit company's brochure, if you can).

Aldebaran Educational has a wonderful kit for *macramé snowflakes* in gold- and silver-metallic thread, which makes up into ten 4" to 6" snowflakes in five different designs. About $10. I used several of these on my tree this Christmas, and they looked *very* pretty.

Arts Array has some 4" to 5½" *needlepoint ornaments* for your tree, under $7 each. The Santas are best. They have a very nice needlepoint stocking, too, 7½" long, which says "Baby's First Christmas." About $9.

Bahlsen has fantastic *gingerbread house/cookie kits.* The kit arrives as an elaborate cardboard cutout that you glue together, then cover with the four bags of cookies provided. The finished house measures about 18" wide x 15" high. Generally under $15.

Judy Bean Crafts of Kirbyville, Tennessee, has a wonderful *patchwork Christmas tree pillow kit,* plus patchwork placemats, pot holders, and 5" to 7" satin tree ornaments. The pillow measures 16" square and is a bargain at under $10.

Cher's Kit and Kaboodle has some of the most original *Christmas stocking kits* I've ever seen. These are made by a combination of patchwork and appliqué and are available in versions depicting a brown workboot (complete with laces), black basketball sneaker with sock, pink-and-white Victorian high-lace shoe, blue-and-white saddle shoes, and others. Great kits at great prices—under $7.

Creative Needler has wonderful 6½"-high *needlepoint tree ornaments.* The designs are for a gingerbread boy, a gingerbread girl, a boot filled with gifts, a Santa, plus a little stocking that you can personalize. Under $5 each.

Cross Patch Quilting Center offers several fine patchwork Christmas decorations, including a *calico patchwork gingerbread house* (about $7) and a fabulous *calico patchwork Della Robbia wreath.* The wreath kit, under $20, includes polyester stuffing and reinforced styrene ring. Their little *calico tree ornaments* come in the shapes of a dove, a tree, a star, a wonderful calico wreath, and a holly wreath. About $5 for three.

Ginger Snap Station of Atlanta, Georgia, can provide you with more calico decorations and ornaments than you may be able to abide. Their *classic calico wreath kits* are especially nice. The 21" wreath kit includes forty-one print squares, reinforced ring, polyester filling. The kit takes six to eight hours. Under $20. Other decorations include a very handsome gingham patchwork stocking (with, I think, a racist name), plus gingham tree angels, gingerbread boys, candy canes, trees, bells, wreaths, stars, hobby horses, and wonderful boy and girl ornaments modeled after the figures in traditional Sunbonnet Girl quilts.

For the past three or four years I've been longing for one of the exquisite pinecone wreaths sold in a shop called Matt McGhee's in Greenwich Village, New York. I never have bought one because I think they're exorbitantly priced. Each is made of a variety of different cones, and they're really very pretty. But this year I've found a source of marvelous *pinecone wreath kits* that sell for a fraction of what they'd bring at retail. You can buy them, too, from **Gloria's Cone Tree** in Sweet Home, Oregon. The kit for a 15" wreath costs about $9; the 19" kit costs about $12. There are candle centerpiece kits, too, very pretty for your holiday table. Since Gloria's Cone Tree has sales, it pays to get on their mailing list.

Some of the prettiest *needlepoint Christmas stockings* I've seen are available from **Harbour Gifts** in Palmyra Harbour, New Jersey. They're moderately expensive, about $20 each, but these will last as long as you do. Stockings depict an elaborate cowboy boot, a downhill ski boot, a ballet slipper with fancy-edged stocking, and sneaker and sport sock. Harbour Gifts has very pretty *needlepoint angels,* too, *for your treetop.* These are expensive, too, about $25 each, but your family will use them for generations.

Here's a traditional *Christmas needlepoint pillow* you'll treasure for the rest of your days. Modeled on a Della Robbia wreath, it's 14" in diameter, and depicts lemons, limes, red berries, and nuts, all interwoven with a bright red ribbon and mixed greenery. Not cheap but a classic . . . available from the **Krick Kit Company.** $48.

Elaine Magnin Needlepoint Designs has some of the best *needlepoint tree ornament kits* I've seen. These really are exceptional. Designs include an old-fashioned Prussian-looking soldier, wise men, a lion and lamb (this one called "Peaceable Kingdom"), angel, Santa riding a reindeer, and more. Prices range from about $8 to $12.50. Magnin has terrific needlepoint stockings, too, but they're expensive.

North Shore Farmhouse has a most unusual wreath kit for your holiday home. It's called the *Spice Wreath Kit,* and it includes whole cloves, nutmeg, stick cinnamon, fennel, mustard, dill, rosemary, and twelve other spices. Bay leaves are used as trim. Pretty, and it smells wonderful. $12 will get you a 6″ and an 8″ wreath. Available individually as well. They have a few nice calico ornaments, too, but you'll find most in other catalogues listed in this section.

Papillon's Christmas catalogue is always interspersed with unusual needlepoint kits for holiday decorating. Items this past year ranged from miniature needlepoint gingerbread houses to very expensive and very beautiful needlepoint Christmas stockings (these range in price from $70 to $95). Most of these kits are more suited to fighting inflation in Chevy Chase, Maryland, or Greenwich, Connecticut, than in Levittown, Long Island.

Peacock Alley has some terrific *needlepoint stocking* kits. My favorite is one that depicts an old-fashioned Santa Claus, a little tree, and a mouse. 16″ long. It costs almost $30, but you and your children will have this stocking forever; it's guaranteed to evoke nostalgia in anyone who looks at it. Their *needlepoint tree ornament kits* are much less expensive, of course, with several under $6. They have a very nice old-fashioned *Santa tree topper ornament,* well under $20; I think that considering the price of other tree-topper kits I've seen, this one is a buy.

Elsa Williams' *needlepoint, cross-stitch, and crewel stocking kits* are some of the most charming designs around. If you like cross-stitch, you'll particularly like their inexpensive Merry Christmas sampler stocking, quite unusual and less than $15. Crewel enthusiasts will probably enjoy the 11″ x 17″ caroler stocking—it's funny. But since I'm crazy about needlepoint, my own choice would be the wonderful 13″-high angel stocking, under $15. They have other nice ones, too, plus *bargello tree ornaments.* Available from **Stitchin' Time** in Rochester, New York.

Studio 35 has some lovely *needlepoint tree ornament* kits. These measure 2″ square and are worked in 6-strand cotton floss and gold metallic yarn on #14 interlock canvas. Designs are of a white dove, an angel, a tree, and a snowflake/star. Each can be used as a pincushion, too. $3.95 each, including shipping. Studio 35 has bargello ball tree ornaments, too.

Paper quilling is a natural for beautiful tree ornaments or *snowflakes for package decorations.* Inexpensive kits for the snowflakes and for larger quilled wreaths are available from **Quill Art, Inc.,** in St. Louis, Missouri. The wreath kits come with quilling paper, pins, patterns, instructions, and ribbons for bows. Snowflake kit #724 makes up into ten to twelve snowflakes, the largest of which measures 4″ across; cost is $2.50 for the kit, plus $1.50 postage and handling.

Lee Ward's Creative Crafts Center produces several dozen Christmas decoration kits each year, but my favorites are their *hooked tree-skirt kits.* These range in price from $20 to $40; they usually have holly, Santa, or poinsettia designs. They offer many other kits of all types, including *unusual hooked stocking kits, needlepoint wreaths, Christmas cross-stitch samplers,* and *patchwork wreaths and angels.*

APPENDIX

A Note About Ordering Kits
from Other Countries

There is United States duty added to most imported kits, but even with postage, insurance, and duty, prices are often lower than some American kits, or the kit is simply not available here. A clearance fee of $1 is always levied by the United States Post Office when U.S. duty must be paid, and your mail deliverer must collect the amount owed. How much the duty will amount to depends upon the merchandise ordered. At this writing, there is no duty on sweater kits. If you're thinking of ordering other types of kits you ought to check with your local post office or call the U.S. Customs Office nearest you.

Generally, foreign kit manufacturers will accept payment in American dollars, but not every manufacturer will accept your personal check. They prefer a bank certified check or a cashier's check (bank money order). Some kit purveyors, like Shannon Free Airport, accept payment by credit card. (Currently, they accept VISA/Master Charge, American Express, and Diners Club.)

Sources of Kits for Furniture

Aldens, Inc.
5000 West Roosevelt Road
Chicago, Illinois 60607
(312) 854-4141
Pine furniture kits, including roll-top desk, storage
bench, bar stools.
CATALOGUE: Free

The Bartley Collection, Ltd.
747 Oakwood Avenue
Lake Forest, Illinois 60045
(800) 621-5199
(800) 972-5855 (in Illinois)
Extraordinary-quality museum reproduction furniture.
CATALOGUE: Free

Bedford Lumber Company, Inc.
P.O. Box 65
Shelbyville, Tennessee 37160
(615) 684-2825
Cedar furniture kits. They're especially good on
plain cedar storage chests.
CATALOGUE: Free

Cohasset Colonials
Cohasset, Massachusetts 02025
(617) 383-0110
Cohasset is another excellent kit manufacturer with
an extraordinary line of Shaker furniture kits and
other kits in the early American tradition.
CATALOGUE: $1.00

Conran's
145 Huguenot Street
New Rochelle, New York 10801
(914) 633-8200
Conran's has had, at times, kits for love seats, chairs,
tubular steel beds, and kitchen cabinets. To see
what's available at the moment, either send for their
catalogue or stop by one of their outlets.
CATALOGUE: $2.50

Custom Art Furniture
Max Durst, Inc.
225 East Twenty-fourth Street
New York, New York 10010
(212) 684-4465
Wooden wall-unit kits, in marvelous designs, of
beautiful veneers.
CATALOGUE: $2.00

Emperor Clock Company
Emperor Industrial Park
Fairhope, Alabama 36532
(205) 928-2316
Kits for cherry furniture, as well as clocks.
CATALOGUE: Free

Garden Way Research
Charlotte, Vermont 05445
(802) 425-2121
Garden Way has kits for park benches, food dehy-
drators, cider presses.
CATALOGUE: 25 cents

Heritage Design
P.O. Box 103
Monticello, Iowa 52310
)lf002(319) 465-3270
Upholstered and caned rocking chair kits.
FREE FLYER

Knot Just Another Knotter
P.O. Box 613
Big Sandy, Texas 75755
No phone listed
Macramé furniture kits.
BROCHURE: 25 cents

Nasco
901 Janesville Avenue
Fort Atkinsville, Wisconsin 53538
(414) 563-2446
Nasco has kits for footstools, looms, bird houses, and other miscellaneous items.
CATALOGUE: Free

H. H. Perkins Company
10 South Bradley Road
Woodbridge, Connecticut 06525
(203) 389-9501
Inexpensive kits for bar stools, ladder-back chairs, child's rocker.
CATALOGUE: 50 cents

Rollingswood
Box 404
Grayslake, Illinois 60030
(312) 223-7655
Excellent quality antique reproduction kits.
CATALOGUE: $1.00

Shaker Workshops
P.O. Box 1028
Concord, Massachusetts 01742
(617) 646-8985
Very fine quality Shaker reproduction furniture kits.
CATALOGUE: 50 cents

SMI
Highway 47 North
Department 21, P.O. Box 360
Bay Minette, Alabama 36507
Bentwood rocker and carved-oak kitchen chair kits.
FREE LEAFLET.

Yield House
North Conway, New Hampshire 03860
(603) 356-5338
An amazing assortment of furniture kits, most of which are constructed of pine.
CATALOGUE: Free

Other Sources of Furniture Kits

Family Circle Kits
P.O. Box 450
Teaneck, New Jersey 07666
No phone listed.
Family Circle periodically offers kits for furniture. One of their best, recently, was a mahogany candlestand table with tray-pull, which sold for about $25. Write for more information.

Naugs
P.O. Box 127
Hamilton, Massachusetts 01936
New England lobster-trap table kits. About $50.

New Moon
7 Lansdowne Street
Boston, Massachusetts 02215
(617) 267-9390
Japanese-style futon mattress kits. Single size costs about $40; $15 less than presewn futon.

Weymouth Woodcrafters
P.O. Box 49
Sandwich, Massachusetts 02563
No phone listed.
This tiny company sells inexpensive kits for old-fashioned solid-pine lap desks. About $20 for the plain lid, $10 more for one hand-carved in rose motif.
No brochure, but write to them if you're interested in the lap desk.

In addition, you ought to check your local department store for knock/down furniture, and for kits. In the New York City area, within the past year Bloomingdale's and Macy's each carried a few furniture kits.

Sources of Kits for Rugs

American Handicrafts
P.O. Box 791
Fort Worth, Texas   76101
(817) 921-9051
American Handicrafts/Marribee Needlearts stores all over the country; look in the phone book near you. If you can't find one, you can order their catalogue and order through the mail. Hooked-rug kits; the best are for children's rooms.
CATALOGUE: 50 cents

American Needlewoman
3806 Alta Mesa Boulevard
Century City I Shopping Center
Fort Worth, Texas   76133
(817) 294-1981
Some very nice hooked-rug kits.
CATALOGUE: Free

Art Needlework Industries, Ltd.
7 St. Michael's Mansions
Ship Street, Oxford, OX1 3DG
England
This extraordinary organization has some of the most beautiful needlepoint and hooked-rug designs available anywhere. The directors are needlework historians, very serious about preserving traditional British and other designs. An excellent source too for needlepoint chair cover graphs.
CATALOGUE: $4.00

Adele Bishop, Inc.
Dorset, Vermont   05251
(800) 867-5989
Magnificent stencil kit designs for floor cloths, plus stencils for walls, furniture, fabrics, and other decorative accessories.
CATALOGUE: $1.00

Braid-Aid
466 Washington Street
Pembroke, Massachusetts   02359
(617) 826-6091
Marvelous braided rug kits.
CATALOGUE: $1.50

CUM Textile Industries, Ltd.
5, Roemersgade
1362 Copenhagen K
Denmark
An excellent source of rya rug kits.
CATALOGUE: $4.00

Elaine Magnin Needlepoint Design
3063 Fillmore Street
San Francisco, California
(415) 931-3063
Fabulous needlepoint rug kits.
CATALOGUE: Free

Mary Maxim
2001 Holland Avenue
Port Huron, Michigan   48060
(313) 987-2000
Hooked-rug kits, plus kits for sweaters, afghans, embroidered tablecloths, etc.
CATALOGUE: 50 cents

Papillon
458 Plasamour Drive
Atlanta, Georgia   30324
(404) 872-0440
Needlepoint rugs, plus other needlepoint and gift items.
CATALOGUE: Free

Peacock Alley
650 Croswell Street, S.E.
Grand Rapids, Michigan   49506
(616) 454-9898
Another excellent source of fine needlepoint rug kits.
CATALOGUE: $2.00

Shillcraft

500 North Calvert Street
Baltimore, Maryland 21202
(301) 539-0430
Hooked-rug kits available only via mail.
CATALOGUE: Free

The Stitchery

Wellesley, Massachusetts 02181
(800) 225-4127
In Massachusetts, if you are ordering you can call 237-7554 collect.
A consistently interesting needlework catalogue, which invariably includes a few needlepoint rug kits.
CATALOGUE SUBSCRIPTION: $1.00

Stitchin' Time

P.O. Box 18063
Rochester, New York 14618
(716) 266-3169
An excellent source of needlepoint and hooked-rug kits from a variety of manufacturers, including Bernat, Elsa Williams, and Spinnerin.
CATALOGUES: $4.00

Wool Design, Inc.

8916 York Road
Charlotte, North Carolina 28224
(704) 588-3128
Very beautiful latch-hooked rug kits.
CATALOGUE: $2.00

Other Sources of Kits for Rugs

Woolcraft, Inc.

North Street
Medfield, Massachusetts 02052
At the time of this writing, I haven't yet seen the Woolcraft, Inc., catalogues ($2.00 for catalogue #153; $2.00 for catalogue #7, special European edition), but they sound *very* promising indeed.

Sources of Kits for Clocks

Barap Specialties

835 Bellows Avenue
Frankfort, Michigan 49635
(616) 352-9863
Barap has just a few clock kits, but they're most attractive.
CATALOGUE: 50 cents

Caldwell Industries

603–609 East Davis Street
P.O. Box 591
Luling, Texas 78648
(512) 875-2654
Wooden gear clock kits, plus other unusual kits for collectors.
CATALOGUE: $1.00

Craft Products Company

2200 Dean Street
St. Charles, Illinois 60174
(312) 584-9600
Kits for grandfather clocks, shelf clocks, and wall clocks.
CATALOGUE: $1.50

Craftsman Wood Service Company

1735 Cortland Court
Addison, Illinois 60101
(312) 629-3100
Several attractive, antique reproduction clock kits.
CATALOGUE: $1.00

Edmund Scientific Company

101 East Gloucester Pike
Barrington, New Jersey 08007
(609) 547-3488
One school clock kit, plus miniature clock kits. Many other technical kits, plus kits for toys.
CATALOGUE: Free

Emperor Clock Company

Emperor Industrial Park
Fairhope, Alabama 36532
(205) 928-2316
Grandfather clock kits.
CATALOGUE: Free

Heritage Clock Company
Heritage Industrial Park
Drawer 1577
Lexington, North Carolina   27292
(704) 956-2113
Grandfather, schoolhouse, and shelf clock kits.
CATALOGUE: $1.00

Kuempel Chime Clock Works and Studio
21195 Minnetonka Boulevard
Excelsior, Minnesota   55331
(612) 474-6177
Hand-crafted grandfather clock kits.
CATALOGUE: Free

Mason & Sullivan Company
39 Blossom Avenue
Osterville, Massachusetts   02655
(617) 428-5726
Excellent quality, extremely attractive kits for wall clocks, shelf clocks, and case clocks.
CATALOGUE: $1.00

The New England Clock Company
P.O. Box 640
Bristol, Connecticut   06010
(203) 677-4253
Their Connecticut Clock Company division has several fine case clock kits, plus a small but interesting selection of shelf and wall clock kits.
BROCHURE: Free

Viking Clock Company
The Viking Building, Box 490
Foley, Alabama   36536
(205) 943-5081
A few grandfather clock kits, plus some Victorian-reproduction wall and shelf clocks.
BROCHURE: $1.00

Westwood Clocks 'n Kits
3210 Airport Way
P.O. Box 2930
Long Beach, California   90801
(213) 595-4981 (for orders)
(213) 595-5411 (showroom)

Grandfather clock kits, plus kits for several smaller clocks.
BROCHURE: $1.00

Other Sources of Kits for Clocks

Hentschel Clock Company
39 Blossom Avenue
Osterville, Massachusetts   02655
(617) 428-3505
Relatively inexpensive yet very handsome grandfather clock kits, of good quality.
BROCHURE: Free

Sources of Kits for Decorative Accessories

Bay Country Woodcrafts, Inc.
U.S. Route 13
Oak Hall, Virginia   23416
(804) 824-5626
Duck decoy and accessory kits.
CATALOGUE: $1.00

Adele Bishop, Inc. *See listing under* Sources of Rug Kits.

James Bliss & Co., Inc.
Route 128 (Exit 61)
Dedham, Massachusetts   02026
(617) 329-2430
Medieval lantern kit, early German clock kits, ship model kits.
CATALOGUE: $1.00

Brookstone
127 Vose Farm Road
Peterborough, New Hampshire   03458
(603) 924-9511 (twenty-four-hour telephone order service)
Picture framing kits, plus many handy hard-to-find tools.
CATALOGUE: Free

Cane & Basket Supply Company
1283 South Cochran Avenue
Los Angeles, California   90019
(213) 939-9644
Chair caning kits, plus kits for inexpensive ladder-back chairs (around $20).
CATALOGUE: $1.00

Conran's. *See listing under* Sources of Kits for Furniture.

Constantine
2050 Eastchester Road
Bronx, New York   10461
(212) 792-1600
Chair caning and duck decoy kits.
CATALOGUE: $1.00

The Country Loft
Mail Order Department
South Shore Park
Hingham, Massachusetts   02043
(800) 225-5408 (toll-free outside Massachusetts)
(617) 749-7766
Lamp kit, plus many interesting, preassembled country American accessories.
CATALOGUE: Free

Craftsman Wood Service Company. *See listing under* Sources of Kits for Clocks.

Double M Marketing Company, Inc.
11220 Talbert Avenue
P.O. Box 8500
Fountain Valley, California   92708
(714) 556-6880
Wall-mural kits.
BROCHURE: Free

Imaginations
61 Kendall Street
Framingham, Massachusetts   01701
(617) 620-1411
Fabric wall-mural kits.
BROCHURE: Free

Lyme Crafts
15 Joshuatown Road
Lyme, Connecticut   06371
No phone listed.
Peg-rack kit.

Mason & Sullivan Company. *See listing under* Sources of Kits for Clocks.

Nasco. *See listing under* Sources of Kits for Furniture.

Old Sturbridge Village Museum Gift Shop
Old Sturbridge Village
Sturbridge, Massachusetts   01566
(617) 347-9843
A wonderful catalogue of fine reproduction tinware, baskets, stoneware, etc. Some kits, including one for a spinning wheel.
CATALOGUE: Free

Patch-It
Box 16A
Waitsfield, Vermont   05673
No phone listed.
Patchwork bird mobile kit.
BROCHURE: 25 cents

H. H. Perkins Company. *See listing under* Sources of Kits for Furniture.

Pickwick Lamps
South Main Street, Route 100
Stowe, Vermont   05672
(802) 253-9291
Lamp kits.
BROCHURE: Free

Shades of Olde
P.O. Box 260
Lyons, Colorado   80540
(303) 823-5153
Fancy lampshade kits. They're now wholesaling only, but if you write to them, they'll send a brochure, plus the address of the nearest store handling their kits.

Other Sources of Kits for Decorative Accessories

Newell Workshop
19 Blaine Avenue
Hinsdale, Illinois   60521
No phone listed.
Inexpensive chair caning kits.
BROCHURE: Free

Preston's at Main Street Wharf
Greenport, Long Island, New York   11944
(516) 477-1990
Duck decoy kits, ship model kits, plus preassembled nautical decorative accessories.
CATALOGUE: 25 cents

Sources of Stained-Glass Accessory Kits

Mary Maxim. *See listing under* Sources of Kits for Rugs.

Spector's Stained Glass
506 Hazelwood Drive
Easton, Maryland   21601
(301) 822-8369
Stained-glass kits for mirrors, lamps, suncatchers.
BROCHURE: $1.00

Studio Design, Inc.
Rainbow Art Glass
49 Shark River Road
Neptune, New Jersey   07753
(201) 922-1090

An exciting range of kits for stained-glass lamps, mirrors, clocks, suncatchers, terrariums.
CATALOGUE: $2.00

Whittemore–Durgin Glass Company
P.O. Box 2065
Hanover, Massachusetts   02339
(617) 871-1743
Stained-glass lamp kits. You cut the glass.
CATALOGUE: Free

H. L. Worden Company
118 Main Street
P.O. Box 519
Granger, Washington   98932
(509) 854-1557
Stained-glass lamp kits. You cut the glass.
CATALOGUE: $1.00

Additional Sources of Stained-Glass Kits

Lee Wards Creative Crafts Center
1200 St. Charles Road
Elgin, Illinois   60120
(800) 621-5809 (twenty-four-hour toll-free order service)
(800) 972-5858 (in Illinois only)
A small selection of stained-glass hanging lamps, suncatchers, wall panels. Mostly needlecrafts kits.
BROCHURE: Free

CHAPTER 2—MUSICAL INSTRUMENTS

Sources of Kits for Dulcimers and Hammered Dulcimers

Alpine Dulcimer Company
P.O. Box 566
Boulder, Colorado   80306
No phone listed.
Dulcimer kits.
BROCHURE: Free

Black Mountain Instruments
16264 Main Street
P.O. Box 779
Lower Lake, California   95457
(707) 994-9315
Dulcimer kits and accessories.
BROCHURE: Free

Country Ways, Inc.
3500 Highway 101 South
Minnetonka, Minnesota 55343
(612) 473-4334
Dulcimer, mandolin, lumberjack, banjo kits—and much more.
CATALOGUE: $1.00

The Dulcimer Shoppe
Drawer E—Highway 9 North
Mountain View, Arkansas 72560
(501) 269-8639
Kits for dulcimers, plus an excellent line of preassembled dulcimers, dulcimer cases, books, tapes, and other folk recordings.
CATALOGUE: $1.00

Elderly Instruments
541 East Grand River
P.O. Box 1795
East Lansing, Michigan 48823
(517) 332-4331
Kits for dulcimers, hammered dulcimers, banjos. An excellent catalogue of music books, records, instruments, and accessories.
CATALOGUE: Free

Guitars Friend
Route 1, Box 200
Sandpoint, Idaho 83864
(208) 263-7640
Kits for dulcimers, guitars, mandolins, banjos. Also, partially assembled hammered dulcimers. Many other fine preassembled instruments.
CATALOGUE: Free

Here, Inc.
29 Southeast Main Street
Minneapolis, Minnesota 55414
(612) 379-4646
Dulcimer, hammered dulcimer, and banjo kits.
BROCHURE: Free

Hughes Dulcimer Company
4419 West Colfax Avenue
Denver, Colorado 80204
(303) 572-3753

Very interesting range of kit instruments, including dulcimers, tomato box instruments, folk harps, hammered dulcimers, guitars, mandolins, and kalimbas.
CATALOGUE: Free

International Luthiers Supply, Inc.
P.O. Box 15444
Tulsa, Oklahoma 74112
(918) 835-4181
Discounted kits for dulcimers, violins, violin bows, mandolins, guitars, hammered dulcimers, and other instruments and supplies for the musician.
CATALOGUE: $1.00 (credited toward purchase)

Other Sources of Kits for Dulcimers and Hammered Dulcimers (Psaltery)

CapriTaurus Folk Music
5497 Highway 9 South
P.O. Box 153
Felton, California 95018
(408) 335-4478
At the time of this writing they are planning to add dulcimer and psaltery kits to their line of custom dulcimers.
CATALOGUE: $3.00

Jean's Dulcimer Shop
P.O. Box 8, Highway 32
Cosby, Tennessee 37722
(615) 487-5543
Dulcimer and hammered dulcimer kits, plus an excellent line of mountain dulcimer and/or hammered dulcimer recording and related books.
BROCHURE: $1.00

Rugg & Jackel Music Co.
P.O. Box 389
Felton, California 95018
(408) 335-3660
Kits for dulcimers, and the mbira African piano. The dulcimer kits are made by Folk Roots, with more than usual attention to the grain of wood used. Excellent dulcimers.
BROCHURE: Free

Sources of Kits for Banjos, Violins, Mandolins, Guitars, Balalaikas, Lutes, and Cellos

Constantine
2050 Eastchester Road
Bronx, New York 10461
(212) 792-1600
Guitar kits, as well as various types of woodworking supplies.
CATALOGUE: Free

Country Ways. *See listing under* Sources of Kits for Dulcimers and Hammered Dulcimers.

Elderly Instruments. *See listing under* Sources of Kits for Dulcimers and Hammered Dulcimers.

Guitars Friend. *See listing under* Sources of Kits for Dulcimers and Hammered Dulcimers.

Here, Inc. *See listing under* Sources of Kits for Dulcimers and Hammered Dulcimers.

International Luthiers Supply, Inc. *See listing under* Sources of Kits for Dulcimers and Hammered Dulcimers.

International Violin Company
4026 West Belvedere Avenue
Baltimore, Maryland 21215
(301) 542-3535
Kits for violins and guitars, plus preassembled instruments, accessories, and supplies for the musician.
CATALOGUE: Free

Stewart–MacDonald Manufacturing Company
Box 900
Athens, Ohio 45701
(614) 592-3021
Excellent quality banjo and mandolin kits.
CATALOGUE: Free

Other Sources of Kits for Banjos, Violins, Mandolins, Guitars, Balalaikas, Lutes, and Cellos

Hughes Dulcimer Company. *See listing under* Sources of Kits for Dulcimers and Hammered Dulcimers.

Sources of Kits for Harpsichords, Spinets, Pianofortes, Clavichords, and Virginals

Burton Harpsichords
4921 North Fifty-seventh Street
Box 80222
Lincoln, Nebraska 68501
(402) 467-1430
Lovely harpsichord, spinet, and clavichord kits.
CATALOGUE: Free

Frank Hubbard Harpsichords, Inc.
185A Lyman Street
Waltham, Massachusetts 02154
(617) 894-3238
Exquisite harpsichord and pianoforte kits.
CATALOGUE: $1.00

The Instrument Workshop
318 North Thirty-sixth Street
Seattle, Washington 98103
(206) 632-7918
(206) 523-6129 (7–9 evenings, Seattle time)
Kits for harpsichords, spinets, virginals, clavichords, fortepianos, based on historical instruments.
CATALOGUE: $1.50

The Williams Workshop
1229 Olancha Drive
Los Angeles, California 90065
(213) 254-2115
Inexpensive kits for a small Flemish harpsichord, triangular spinet, Italian virginal, and portable clavichord.
CATALOGUE: 50 cents

Other Sources of Kits for Harpsichords

Hughes Dulcimer Company. *See listing under* Sources of Kits for Dulcimers and Hammered Dulcimers.

Sources of Kits for Organs, Guitar Amplifiers, and Synthesizers

Devtronix Organs, Inc.
6101 Warehouse Way
Sacramento, California 95826
(916) 381-6203
Electronic organ kits.
CATALOGUE: $2.00

Heath Company
Benton Harbor, Michigan 49022
(616) 982-3411
Electronic organ kits, plus an amazing variety of kits for virtually every type of electronic equipment for home and business use.
CATALOGUE: Free

PAIA Electronics, Inc.
P.O. Box 14359
Oklahoma City, Oklahoma 73116
(405) 843-9626
Kits for synthesizer systems.
BROCHURE: Free

Radio Shack
For the store near you, look in your local phone book; Radio Shack has about six thousand stores. You have to pick up the free catalogue there. If you can't find a store near you, write to:
Radio Shack
Tandy Corporation
500 One Tandy Center
Fort Worth, Texas 76102
(817) 390-3011 (main office)
Electronic organ kits suitable for children.

Schober Organ Corporation
43 West Sixty-first Street
New York, New York 10023
(212) 586-7552
Organ kits.
CATALOGUE: Free

Wersi Electronics, Inc.
Box 5318
Lancaster, Pennsylvania 17601
(717) 299-4327
Electronic organ kits.
CATALOGUE: $2.00

Sources of Kits for Folk Harps, Kalimbas, Lyres, and Other Instruments

Country Ways, Inc. *See listing under* Sources of Kits for Dulcimers and Hammered Dulcimers.

Here, Inc. *See listing under* Sources of Kits for Dulcimers and Hammered Dulcimers.

Hughes Dulcimer Company. *See listing under* Sources of Kits for Dulcimers and Hammered Dulcimers.

International Luthiers Supply, Inc. *See listing under* Sources of Kits for Dulcimers and Hammered Dulcimers.

Lee Music Manufacturing Company
P.O. Box 308
Culver, Oregon 97734
(503) 546-4851
Electric player adapters in kit form for player pianos.
BROCHURE: Free

Rugg & Jackel Music Co. *See listing under* Sources of Kits for Dulcimers and Hammered Dulcimers.

Chapter 3—SPORTING GOODS AND SPORTING CLOTHING

Sources of Backpacking, Camping and Mountaineering Equipment and Clothing

Altra, Inc.
5541 Central Avenue
Boulder, Colorado 80301
(303) 449-2401
An excellent line of kits for tents, gaitors, day packs, booties, etc. Available by mail from the manufacturer or through retail stores all over the country. They'll send a list of dealers in your part of the country when you request their catalogue.
CATALOGUE: Free

Atlanta Cutlery Corp.
P.O. Box 839
Conyers, Georgia 30207
(404) 922-3700
Sporting knife kits.
BROCHURE: $1.00

Bingham Projects, Inc.
P.O. Box 3013-3400 South 1350 W.
Ogden, Utah 84409
(801) 731-2735
Kits for bows, arrows, knives, skateboards, cross-country skis, etc. These seem to be best as school shop/industrial arts projects.
BROCHURE: $1.00

Country Ways, Inc.
3500 Highway 101 South
Minnetonka, Minnesota 55343
(612) 473-4334
Snowshoe kits, knife kits, plus kits for day packs, sleeping bags, rain gear, panniers, and outdoor equipment of most kinds. An extraordinary company with fair prices, personal attention when you need it, and imaginative gear.
BROCHURE: $1.00

Custom Knifemaker's Supply
P.O. Box 308
Emory, Texas 75440
(214) 473-3330
At least one expensive but exquisite knife kit, plus other knife-making supplies.
CATALOGUE: $2.00

Frostline Kits
Frostline Circle
Denver, Colorado 80241
(303) 451-5600
A truly remarkable line of kits for tents, sleeping bags, booties, parkas, vests, packs, downhill ski clothing, etc.
CATALOGUE: Free

KlimaKraft
316 East Drive
Oak Ridge, Tennessee 37831
No phone listed.
Manufacturers of very inexpensive wood-and-nylon pack frame kits suitable for Cub or Brownie Scout use.
FLYER: Free

Plain Brown Wrapper, Inc.
2200 West Alameda No. 35
Denver, Colorado 80223
(303) 936-2377
A fine line of kits for parkas, wind shirts, rain gear, down booties, sleeping bags. Their kits do not require you to sear the edges of the fabric used.
CATALOGUE: $1.00

Sherpa, Inc.
2222 West Diversey Parkway
Chicago, Illinois 60647
(312) 772-6200
Aluminum-frame snowshoe kits.
CATALOGUE: Free

SunDown Kits
14850 Northeast Thirty-first Circle
Redmond, Washington 98052
(206) 883-3997
A full line of kits for sleeping bags, vests, parkas, tents, rain gear, etc. SunDown is known for the high-quality goose down used in its kits.
CATALOGUE: $1.00

Allen J. Valero
Failing Spring Hollow
R.D. #1, Box 199
Monroetown, Pennsylvania   18832
(717) 364-5160
Excellent kits for sheepskin vests, jackets and other items.
CATALOGUE: $3.00

Vermont Tubbs, Inc.
Sales Office
P.O. Box 98
Ashford, Connecticut   06278
In Vermont: (802) 247-3414
Excellent traditional ash and neoprene snowshoe kits.
BROCHURE: Free

Sources of Kits for Rods, Fly-tying, and Other Fishing Tackle and Accessories

The Angler's Supply House, Inc.
815 Railway Street
P.O. Box 996
Williamsport, Pennsylvania   17701
(717) 323-7564
Kits for spin-cast rods, spinning rods, fly- and leader-tying kits, plus fish-mounting kits.
CATALOGUE: Free

Bedford Lumber Company, Inc.
P.O. Box 65
Shelbyville, Tennessee   37160
(615) 684-2825
Kits for fishing-rod racks, gun cabinets and racks, archery racks, as well as all varieties of cedar furniture.
CATALOGUE: Free

Buz's Fly and Tackle Shop
805 West Tulare Avenue
Visalia, California   93277
(209) 734-7547
Fly-tying kits, plus preassembled Fenwick and Cortland rods, fly-tying supplies, hooks, etc.
CATALOGUE: Free

Cascade Lakes Tackle
3 Mill Road
P.O. Box 147
Ballston Lake, New York   12019
(518) 399-3945
Landing net kits.
BROCHURE: Free

Coren's Rod & Reel Service
6619 North Clark Street
Chicago, Illinois   60626
(312) 743-2980
Rod kits.
CATALOGUE: $1.00

Frostline Kits. *See entry under* Sources of Backpacking, Camping, and Mountaineering Equipment and Clothing.

Gander Mountain, Inc.
P.O. Box 248
Wilmot, Wisconsin   53192
(800) 558-9410 (toll-free)
(414) 862-2331 (orders from Alaska, Hawaii, and Wisconsin)
Fenwick rod-building kits, plus all kinds of preassembled gear for the sportsman or sportswoman.
CATALOGUE: Free

Gene's Tackle Shop
P.O. Box 7701
Rochester, New York   14622
No phone number listed.
Fly-tying kits and supplies.
CATALOGUE: Free

Lure-Craft
P.O. Box 1418
Bloomington, Indiana   47401
(812) 825-9088
Worm-making kits.
CATALOGUE: $1.00

The Netcraft Co.
2800 Tremainsville Road
Toledo, Ohio 43613
(419) 472-9826
Fly-tying and other kits.
CATALOGUE: Free

Orvis
10 River Road
Manchester, Vermont 05254
(802) 362-1300
Extensive line of fishing-rod kits. Orvis's catalogue is full of fascinating items for the outdoorsperson— beautiful Rambouillet tableware, for example, the service in use at the Château de Rambouillet, the hunting residence of the President of France.
CATALOGUE: Free

Steckler-Tibor
P.O. Box 607
Stoneboro, Pennsylvania 16153
(412) 376-3358
Fishing-rod kits, landing-net kits, and other supplies for the fly-angling enthusiast.
CATALOGUE: $1.00

Additional Sources of Kits for Fly-tying

Universal Vise Corp.
16 Union Avenue
P.O. Box 626
Westfield, Massachusetts 01085
(413) 568-0964
Fly-tying kits, ranging in price from $9.95 to $49.95.
CATALOGUE: Free

Yakima Bait Company
P.O. Box 310
Granger, Washington 98932
(509) 584-1311
Yakima makes a drift-bobber kit in several sizes. Write to them if you would like a list of distributors in your area.
CATALOGUE: 25 cents

Sources of Kits for Black-Powder Firearms

The Armoury, Inc.
Route 202
New Preston, Connecticut 06777
(203) 868-0001
Muzzle-loading replica-firearms kits.
CATALOGUE: $1.00

Dixie Gun Works, Inc.
Gunpowder Lane
Union City, Tennessee 38261
(901) 885-0561
Black-powder firearms kits.
CATALOGUE: $2.00 bulk rate or $3.00 U.P.S.

Hopkins & Allen Arms
3 Ethel Avenue
Hawthorne, New Jersey 07507
(201) 427-1165
Black-powder firearms kits.
CATALOGUE: Free

Lyman Products
Route 147
Middlefield, Connecticut 06455
(203) 349-3421
Black-powder firearms kits.
CATALOGUE: $1.00

Navy Arms Company
689 Bergen Boulevard
Ridgefield, New Jersey 07657
(201) 945-2500
Black-powder firearms kits.
CATALOGUE: $1.00

Other Sources of Kits for Muzzle-loading Firearms

Connecticut Valley Arms, Inc.
Saybrook Road
Haddam, Connecticut 06438
(203) 345-8511
Muzzle-loading firearms kits.
CATALOGUE: Free

Parker Distributors of Florida
P.O. Box 4960
Hialeah, Florida 33014
(800) 327-5088
Black-powder firearms kits.
CATALOGUE: Free

Sources of Bicycle Bags, Tennis and Running Clothing, Gun Racks, Trampolines, Crossbow Kits, and Other Sporting Goods Kits

Bedford Lumber Company, Inc. *See listing under* Sources of Kits for Rods, Fly-tying, and Other Fishing Tackle and Accessories.

Bingham Projects, Inc. *See listing under* Sources of Backpacking, Camping, and Mountaineering Equipment and Clothing.

Frostline Kits. *See listing under* Sources of Backpacking, Camping, and Mountaineering Equipment and Clothing.

Gander Mountain, Inc. *See listing under* Sources of Kits for Rods, Fly-tying, and Other Fishing Tackle and Accessories.

Golf Day Products, Inc.
3015 Commercial Avenue
Northbrook, Illinois 60662
(312) 498-1400
Golf wood-refinishing kits, plus other do-it-yourself golf supplies.
CATALOGUE: $1.75

Doug Kittredge Bow Hut
P.O. Box 598
Mammoth Lakes, California 93546
(714) 934-8355
Arrow kits and other archery supplies.
ARCHER'S BIBLE: Free

Gerald D. Miller
P.O. Box 2159
Petaluma, California 94952
No phone listed.
Crossbow kits.
BROCHURE: $1.00

Patch-It
P.O. Box 16A
Waitsfield, Vermont 05673
(802) 496-2027
Patchwork tennis racquet covers.
CATALOGUE: 25 cents

SMI
Highway 47N.
P.O. Box 360
Bay Minette, Alabama 36507
No phone listed.
Gun cabinet kit.
LEAFLET: Free

Teco
1122 Industrial Drive
P.O. Box 706
Matthews, North Carolina 28105
(704) 847-4455
Trampoline kits.
LITERATURE: Free

Trampoline Kits and Supplies, Inc.
1367 Highway 138
Riverdale, Georgia 30296
(404) 461-9941
(404) 478-3933
Trampoline kits.
BROCHURE: Free

An Additional Source of Gun Rack Kits

Coladonato Brothers
P.O. Box 156
Hazleton, Pennsylvania 18201
(717) 455-2431
Many gun-cabinet kits.
CATALOGUE: $3.25

Chapter 4—HIGH TECHNOLOGY AND SCIENTIFIC KITS

Sources of High Technology and Scientific Kits

ATV Research
Thirteenth & Broadway
Dakota City, Nebraska   68731
(402) 987-3771
Solid-state TV camera kits.
Brochure: Free

Bigelow Electronics
P.O. Box 125
Bluffton, Ohio   45817
(419) 358-7851
A distributor that carries the Philmore line of small electronics kits, including their aerial kit.
Catalogue: $1.00

Burstein-Applebee
3199 Mercier Street
Kansas City, Missouri   64111
(816) 474-7170
(800) 821-3686 (outside Missouri)
Solar-energy lab kits for youngsters.
Catalogue: $1.00

Chaney Electronics, Inc.
P.O. Box 27038
Denver, Colorado   80227
(303) 781-5750
Kits for electronic warning flashers.
Catalogue: Free

Coulter Optical Company
P.O. Box K
Idyllwild, California   92349
(714) 659-2991
Telescope kits.
Brochure: Free

Edmund Scientific
7082 Edscorp Building
Barrington, New Jersey   08007
(609) 547-8900
Kits for solar ovens, sextants, crystal radios, hot-air balloons, etc. A marvelous scientific catalogue, particularly suited for families encouraging an interest in astronomy.
Catalogue: Free

Educational Design, Inc.
47 West Thirteenth Street
New York, New York   10011
(212) 255-7900
Science learning kits.
Brochure: Free

Graymark International
P.O. Box 17359
Irvine, California   92713
(714) 540-5480
Kits for transistor radios, tachometers, digital clocks, and more.
Catalogue: Free

The Heath Company
Benton Harbor, Michigan   49022
(616) 983-3961
An outstanding range of technical kits, ranging from light dimmers to 16-byte home computers.
Catalogue: Free

Inter-Tronics, Inc.
P.O. Box 1021
Oak Brook, Illinois   60521
(312) 344-5063
Electronic auto alarm systems kit.
Brochure: Free

Paul MacAlister & Associates
P.O. Box 157
Lake Bluff, Illinois   60044
Magnificent kits for a perpetual calendar, a nocturnal, sundial, and astrolabe.
Literature: Free

The Macrocoma Company
15 North Main Street
Washington Crossing, Pennsylvania 18977
No phone listed.
TV projector kits.
FLYER: Free

PAIA Electronics
1020 West Wilshire Boulevard
Oklahoma City, Oklahoma 73116
(405) 843-9626
Kits for surf synthesizers, electronic wind chimes, etc.
BROCHURE: Free

Radio Shack
Tandy Corporation
500 One Tandy Center
Fort Worth, Texas 76102
(817) 390-3011
They have almost six thousand stores across the country; look in the phone book for the store nearest your home. Educational toy kits, plus kits for small items like strobe light and electronic bike speedometer.
CATALOGUE: Free at stores

Rocky Mountain Science Supply, Inc.
3093 Walnut Street
Boulder, Colorado 80301
(303) 449-3350
Miniature solar-power kit, plus other Skilcraft kits.
CATALOGUE: $2.00

Speakerlab
735 North Northlake Way
Seattle, Washington 98103
(800) 426-7736
(206) 633-5020 (In Washington state, Alaska, and Hawaii, you may call collect to place your order.)
Top-quality speaker kits for your hi-fi system.
CATALOGUE: Free

Other Sources of High Technology and Scientific Kits

Dage Scientific Instruments
P.O. Box 1054
Livermore, California 94550
(415) 447-3433
Kits for test equipment, including a function generator, digital autorange capacitance meter, electronic thermometer, thermo-couple signal processor, and more.
BROCHURE: Free

King Research Labs, Inc.
801 South Eleventh Avenue
Maywood, Illinois 60153
(312) 344-7877
Keyless, do-it-yourself alarm system for automobile, boat, or home. At the time of this writing, these are not yet in mass production, but they look good. Worth an inquiry.

N. Remer Optics
P.O. Box 306
Southampton, Pennsylvania 18966
(215) 355-3086
Mirror-making kits for constructing your own telescope.
LEAFLET: Free

Telescopics
P.O. Box 98
La Canada, California 91011
(213) 885-0846
Mirror-making kits for constructing your own telescope.
CATALOGUE: 50 cents

CHAPTER 5—HOMES FROM KITS

Sources of Log Home Kits

Alpine Log Homes, Inc.
P.O. Box 85
Victor, Montana 59875
(406) 642-3451
Hand-peeled, nonmilled log home kits.
CATALOGUE: $3.00

Alta Industries Ltd.
Route 30
P.O. Box 88
Halcottsville, New York 12438
(914) 586-3336
Pine log home kits.
CATALOGUE: $3.00

American Log Homes, Inc.
P.O. Box 535
Bourbon, Missouri 65441
(314) 732-5206
Dry pine or spruce log home kits.
CATALOGUE: $1.00

L. C. Andrew, Inc.
28 Depot Street
South Windham, Maine 04082
(207) 892-8561
Northern white cedar log home kits.
CATALOGUE: $4.00

Beaver Log Homes
Chisum Industries, Inc.
518 North J. M. Davis
P.O. Box 1145
Claremore, Oklahoma 74017
(918) 341-5932
Log home kits.
CATALOGUE: $4.50

Bellaire Log Cabin Manufacturing Co.
P.O. Box 322
Bellaire, Michigan 49615
(616) 533-8633
White cedar log home kits. All Bellaire kits are complete with the exception of the foundation, electric wiring, plumbing, heating, or fireplaces.
CATALOGUE: $2.00

Boyne Falls Log Homes, Inc.
Boyne Falls, Michigan 49713
(616) 549-2421
Northern white cedar sill and post partially preassembled log home kits. Boyne Falls's kits are very complete, offering everything from oak flooring to closet hardware.
PORTFOLIO: $3.00

Green Mountain Cabins, Inc.
P.O. Box 190
Chester, Vermont 05143
(802) 875-2163
Spruce log home kits.
INITIAL SMALL CATALOGUE: Free
COMPLETE CATALOGUE AND "DESIGN YOUR OWN HOME" KIT: $4.00

Green River Trading Co.
Boston Corners Road
Millerton, New York 12546
(518) 789-3311
White pine log home kits.
BROCHURE: Free

Heritage Log Homes
P.O. Box 610
Gatlinburg, Tennessee 37738
(615) 436-9331
Southern yellow pine log home kits.
BROCHURE: $5.00

Katahdin Forest Products Co.
P.O. Box 145
Oakfield, Maine 04763
(207) 757-8278
Hand-peeled Northern white cedar or spruce, complete or shell log home kits.
BROCHURE: $4.00

Liberty Log Homes
P.O. Box 398
Centreville, Alabama   35042
(205) 926-4631
Yellow pine log home kits.
BROCHURE: $3.00

National Beauti-Log Cedar Homes, Inc.
1250 South Wilson Way
Stockton, California   95205
(209) 465-3437
Precut cedar home kits.
CATALOGUE: $1.00

New England Log Homes
2301 State Street
P.O. Box 5056
Hamden, Connecticut   06518
(203) 562-9981
Pine log home kits.
PLANNING KIT: $4.00

Northeastern Log Homes, Inc.
P.O. Box 46
Kenduskeag, Maine   04450
(207) 884-7000
Milled Eastern white pine log home kits.
BROCHURE: $3.00

Northern Products Log Homes, Inc.
Bomarc Road
P.O. Box 616
Bangor, Maine   04401
(207) 945-6414
Eastern white pine tongue-and-groove, milled-log home kits.
CATALOGUE: $4.00

Rocky Mountain Log Homes
Route 1
P.O. Box 1255
Hamilton, Montana   59840
(406) 363-5680
Log home kits employing the "Swedish Cope" method of construction.
BROCHURE: $3.00

Southern Log Homes
P.O. Box 236
Andrews, North Carolina   28901
(704) 321-4173
Southern yellow pine log home kits.
CATALOGUE: $3.00

Timber Log Homes, Inc.
Austin Drive
Marlborough, Connecticut   06447
(203) 295-9529
Log home kits constructed of uniformly milled white pine logs. Blueprints available at $20.00 per set. Construction manuals available at $5.00 each.
BROCHURE: $3.00

Wilderness Log Homes
R.R. #2
Plymouth, Wisconsin   53073
(414) 893-8416 (Wisconsin residents)
(800) 558-5881 (toll-free)
Pine or cedar full or half log home kits.
BROCHURE/PLAN BOOK: $4.00

Yellowstone Log Homes
Route 4
P.O. Box 2
Rigby, Idaho   83442
(208) 745-8110
Lodgepole pine log home kits.
CATALOGUE: $3.00

Additional Sources of Log Home Kits

Authentic Homes Corp.
P.O. Box 1288
Laramie, Wyoming   82070
(307) 742-3786
Pine log home kits.
CATALOGUE: $3.00

Building Logs, Inc.
P.O. Box 300
Gunnison, Colorado   81230
(303) 641-1844
Uniformly milled pine or spruce log home kits.
CATALOGUE: $3.00

Cedar Homes, Inc.
555-116 Avenue N. E.
Suite 150
Bellevue, Washington 98004
(206) 454-3966
Western red cedar log home kits.
CATALOGUE: $10.00

Crockett Log Homes
Route 9
West Chesterfield, New Hampshire 03466
(603) 256-8750
CATALOGUE: $3.00

Hainesway II Log Homes
Sylvan Products, Inc.
4729 State Highway No. 3, S.W.
Port Orchard, Washington 98366
(206) 674-2511
Douglas fir or pine outer log shells; doors and window frames provided.
BROCHURE: Free

Justus Company, Inc.
P.O. Box 91515
Tacoma, Washington 98491
(206) 582-3404
Western red cedar log home kits.
BROCHURE: $4.00

Lodge Logs by MacGregor
3200 Gowen Road
P.O. Box 5058
Boise, Idaho 83705
(208) 336-2450
Lodgepole pine milled log home kits.
PLAN BOOK: $5.00

Log Systems, Inc.
2923 Jahn Avenue, N.W.
Gig Harbor, Washington 98335
(206) 858-8202
Post-and-beam red cedar log home kits. Fir or pine are available as well.
BROCHURE: $2.00

Lok-N-Logs, Inc.
Route 80
R.D. #2, Box 212
Sherburne, New York 13460
(607) 674-4447
BROCHURE: $3.00

Moba-Log Homes
P.O. Box 1253
Hamilton, Montana 59840
(406) 363-2550
Until recently Moba-Log sold only completely finished log mobile homes. Recently, they've begun to sell fully constructed shells, the interior of which the customer can finish him or herself.
BROCHURE: Free

Model Log Lumber Enterprises, Inc.
75777 Gallatin Road
Bozeman, Montana 59715
(406) 763-4411
Homes of lodgepole pine and Douglas fir.
CATALOGUE: $5.00

Mountain Logs
P.O. Box 1128
Hamilton, Montana 59840
(406) 961-3222
Log home kits. They periodically run workshops for customers interested in constructing their own log homes.
BROCHURE: Free

National Log Construction Company, Inc.
P.O. Box 69
Thompson Falls, Montana 59873
(406) 827-3521
Air Lock log home kits.
BROCHURE: $2.50

Pan Abode Cedar Homes
4350 Lake Washington Boulevard N.
Renton, Washington 98055
(206) 255-8261
Cedar tongue-and-groove log home kits.
BROCHURE: $7.50

Pioneer Log Homes
P.O. Box 267
Newport, New Hampshire   03773
(603) 863-1050
Log home kits featuring preassembled exterior walls, interior partitions, and roof trusses. They claim their kits average around $1,000 less than the competition.
BROCHURE: $3.50

R & L Log Building, Inc.
Mount Upton, New York   13809
(607) 764-8118
Milled red pine log home kits.
CATALOGUE: $3.00

Real Log Homes, Inc.
Missoula, Montana   59807
(406) 721-1600
Lodgepole pine log home kits. Cedar available as well.
CATALOGUE: $5.00

Rustic Log Structures
14000 Interurban Avenue S.
Seattle, Washington   98168
(206) 246-1332
Lodgepole pine log home kits.
CATALOGUE: $3.00

Rustics of Lindbergh Lake
Condon, Montana   59826
(406) 754-2222
Hand-peeled log home kits. Available either as log-frame kits or more complete kits. They will also custom-design homes.
BROCHURE: $3.00

Shawnee Log Homes, Inc.
Route 8
P.O. Box 449
220 South
Roanoke, Virginia   24014
(703) 989-5400
Hand-peeled log home kits.
Log Home Planning Guide: $3.00

Sylvan Products, Inc.
4729 State Highway #3, S.W.
Port Orchard, Washington   98366
(206) 674-2511
Douglas fir or pine log home kits.
BROCHURE: Free

Vermont Log Buildings, Inc.
Hartland, Vermont   05048
(802) 436-2121
Pine log home kits; more than thirty models available.
BROCHURE: $5.00

Ward Cabin Company
P.O. Box 152
Lisbon, New Hampshire   03585
(603) 838-6664
Cedar log home kits by one of the oldest and most respected manufacturers of this kind of home.
BROCHURE: $5.00

Western Valley Log Homes
P.O. Box 254
Victor, Montana   59875
(406) 961-4421
Machine-milled and peeled-log home kits.
CATALOGUE: $3.00

Youngstrom Log Homes
Blackfoot, Idaho   83221
(208) 785-0632
Pine log home kits.
CATALOGUE: $2.00

Sources of Post-and-Beam Home Kits

Bow House, Inc.
Bolton, Massachusetts   01740
(617) 779-6464
Marvelous frame homes with Cape Cod-style bent-roof beams, unusual reproduction hardware, plus other details evocative of two-hundred-old Cape homes.
BROCHURE: $4.00

Miles Homes
4500 Lyndale Avenue N.
Minneapolis, Minnesota 55412
(612) 588-9700
Many house kits, ranging from rather suburban-looking split-levels, to interesting chalet-type designs. Financing available from the manufacturer.
BROCHURE: Free

Sawmill River Post & Beam, Inc.
P.O. Box 227
Leverett, Massachusetts 01054
(413) 367-9969
Very beautiful traditional or modern-design home kits. Interiors are light and rustic yet contemporary.
BROCHURE: $4.00

Shelter-Kit, Inc.
22 Mill Street
P.O. Box 1
Tilton, New Hampshire 03276
(603) 934-4327
Modular houses in kit form, designed expressly for amateur builders.
BROCHURE: $3.00

Timber Kit
P.O. Box 704
Amherst, Massachusetts 01002
(413) 665-2210
Attractive, ready-for-solar post-and-beam home kits.
CATALOGUE: $1.00

Yankee Barn Homes, Inc.
Drawer A
Grantham, New Hampshire 03753
(603) 863-4545
Sturdy, attractive homes with old yellow pine beams and the commodious life-style of barn living.
BROCHURE: $4.00

Other Sources of Post-and-Beam Home Kits

E. F. Bufton & Son
P.O. Box 581
Mill Street
South Lancaster, Massachusetts 01561
We recently saw one of their post-and-beam commercial buildings in Hampton Bays, New York: magnificent.
BROCHURE: Free

House of Thoreau
P.O. Box 91
Concord, Massachusetts 01742
(617) 259-8709
Magnificent reproductions of Thoreau's 10' x 15' cabin. At the time of this writing, the complete package of materials costs only $4,000.

Standard Homes
U.S. Highway 169 and I-35
P.O. Box 1900
Olathe, Kansas 66061
(913) 782-4220
Sturdy brick or brick-and-wood ranch or split-level home kits. Most have three bedrooms and no-nonsense designs.
BROCHURE: $1.00

Vestal Villas
RFD #1
Exeter, New Hampshire 03833
(603) 679-5649
Pine frame house kits.
BROCHURE: Free

Wickes Lumber
515 North Washington Avenue
Saginaw, Michigan 48607
(517) 753-9121
Wickes's year-round houses tend toward the suburban tract look, but their vacation homes, especially the Chalet and Heritage models, are easily constructed, very attractive building packages, with some parts already preassembled.
BROCHURE: Free

Sources of Kit Companies That Sell Dome Homes, Round Homes and Tipis

Cathedralite Domes
P.O. Box 880
Aptos, California 95003
(408) 462-2210
Classic geodesic dome home kits with preassembled triangles.
CATALOGUE: $4.00

Earthworks
R.D. #1
North Ferrisburg, Vermont 05473
No phone listed.
Earthworks is a tiny company that produces beautiful tipi kits at reasonable prices.
BROCHURE: Free

Geodesic Domes, Inc.
10290 Davison Road
Davison, Michigan 48423
(313) 653-2383
Geodesic dome home kits with preassembled triangles.
BROCHURE: $3.00

Meyer Round Structures
27649 Industrial Boulevard
Hayward, California 94545
(415) 785-1688
Prefabricated circular homes.
BROCHURE: $2.00

Monterey Domes, Inc.
1855-W Iowa Avenue
P.O. Box 55116-W
Riverside, California 92517
(714) 684-2601
Precut, predrilled, color-coded geodesic home kits.
CATALOGUE: $4.00
ASSSEMBLY MANUAL: $5.00

Nomadics—Tipi Makers
17671 Snow Creek Road
Bend, Oregon 97701
(503) 389-3980
Tipi and liner kits.
CATALOGUE: $1.00

Polydome, Inc.
1238 Broadway
El Cajon, California 92021
(714) 547-1400
Prefabricated dome home kits using both triangles and trapezoids.
LEAFLET: Free

Rondo Homes, Inc.
P.O. Box 1679
Tahoe City, California 95730
(916) 583-5804
Shell package kits designed to meet your requirements.
LEAFLET: Free

Sources of Solar Home Kits and Companies Manufacturing Solar Panel Kits

Beaver Log Homes. *See listing under* Sources of Log Home Kits.

Contemporary Structures, Inc.
1102 Center Street
Ludlow, Massachusetts 01056
(413) 583-8300
Energy-efficient post-and-beam homes designed to accommodate passive or active solar-energy systems.
LEAFLET: Free

Heritage Log Homes. *See listing under* Sources of Log Home Kits.

Monterey Domes, Inc. *See listing under* Sources of Dome Home Kits.

Shelter Kit, Inc. *See listing under* Sources of Post-and-Beam Home Kits.

Suntree Solar Company
20 Austin Avenue
Greenville, Rhode Island   02828
(401) 949-2972
Domestic solar-collector kits.
LEAFLET: Free

Timber Kit. *See listing under* Sources of Post-and-Beam Home Kits.

Yellowstone Log Homes. *See listing under* Sources of Log Home Kits.

Sources of Greenhouses, Storage Sheds, Gazebos, Storm Windows, and Other Kits for Your Home

Greenhouses

Four Seasons Solar Products Corp.
910 Route 110
Farmingdale, New York   11735
(516) 694-4400
Everything from small solar lean-to greenhouses to add-a-room home spas.
CATALOGUE: Free

J. A. Nearing Co., Inc.
9390 Davis Avenue
Laurel, Maryland   20810
(301) 498-5700
Easy to assemble, do-it-yourself greenhouses for everything from your co-op kitchen window to your suburban estate.
CATALOGUE: Free

Peter Reimuller, The Greenhouseman®
980 Seventeenth Avenue
Santa Cruz, California   95062
(408) 476-3145
Acrylic and redwood greenhouses to be assembled using heavy-gauge galvanized steel brackets and steel bolts, nuts, washers.
CATALOGUE: $1.00

Texas Greenhouse Co., Inc.
2717 St. Louis Avenue
Fort Worth, Texas   76110
(817) 926-5447
Redwood and fiberglass, redwood and glass, or steel and glass greenhouses. Excellent variety and reasonable prices. They've been in business since 1948, so you'll probably be able to get replacement parts for a while yet.
CATALOGUE: Free

Turner Greenhouses
Highway 117 South
P.O. Box 1260
Goldsboro, North Carolina   27530
(919) 734-2351
(800) 672-4770 (in North Carolina)
Sturdy, "slant-side" greenhouses that need no foundation. Reasonably priced.
CATALOGUE: Free

Outbuildings

Bow House, Inc. *See listing under* Sources of Post-and-Beam Home Kits.

Jer Manufacturing, Inc.
7205 Arthur Drive
Coopersville, Michigan   49404
(616) 837-8174
Little barns or storage sheds from kits.
LEAFLET: Free

Sears, Roebuck & Co.
Adams and Whitaker Streets
Philadelphia, Pennsylvania   19132
(215) 533-4800
Storage buildings in kit form.
CATALOGUE: $2.00

Stairs, Storm Windows, and Other Useful Kits

American General Products, Inc.
1735 Holmes Road
Ypsilanti, Michigan   48197
(313) 483-1833
Studio Stair® spiral-stair kits.
BROCHURE: Free

Bay Country Woodcrafts, Inc.
U.S. Route 13
Oak Hall, Virginia   23416
(804) 824-5626
Flying Duck weathervane kit, plus other attractive wildfowl-oriented kits.
CATALOGUE: $1.00

Elgar Products, Inc.
P.O. Box 22348
Beachwood, Ohio   44122
(216) 831-1558
Storm window kits.
LEAFLET: Free

Fisher's Products, Inc.
Route 1, P.O. Box 63
Conifer, Colorado   80433
(303) 838-2371
Glass door barrel stove kit.
CATALOGUE: $1.00

The Iron Shop
400 Reed Road
P.O. Box 128
Broomall, Pennsylvania   19008
(215) 544-7100
Attractive spiral-stair kits.
CATALOGUE: Free

Maskolite
1770 Joyce Avenue
P.O. Box 1497
Columbus, Ohio   43216
No phone listed.
In-Sider® Storm windows.
LEAFLET: Free

Mylen Industries, Inc.
650 Washington Street
Peekskill, New York   10566
(914) 739-8486
(212) 585-6767
Spiral-stair and open-riser straight-stair kits.
BROCHURE: Free

Plaskolite
1770 Joyce Avenue
Columbus, Ohio   43219
(614) 294-3281
Storm window kits.
LEAFLET: Free

Tyz-all® Plastics, Inc.
240 Glen Head Road
Glen Head, New York   11545
(516) 676-2470
Storm-window kits, plus screen and frame kits.
LEAFLET: Free

Yardlighting Systems, Inc.
1039 Charles Avenue
Saint Paul, Minnesota   55104
(612) 644-3390
Gaslight-conversion kits.
BROCHURE: Free

CHAPTER 6—TOYS

Sources of Kits for Dolls, Doll Clothing, and Stuffed Animals

Charing Cross Kits
Main Street
P.O. Box 798
Meredith, New Hampshire   03253
(603) 279-8449
Wonderful kits for children's and adults' clothing, plus stuffed dolls and doll clothing.
CATALOGUE: $2.00

Cross Patch Quilting Center
Route 9
Garrison, New York   10524
(914) 424-3443
Calico patchwork Mother Goose kit, as well as other patchwork kits and supplies.
CATALOGUE: $1.00

The Enchanted Doll House
Manchester Center, Vermont   05255
(802) 362-3030
Dollhouse and dollhouse furniture kits, doll kits, plus more; a marvelous toy catalogue.
CATALOGUE: $2.00

Eva Mae Doll Company
1931 Fifteenth Street
San Pablo, California   94806
(415) 235-3056
A wide selection of antique reproduction doll kits, plus a few magnificent original doll kits.
CATALOGUE: 35 cents

Mark Farmer Company, Inc.
38 Washington Avenue
P.O. Box 428
Point Richmond, California   94807
China, bisque, porcelain doll kits—and lots of them. Dollhouse doll kits as well.
CATALOGUE: $2.00

Haan Crafts Corporation
185 South Main Street
Otterbein, Indiana   47970
(317) 583-4496
Marvelous stuffed animal kits.
CATALOGUE: $1.00

Larry Houston Studio
2101 Estero Boulevard
Fort Myers Beach, Florida   33931
(813) 463-6655
Many excellent doll kits, mostly bisque reproductions. Some more modern kits, including a doll that resembles Elvis.
BROCHURE: $1.00 (refundable with first order)

Marie Louise Originals
P.O. Box 5785
Huntington Beach, California   92646
No phone listed.
Exquisite boy and girl cloth doll kits.
LEAFLET: Free

Mary Maxim
2001 Holland Avenue
Port Huron, Michigan   48060
(313) 987-2000
Kits for stuffed animals, plus rag dolls.
CATALOGUE: 50 cents

Needlepunch
1409 Fifth Street
Berkeley, California   94710
(415) 527-4561
Folk art stuffed animal kits.
BROCHURE: Free

Pattern Plus
21 Mountain View Avenue
New Milford, Connecticut   06776
(203) 354-1894
Terrific cloth doll kits.
CATALOGUE: $1.25

H. H. Perkins Company
10 South Bradley Road
Woodbridge, Connecticut   06525
(203) 389-9501
Reed doll cradle kit.
BROCHURE: 50 cents

Standard Doll Company
23-83 Thirty-first Street
Long Island City, New York   11105
(212) 721-7787
A huge variety of China doll kits, porcelain bisque kits, apple-head doll kits, and more.
CATALOGUE: $1.50

*Other Sources of Kits for Dolls
and Doll Furniture*

Amerillis Brookshire
Sunshine Doll Hospital
Route 2
P.O. Box 161
Columbus, Kansas   66725
(316) 674-3691 Call after 5:00 P.M.
Antique reproduction doll kits.
FLYER: 50 cents

Bill Harmon
439 South Scraper
Vinita, Oklahoma   74301
(918) 256-2762
Antique reproduction doll kits.
LEAFLET: Free

Weymouth Woodcrafters
P.O. Box 49
Sandwich, Massachusetts   02564
No phone listed.
They have a $16.95 (postpaid) kit for a pine reproduction of a Shaker doll cradle: 22″ long x 11½″ wide x 11½″ deep. Quilt, pad, and pillow kit available for an additional $4.95.
DESCRIPTIVE MATERIAL: Free

*Sources of Kits for Cardboard Houses,
Buildings, and Villages*

Brentano's
Department 1021
Tinton Falls, New Jersey   07724
(800) 228-2028, Extension 130
They carry Putnam's *Build Your Own* series of cut-out buildings.
CATALOGUE: Free

Dover Publications, Inc.
180 Varick Street
New York, New York 10014
(212) 255-3755
Cut-and-assemble cardboard towns.
CATALOGUE: Free

The Metropolitan Museum of Art Gift Shop
255 Gracie Station
New York, New York 10028
(212) 362-3335
Cardboard towns.
CATALOGUE: Published at Christmas only, $1.00 (at the time of this writing)

Monte Models
P.O. Box 2391
New Bern, North Carolina   28560
(919) 637-5803
A huge and fascinating selection of paper models of fine American architecture, as well as some models of buildings in Holland, Germany, England, Switzerland, Denmark.
CATALOGUE: Free

*Additional Source of Kits for
Cardboard Houses and Villages*

Grandy's Workshop
9702 Amberton Parkway
Dallas, Texas   75243
No phone listed.
Model castle kit, 42″ x 42″.
BROCHURE: $1.00

Sources of Dollhouses and Dollhouse Furniture

Artply Company, Inc.
907 Shepherd Avenue
Brooklyn, New York   11208
(212) 649-2440
Dollhouse kits.
Write for information.

Bee Jay's Little World
Route 4
Northwood, New Hampshire   03261
(603) 942-8380
Dollhouse kits.
BROCHURE: 50 cents

James Bliss & Company, Inc.
Route 128 (Exit 61)
Dedham, Massachusetts   02026
(617) 329-2430
Dollhouse furniture kits, sailing ship kits, and more.
CATALOGUE: Free

Chrysolite, Inc.
5118 Midfield Drive
Portage, Michigan   49081
No phone listed.
Tiny 12-volt 1":1' lighting fixtures for your doll-house.
Free flyer usually available at your local miniatures store. If not, write to them directly.

Cir-Kit Concepts, Inc.
612 North Broadway
Rochester, Minnesota   55901
(507) 288-8237
Kits for electrifying your dollhouse, plus kits for tiny porcelain ceiling fixtures.
BROCHURE: $2.00

Constantine
2050 Eastchester Road
Bronx, New York   10461
(212) 792-1602
A nice selection of dollhouse furniture kits. One dollhouse kit.
CATALOGUE: Free

Country Stitching
P.O. Box 119
Willow Grove, Pennsylvania   19090
(215) 576-7835
Marvelous kits for counted cross-stitch miniature rugs.
BROCHURE: Free

Craft Products Miniatures
2200 Dean Street
Saint Charles, Illinois   60174
(312) 584-9600
Dollhouse and dollhouse furniture kits and accessories.
DOLLHOUSE CATALOGUE: $1.50

The Enchanted Doll House. *See listing under* Sources of Kits for Dolls, Doll Clothing, and Stuffed Animals.

Mark Farmer Company, Inc. *See listing under* Sources of Kits for Dolls, Doll Clothing, and Stuffed Animals.

Favorites from the Past
2951 Harris Street
Kennesaw, Georgia   30144
(404) 427-3921
Wide selection of dollhouse furniture and accessory kits. A few stripped-down dollhouse kits.
CATALOGUE: $1.00

Hill's Dollhouse Workshop
9 Mayhew Drive
Fairfield, New Jersey   07006
(201) 226-3550
Dollhouse kits.
BROCHURE: Free

House of Miniatures®
X-Acto®
45-35 Van Dam Street
Long Island City, New York   11101
(516) 485-5544 (Bob Corey Associates. They handle House of Miniatures mail orders.)
Fine dollhouse furniture kits and fabulous needle-point dollhouse rug kits.
CATALOGUE: $1.00

Illinois Hobbycraft, Inc.
Mail Order Division
605 North Broadway
Aurora, Illinois   60505
(312) 892-9310
Excellent-quality electric fixture kits and wiring kits.
Dollhouse furniture kits. Many nonkit dollhouse
building supplies and plans.
CATALOGUE: $3.50

Mildon, Inc.
Dock Shipping Center
955 Ferry Boulevard
Stratford, Connecticut   06497
(203) 378-0451
Fantasy Island dollhouse kit.
FLYER: Free

My Uncle, Inc.
133 Main Street
Fryeburg, Maine   04037
(207) 935-2109
Excellent dollhouse kits.
CATALOGUE: Free

Perfection Products Company
1375 Headquarters Drive
P.O. Box 6871
Greensboro, North Carolina   27405
(919) 272-7200
Fine dollhouse furniture kits.
BROCHURE: 50 cents

Quill Art, Inc.
11762 Westline Drive
Saint Louis, Missouri   63141
(314) 872-3181
Charming dollhouse furniture made by quilling
technique.
CATALOGUE: $1.00

Scientific Models, Inc.
340 Snyder Avenue
Berkeley Heights, New Jersey   07922
(201) 464-7070
Dollhouse furniture kits.
CATALOGUE: 50 cents

Skil-Craft
Division of Western Publishing Company, Inc.
P.O. Box 705
Racine, Wisconsin   53401
(414) 633-2431
Dollhouse and dollhouse furniture kits.
Write for more information; they generally sell to
the trade only.

Woodline Products, Inc.
245 East Adele
Villa Park, Illinois   60181
(312) 833-8521
Dollhouse kits.
BROCHURE: Free

Additional Sources of Dollhouses and Dollhouse Furniture

Miniature Homes & Furnishings, Inc.
P.O. Box 205
Everett, Massachusetts   02149
(617) 389-7636
Dollhouse and dollhouse furniture kits.
CATALOGUE: $2.50

Nora Nelson & Associates
621 Sixth Avenue
New York, New York, 10011
(212) 691-3992
Relatively inexpensive dollhouse kits.
LEAFLET: Free

Sources of Rocking Horses, Wooden Trains, Backgammon Boards, and Other Toy Kits

The American Museum of Natural History
Museum Shop Catalogue Department
Central Park West at Seventy-ninth Street
New York, New York 10024
(212) 799-8958
Fossil dig kits.
CATALOGUE: 50 cents for postage and handling

The Bartley Collection, Ltd.
747 Oakwood Avenue
Lake Forest, Illinois   60045
(312) 295-2535
Rocking horse kit, plus *many* fine furniture kits.
CATALOGUE: Free

Dick Blick Company
P.O. Box 1267
Galesburg, Illinois   61401
(309) 343-6181 (Galesburg store)
(215) 965-6051 (Allentown, Pennsylvania store)
Craft kits.
CATALOGUE: Free

Educational Design, Inc.
47 West Thirteenth Street
New York, New York   10011
(212) 255-7900
Fingerprint and other science kits.
CATALOGUE: Free

Stephen Ellis
805 East University Avenue
Gainesville, Florida   32601
(904) 378-1304
Wooden toy kits.
FLYER: Free

Nick Lecakes
303 Park Avenue South
New York, New York   10016
(212) 533-6767
Wooden train kits.
FLYER: Free

Nasco
901 Janesville Avenue
Fort Atkinsville, Wisconsin   53538
(414) 563-2446
Silk-screen printing kits, plus other craft supplies.
CATALOGUE: Free

The New York Botanical Garden Gift Shop
Bronx, New York   10458
(212) 220-8700
Sun-print kits.
CATALOGUE: Free

Oldstone Enterprises
77 Summer Street
Boston, Massachusetts   02110
(617) 542-4112
Rubbing kits and materials.
BROCHURE: Free

The Woodworkers Store®
21801 Industrial Park
Rogers, Minnesota   55374
(612) 428-4101
Kits for backgammon board, checkerboard, rocking horse; plus other wood-working supplies.
CATALOGUE: $1.00

Additional Sources of Toy Kits

Abbey Press Christian Family Catalog
Hill Drive
Saint Meinrad, Indiana   47555
(812) 357-8251
A general gift catalogue, which periodically includes toy kits.
CATALOGUE: Free

Just For Kids
Primrose Lane
Laconia, New Hampshire   03246
(603) 524-6004
A general (and interesting) toy catalogue, which usually includes a few kits for toys.
CATALOGUE: Free

Charles Zadeh
225 Fifth Avenue
New York, New York   10010
(212) 689-4154
Easy-to-assemble wooden model of an antique tricycle. Zadeh is a wholesaler, but an inquiry could help locate a source near you for this attractive kit.

Sources of Kite Kits

Frostline Kits
Frostline Circle
Denver, Colorado   80241
(303) 451-5600
In addition to their fine line of outdoor clothing kits, Frostline carries several kite kits.
CATALOGUE: Free

Go Fly a Kite
1434 Third Avenue
New York, New York   10028
(212) 988-8885
Kite kits, plus many very beautiful preassembled kites.
CATALOGUE: $1.00

RAFCO
3136 Kashiwa Street
Torrance, California   90509
(213) 539-4700
Rotating airfoil kite kits.
FLYER: Free

Sources of Kits for Backyard Playground Equipment

Big Toys®
Northwest Design Products, Inc.
3113 South Pine Street
Tacoma, Washington   98404
(206) 572-7611
Cedar backyard gyms.
CATALOGUE: Free

Child Life Play Specialties, Inc.
55 Whitney Street
Holliston, Massachusetts   01746
(617) 429-4639
Backyard play equipment kits.
CATALOGUE: Free

Sources of Kits for Model Ships

James Bliss & Company, Inc. *See listing under* Sources of Kits for Dollhouses and Dollhouse Furniture.

Bluejacket Ship Crafters
50 Water Street
South Norwalk, Connecticut   06854
(203) 853-3353
Marvelous model-ship kits and model-ship fittings.
CATALOGUE: $2.00

The Brookstone Company
127 Vose Farm Road
Peterborough, New Hampshire   03458
(603) 924-9511
Museum-quality showcase kits for ship models.
CATALOGUE: Free

The Dromedary
6324 Belton Road
El Paso, Texas   79912
(915) 584-2445
Model-ship kits, plus handmade and custom-built models.
CATALOGUE: $5.00

Dumas Products, Inc.
909 East Seventeenth Street
Tucson, Arizona   85719
(602) 623-3742
Radio-control model sailboats, cabin cruisers, powerboats, racing hydroplanes, etc.
CATALOGUE: Free

A. J. Fisher, Inc.
1002 Etowah Avenue
Royal Oak, Michigan   48067
(313) 541-0352
Many fine model-ship kits.
CATALOGUE: $2.00

Model Expo, Inc.
230 Second Street
Dunellen, New Jersey   08812
No phone listed.
Many fine model-ship kits.
CATALOGUE: $1.00

Model Shipways, Inc.
39 West Fort Lee Road
Bogota, New Jersey 07603
(201) 342-7920
Excellent model-ship kits.
CATALOGUE: $1.50

Preston's at Main Street Wharf
Greenport, Long Island, New York 11944
(516) 477-1990
Catalogue lists more than fifty ship models, including some that can be motorized.
CATALOGUE: 25 cents

Replica Creations, Inc.
R.D. #4, P.O. Box 279
Middletown, New York 10940
(914) 355-1430
Interesting ship models, constructed by using techniques employed in construction of full-size boats built of ferrocement and fiberglass.
BROCHURE: Free

Scientific Models, Inc.
340 Snyder Avenue
Berkeley Heights, New Jersey 07922
(201) 464-7070
Excellent-quality ship models found in almost every mail-order catalogue dealing with this subject, as well as in hobby shops across the country.
BROCHURE: 50 cents

The South Street Seaport Museum Model Shop
203 Front Street
New York, New York 10038
(212) 766-9039
Top-quality ship models.
CATALOGUE: $1.00 (refundable on first order)

Sterling Models, Inc.
Sterling Building
3620 "G" Street
Philadelphia, Pennsylvania 19134
(215) 426-4100
Very interesting line of R/C boats, as well as many R/C airplane kits.
CATALOGUE: 50 cents

Other Sources of Kits for Model Ships

Curacao Modelbouw
P.O. Box 470
Curacao, Netherlands Antilles
Caribbean
Fabulous selection of model ships, R/C boats, and R/C airplanes mostly from German manufacturers.
CATALOGUE: $5.00

International Marine Exchange
Route 1
P.O. Box 207
Hendersonville, North Carolina 28739
(704) 685-8645
A fine line of R/C boat kits.
CATALOGUE: $2.00

Shipyard Crafts
P.O. Box 171
San Lorenzo, California 94580
(415) 357-3988
Ship-in-bottle kits, plus several fine model-ship kits, including one for Captain Ahab's *Pequod.*
CATALOGUE: Free

Staubitz of Buffalo
105 Hollybrook Drive
Williamsville, New York 14221
(716) 634-7231
Fiberglass ships in miniature. Not for beginners. Includes models for an LCM (landing craft for mechanized equipment) and the battleship *Fletcher.*
BROCHURE: Self-addressed stamped envelope.

Sources of Kits for Model Airplanes, including Kits for Radio-control Aircraft

Bridi Hobby Enterprises
1611 East Sandison Street
Wilmington, California 90744
(213) 549-4971
Super R/C airplane kits.
CATALOGUE: $1.00

Fliteglas Models
R.D. 1, P.O. Box 324
Neoga, Illinois 62447
(217) 895-2533
Excellent-quality R/C airplane kits.
BROCHURE: 50 cents

Majestic Models
3273 West 129th Street
Cleveland, Ohio 44111
(216) 251-4176
Large selection of rubber powered models and free-flight gliders.
BROCHURE: $1.00

Bud Nosen Models
P.O. Box 105
Two Harbors, Minnesota 55616
(218) 834-4544
Terrific selection of R/C airplane kits.
CATALOGUE: 50 cents

Rockford Model Aircraft
P.O. Box 6024
Rockford, Illinois 61125
(815) 874-7891 (ask for Dennis Ebans)
Very realistic plastic airplane models.
COMMERCIAL AND CIVILIAN AIRCRAFT MODELS
CATALOGUE: $1.00

Sig Manufacturing, Inc.
Route 1
P.O. Box 1
Montezuma, Iowa 50171
(515) 623-5154
A huge selection of R/C airplane kits.
CATALOGUE: $2.00

Sterling Models, Inc. *See listing under* Sources of Kits for Model Ships.

Williams Brothers, Inc.
181 Pawnee Street
San Marcos, California 92069
(714) 744-3082
Plastic airplane models.
BROCHURE: $1.00

Additional Sources of Kits for Model Airplanes, including Kits for Radio-control Aircraft

America's Hobby Center, Inc.
146 West Twenty-second Street
New York, New York 10011
(212) 675-8923
A very large selection of model-airplane kits from SIG, Soarcraft, Jack Stafford, Sterling, Southern R/C Products, Champion, Star, Sturdi-Built, Sure Flite, J. L. Modelcraft, Tern AeroCo., Testors, and Southwestern Sailplanes.
CATALOGUE: $1.50

Johannes Graupner
Postfach 48
D-7312 Kirchheim-Teck
Germany
A stunning selection of model boats, planes, and cars, including many for R/C operation. Some of these are really unbelievably beautiful. If you don't want to order direct from Germany, you can get their catalogue and order from Curacao Modelbouw, address listed under Other Sources of Kits for Model Ships. If you order from Curacao, you're assured of getting instruction sheets in English.

Model Merchant
P.O. Box 3792
Irving, Texas 75061
No phone listed.
Fine selections of relatively inexpensive R/C airplane kits.
FLYER: Free

Polk's Hobby Department Store
314 Fifth Avenue
New York, New York 10001
(212) 279-9034
Just about *everything* for the model builder. More than three hundred kits included. Includes kits for automobiles, airplanes, ships, model railroads. Prices range from under $5.00 to over $750 (for a live steamboat model).
CATALOGUE: $5.00

Sporty's Pilot Shop

Cleremont County Airport
Batavia, Ohio 45103

(513) 732-2411

This catalogue for pilots always contains a few plastic scale models. The current catalogue contains kits for Howard Hughes's infamous *Spruce Goose* and for the space shuttle *Enterprise*.

CATALOGUE: $1.00

Tower Hobbies

P.O. Box 778
Champaign, Illinois 61820

(217) 384-1010

A huge selection of R/C airplanes, as well as gliders from a wide range of manufacturers. Some R/C racing automotiles and R/C boats.

CATALOGUE: $2.50

Sources of Model Railroad Kits

Herkimer Tool and Model Works, Inc.

Herkimer, New York 13350

(315) 866-2110

All-metal passenger-car kits.

FLYER: Free

Little Engines Shop

2135-37 250th Street
Lomita, California 90717

(213) 326-2434

Steam-driven locomotives big enough to pull your children along as passengers.

CATALOGUE: $3.00

Quality Craft Models, Inc.

177 Wheatley Avenue
Northumberland, Pennsylvania 17857

(717) 473-9333

Metal and plastic N-, O-, and HO-scale kits for RR car kits.

BROCHURE: Free

R & R Distributors

P.O. Box 2236
City of Industry, California 91746
No phone listed.
Kits for railway-car wall-display boxes.
Write for information.

Walthers, Inc.

5601 West Florist Avenue
Milwaukee, Wisconsin 53218

(414) 527-0770

HO- and N-scale kits of all types.

N-SCALE CATALOGUE: $3.00
HO-SCALE CATALOGUE: $5.00

Thirty-Five Additional Sources of Model Railroad Kits

America's Hobby Center, Inc. *See listing under* Additional Sources of Kits for Model Airplanes, Including Radio-Control Aircraft. Be sure to ask for their HO- and N-Model Railroad Catalogue.

Bowser Manufacturing Company

21 Howard Street
P.O. Box 322
Montoursville, Pennsylvania 17754

(717) 368-2516

All-metal tender-and-engine kits.

BROCHURE: $3.50

Chooch Enterprises, Inc.

P.O. Box 3882
Glendale, California 91201
No phone listed.
Beautiful limited-production kits for freight stations, etc.

CATALOGUE: $1.00, plus SASE

CM Shops

P.O. Box 49
Newfoundland, New Jersey 07435
No phone listed.
HO boxcar kits.

CATALOGUE: 25 cents

Diamond Scale Construction
P.O. Box 691
Oakridge, Oregon 97463
(503) 782-3903
Turntable kits.
CATALOGUE: 50 cents

Dyna-Model Products Company
Sangerville, Maine 04479
No phone listed.
Fabulous HO-scale kits, including 1947 Ford pickup truck, plumbing supply house, boardinghouse, barns, etc.
CATALOGUE: 50 cents

E & B Valley Railroad Company
14 Soundview Avenue
White Plains, New York 10606
No phone listed.
Fabulous injection-molded plastic kit for Rio Grande Southern caboose in HOn3. Many other kits.
BROCHURE: Free

Etcetera
19 Daniels Road
Saint Louis, Missouri 63124
No phone listed.
HO- and O-scale bargains, including some kits.
LIST: Free

Heljan Kits
1025 Industrial Drive
Bensenville, Illinois 60106
(312) 595-0210
One of the major manufacturers of plastic kits.
HO CATALOGUE: $5.00
N CATALOGUE: $5.00

Helmut's Hobby Specialties
2728 Esplanade Avenue
Davenport, Iowa 52803
(319) 324-9334
They have the Marklin of Germany catalogue; includes some kits.
CATALOGUE (ask for the English edition): $2.50

Hobbies for Men, Inc.
341 Main Street
P.O. Box 149
Beacon, New York 12508
(800) 431-9986
A large discount store carrying many kits. If you know what you want, you can call them toll-free, 10 A.M. to 7 P.M., seven days a week. C.O.D., Master Charge, or VISA accepted. $30 minimum order. Many locomotives, etc., including HO brass, as well.

Hobby Surplus Sales
P.O. Box 1319
New Britain, Connecticut 06050
No phone listed.
Bargains in kits and other railroading supplies.
CATALOGUE: $1.00

HO Craft World
P.O. Box 58012
Louisville, Kentucky 40258
No phone listed.
More than thirty-six hundred kits.
BROCHURE: 50 cents

House of Hobbies
P.O. Box 432
Fair Lawn, New Jersey 07410
No phone listed.
N-scale kits.
CATALOGUE: Free

Juneco Scale Models
Inter-Hobbies Distributors
R. R. #1
Martintown, Ontario KOC 1SO
Canada
No phone listed.
Kits for wood and metal railroad bridges, plus other HO-scale models.
PRICE LIST: 50 cents

Mail Train
P.O. Box 4518
Panorama City, California   91412
(213) 366-3606
Remember that they're on Pacific Daylight Time.
Open seven days a week. Monday–Thursday, 11–6.
Friday until 9. Saturday and Sunday, 10–6. Substantial discounts on kits and other model-railroad supplies and equipment. Minimum order $30. They accept VISA, Master Charge, C.O.D. orders.
No catalogue, but you can call them and specify what you want.

Main Line Models
P.O. Box 565
Pleasant Garden, North Carolina   27313
No phone listed.
O and On3 Precision Wood car kits.
BROCHURE: $1.00 (refundable on first order)

Sal Marino's Model Railroad Center
48 Greenleaf Avenue
Staten Island, New York   10310
(212) 273-9699
HO plastic building kits, N plastic kits; a huge selection of kits.
They'll send latest kit flyers if you'll send self-addressed stamped envelope.

Model Die Casting
3811-15 West Rosecrans
P.O. Box 926
Hawthorne, California   90250
(213) 678-3131
Rolling-stock kits.
MINI-CATALOGUE: 50 cents

Muir Models, Inc.
2020 M South Susan
Santa Ana, California   92704
(714) 540-2364
World's largest manufacturer of N-scale craftsman kits.
CATALOGUE: Send self-addressed stamped envelope

Period Miniatures
P.O. Box 1332
Hawthorne, California   90250
No phone listed.
N- and HO-scale kits for late nineteenth-century depots, hotels, etc.
FLYER: Free

Polk's Hobby Department Store. *See listing under* Additional Sources of Kits for Model Airplanes, Including Radio-Control Aircraft.

Rails West
P.O. Box 1194
Arcadia, California   91006
No phone listed.
Model railroad kits of all types.
CATALOGUE: $2.00 (refunded on first order)

Railway Equipment Company
2010 Elkins Street
Saint Louis, Missouri   63136
No phone listed.
One-quarter-inch-scale kits for two-foot-gauge railroads.
BROCHURE: Send self-addressed stamped envelope

Reynold Railroad Products
4711 East Washington Street
Indianapolis, Indiana   46201
No phone listed.
Athearn O-scale kits.
BROCHURE: Send self-addressed stamped envelope

Sequoia Scale Models
P.O. Box 3521
Fullertown, California   92634
No phone listed.
Wood kits of, for example, tiny blacksmith shop.
CATALOGUE: 50 cents

The Structure Company
P.O. Box 6375
Washington Station
Reno, Nevada   98513
No phone listed.
HO-scale kits.
BROCHURE: Send self-addressed stamped envelope

Sugar Creek Specialties
8000 Belinder Avenue
Leawood, Kansas 66205
No phone listed.
O-scale turnout kits for Atlas flex track.
Write for information.

E. Suydam & Company
P.O. Box 55
Duarte, California 91010
No phone listed.
Structure kits, HO-scale.
CATALOGUE OF STRUCTURES AND BUILDING
MATERIALS: $1.50

Terminal Hobby Shop
5619 West Florest Avenue
P.O. Box 18676
Milwaukee, Wisconsin 53218
(414) 461-1050
A very wide range of model railroading kits.
CATALOGUE: $1.50

Train Master
6 Highland Avenue
Albany, New York 12205
(518) 489-4777
N-scale kits, including Muir models and Heljan kits.
BROCHURE: Send self-addressed stamped envelope
with 28 cents postage attached.

Train Tronics
P.O. Box 38
Goshen, Kentucky 40026
(502) 228-8335
Model railroad light kits.
CATALOGUE: Free

Vanguard Models
102-104 Queens Drive
Liverpool L 130 AR
England
Some interesting kits.
CATALOGUE: $4.00 (airmail)

Woodland Scenics
P.O. Box 266
Shawnee Mission, Kansas 66201
No phone listed.
Landscaping kits.
BROCHURE: 50 cents

Ye Olde Huff N Puff
4820 West Whitehall Road
Furnace, Pennsylvania 16865
No phone listed.
HO kits.
BROCHURE: 50 cents

CHAPTER 7—NEEDLEWORK

Sources of Kits for Knitted Sweaters and Knitted and Crocheted Afghans

Alma's Original Alaska Patterns
Alma Henry
Route 1—277 D3
Salmon, Idaho 83467
(208) 756-4369
Jacket-type patterned sweaters in bulky yarn.
BROCHURE: $1.00

American Handicrafts
Merribee Needlearts
P.O. Box 791
Fort Worth, Texas 76101
See phone book for store near you. If there isn't one
near you, you can order a catalogue from the address
above.
CATALOGUE: Free

Annie's Attic
Route 2
P.O. Box 212
Big Sandy, Texas 75755
(214) 636-4412
Crib- and standard-size afghans and quilting kits.
BROCHURE: $1.00

Better Homes and Gardens Crafts Kits
Locust at Seventeenth
P.O. Box 374
Des Moines, Iowa 50336
(800) 247-2516 (In Nebraska only)
(800) 228-3300
A very fine selection of needlework kits for all types.
CATALOGUE: Free

Emerald Mail Order
Ballingeary
County Cork
Ireland
Kits for Aran fisherman sweaters.
CATALOGUE: $2.00

Icemart
P.O. Box 23
Keflavik Airport
235 Iceland
Fabulous icelandic sweater kits using traditional LOPI wool.
CATALOGUE: $1.00

Janknits
Ingomar, Montana 59039
(406) 358-3826
100 percent wool kits in gorgeous patterns.
BROCHURE: $1.00

La Knitterie
70 Middle Neck Road
Great Neck, New York 11021
No phone listed.
Relatively expensive ribbon-knit sweaters.
Write for additional information.

Mary Maxim
2001 Holland Avenue
Port Huron, Michigan 48060
(313) 987-2000
Excellent-quality sweater and afghan kits—and lots of them.
CATALOGUE: 50 cents

David Morgan
P.O. Box 70190
Seattle, Washington 98107
(206) 282-3300
Interesting catalogue of rugged outdoor clothing; includes one fine sweater kit.
CATALOGUE: 25 cents

Patternworks
P.O. Box 1690
Poughkeepsie, New York 12601
No phone listed.
Chenille sweater kits.
CATALOGUE: $1.00

The Pirate's Cove
P.O. Box 57
Babylon, New York 11702
(516) 661-8663
Excellent-quality imported Irish wool, traditional Aran patterns, plus at least one stunning afghan kit.
BROCHURE: $1.00

The Scottish Lion
North Conway, New Hampshire 03860
(603) 356-2461
Fair Isle sweater kits.
BROCHURE: 50 cents

Shannon Mail Order
Shannon International Airport
Ireland
Aran sweater kits.
CATALOGUE: $1.00

Snowflake Kit
N-1315 Nesøya
Norway
Stunning Scandinavian patterned sweater kits.
Catalogue and wool samples: $3.50

P. Straker, Ltd.
53 School Street
South Dartmouth, Massachusetts 02748
(617) 996-4804
Terrific range of sweater kits for men and women.
CATALOGUE: $2.75

Additional Source of Afghan Kits

Lee Wards Creative Crafts Center
1200 Saint Charles Road
Elgin, Illinois 60120
(800) 621-5809
(800) 972-5858 (for orders in Illinois only)
A general needlework and crafts catalogue that will always include a few afghan kits, very inexpensively priced, in acrylic yarns.
CATALOGUE: Free

Sources of Needlepoint Kits

The American Museum of Natural History
Museum Shop Catalogue
Central Park West at Seventy-ninth Street
New York, New York 10024
(212) 799-8958
Their catalogue usually contains at least one or two needlepoint kits.
CATALOGUE: 50 cents for postage and handling

Bay Country Woodcrafts, Inc.
U.S. Route 13
Oak Hall, Virginia 23416
(804) 824-5626
One or two needlepoint pillow kits featuring wildfowl designs. Other kits in this catalogue include many duck decoys, plus other wildfowl design kits.
CATALOGUE: $1.00

Better Homes and Gardens Kits. *See listing under* Sources of Kits for Knitted Sweaters and Knitted and Crocheted Afghans

Boston Museum Shop
Museum of Fine Arts
29 Sleeper Street
Boston, Massachusetts 02210
(617) 427-1111
Always a few needlepoint kits.
CATALOGUE: Free

Canvas Creations
P.O. Box 84
Arnold, Maryland 21012
(301) 757-4682
Needlepoint nautical maps.
BROCHURE: Free

Everlume Corporation
134 West Hills Road
Huntington Station, New York 11746
(516) 421-1222
Postage-stamp-design pillow kits.
CATALOGUE: 30 cents

The Freer Gallery of Art
Smithsonian Institution
Twelfth Street at Jefferson Drive, S.W.
Washington, D.C. 20560
(202) 357-2104 (ask for the shop)
Their catalogue usually contains a few fascinating and complex needlepoint designs.
CATALOGUE: $1.00

The Horchow Collection
P. O. Box 34257
Dallas, Texas 75234
In Dallas: 385-2719
In Texas: (800) 442-5806
All Others: (800) 527-0303
Luxury goods of all types, including some needlepoint kits.
CATALOGUE SUBSCRIPTION: $2.00

The Krick Kit Company
31 North Brentwood Boulevard
Saint Louis, Missouri 63105
(314) 862-3188
Kits for needlepoint belts, duck doorstops, etc. They'll create a needlepoint design of your home.
CATALOGUE: $2.00

Elaine Magnin Needlepoint Design
3063 Fillmore Street
San Francisco, California   94123
(415) 931-3063
Many needlepoint kits.
CATALOGUE: $2.50

The Metropolitan Museum of Art Gift Shop
255 Gracie Station
New York, New York   10028
(212) 362-3335
One of the finest mail-order catalogues of all time.
Always a few fine needlepoint kits.
CATALOGUE: $1.00

The Met by Mail
Metropolitan Opera Guild
1865 Broadway
New York, New York   10023
(800) 228-5656
The opera lover's wishbook. Very nice needlepoint
kits.
CATALOGUE: 50 cents for mailing and postage.

The Mystic Seaport Museum Store
Mystic, Connecticut   96355
(203) 536-9688
Needlepoint pillow kits, plus much fine nautically
inspired gear and gifts.
CATALOGUE: $1.00

Needlepoint Portraits
P.O. Box 9
Greens Farms, Connecticut   06439
(212) 582-2030 (for information only)
Needlepoint portraits of loved ones or pets.
Write for additional information.

Papillon
458 Plasamour Drive
Atlanta, Georgia   30376
(404) 872-0440
(800) 228-1244 (toll-free)
A marvelous gift catalogue with many needlepoint
items.
CATALOGUE: $1.00

Mrs. Kitty Parfet
1487 Seventieth Street, W.
Invergrove Heights, Minnesota   55075
(612) 454-7090
Custom needlepoint kits.
Write for more information, stating what your
idea is.

Eva Rosenstand Corporation
P.O. Box 775
Kennebunk, Maine   04043
(207) 985-7089
Fantastic Danish embroidery and needlepoint kits.
CATALOGUE: $3.00

Sandeen's Scandinavian Gift Shop
1315 White Bear Avenue
Saint Paul, Minnesota   55106
(612) 776-7012
Marvelous hard-to-find Scandinavian needlework
kits.
CATALOGUE: $2.00

The School of Needlepoint/La Stitcherie
70 Middle Neck Road
Great Neck, New York   11021
(516) 487-2389
Needlepoint vest kits, tennis racquet covers, pillows,
and more.
CATALOGUE: $2.00

Sign of the Peacock, Ltd.
Cashiers, North Carolina   28717
(704) 743-3212
Some unusual needlepoint kits.
CATALOGUE: Free

The Stitchery
Wellesley, Massachusetts   02181
(617) 237-7554
(800) 225-4127 (orders only)
A very large selection of needlepoint kits for everything from pillows to hand mirrors.
CATALOGUE SUBSCRIPTION: $1.00

Stitchin' Time
P.O. Box 18063
Rochester, New York   14618
(716) 271-6884
A variety of catalogues from various manufacturers
CATALOGUE PACKAGE: $5.00

Jane Whitmire
2353 South Meade Street
Arlington, Virginia   22202
(703) 684-8036
Some of the finest needlepoint kits available.
CATALOGUE: $1.00

World Arts
P.O. Box 2008
Covina, California   91722
(213) 331-4604
Kits for needlepoint portraits of your home.
BROCHURE: 25 cents

Additional Sources of Needlepoint Kits

Deluxe Saddlery Importers
1817 Whitehead Road
Baltimore, Maryland   21207
(301) 265-6975
Their catalogue usually includes a few unusual needlepoint items. Recent catalogues had personalized needlepoint pet collars and college seal pillows or wall hangings. Some horsier needlepoint gifts, too, such as needlepoint hunt scene.
GIFT CATALOGUE: Free

Harbour Gifts, Inc.
1070 Harbour Drive
Palmyra Harbour, New Jersey   08065
No phone listed.
Best for their Christmas needlepoint kits, but they have a beautiful tea-cozy kit with exotic dragon design (around $30) and a needlepoint pocket kit (around $8), which says: "The Best Man for the Job May be a Woman."
BROCHURE: Free

Mona Spoor Associates
P.O. Box 285
Montvale, New Jersey   07645
(201) 391-1382
Custom-designed needlepoint designs.
CATALOGUE: $2.00

Sources of Kits for Patchwork and Appliqué

Barbara Allen Quilts
10 Brewster Lane
Oak Ridge, Tennessee   37830
No phone listed.
LEAFLET: Free

Annie's Attic. *See listing under* Sources of Kits for Knitted Sweaters and Knitted and Crocheted Afghans

Judy Bean Crafts
P.O. Box 281
Kirbyville, Texas   75956
(713) 384-9477
Patchwork pillow, wall hanging, and tote kits.
CATALOGUE: $1.00

Better Homes and Gardens Crafts Kits. *See listing under* Sources of Kits for Knitted Sweaters and Knitted and Crocheted Afghans

Cher's Kit and Kaboodle
P.O. Box 71
Vernon Hills, Illinois   60061
(312) 438-4242
Amusing appliqué kits.
BROCHURE: 75 cents

Cross Patch Quilting Center
Route 9
Garrison, New York   10524
(914) 424-3443
Quilting supplies, plus a few kits.
CATALOGUE: $1.00

Ginger Snap Station
P.O. Box 81086
Atlanta, Georgia 30366
(404) 455-4104
Excellent and varied patchwork kits for pillows and other items.
CATALOGUE: 50 cents

Hearthside Mail Order
Quilting Supplies
P.O. Box 24
Milton, Vermont 05468
(802) 893-7811
Extraordinary patchwork-quilt kits.
CATALOGUE: $1.00

Mary Maxim. *See listing under* Sources of Kits for Kits for Knitted Sweaters and Knitted and Crocheted Afghans

Newstalgia® Designs
4254 Boardman-Canfield Road
P.O. Box 494
Canfield, Ohio 44406
(216) 533-7943
A few quilt kits.
BROCHURE: 50 cents

Patch-It
P.O. Box 16A
Waitsfield, Vermont 05673
(802) 496-2027
Patchwork pillows, placemats, other novelty items.
Catalogue: 25 cents

Quilts and Other Comforts
Leman Publications, Inc.
P.O. Box 394
6700 West Forty-fourth Avenue
Wheatridge, Colorado 80033
(303) 420-4272
Extraordinarily fine quilt kits.
CATALOGUE: $1.00

Saddle Valley Stitchery
P.O. Box 144
Saddle Valley, New Jersey 07458
(800) 323-1717
Fabulous embroidered and pieced quilts, plus extraordinary cross-stitch samplers.
CATALOGUE: Free

Salter Path
Shandy Lane
Route 3
P.O. Box 346 B
Wilmington, North Carolina 28406
(919) 256-2806
Very nice quilted pillow kits featuring Audubon prints, and other botanical and bird prints.
Write for additional information.

The Stitchery. *See listing under* Sources of Needlepoint Kits

Thompson & Thompson
P.O. Box 461
Boca Grande, Florida 33921
No phone listed.
Unusual appliqué quilt kits.
Write for free leaflet.

Other Sources of Kits for Patchwork and Appliqué

Handworks
P.O. Box 545
Smithtown, New York 11787
No phone listed.
Fine appliqué crib quilt kits.
CATALOGUE: 75 cents

North Shore Farmhouse
Greenhurst, New York 14742
(716) 484-1430
Several patchwork kits for pillows, quilts, totes, hats.
CATALOGUE: 50 cents

The Patchwork Place, Inc.
19314 183rd Avenue, N.E.
Woodinville, Washington 98072
(206) 485-8638
Very attractive patchwork vest, purse, and stuffed animal kits.
BROCHURE: $2.00

The Quilting Bee
16411 Dezavalla
Channelview, Texas 77530
No phone listed.
Tumbling blocks quilt top kit. Very inexpensive. Write for additional information.

Quilts, Kits & Caboodles
726 Beach Street
Flint, Michigan 48502
(313) 232-5722
Calico patchwork kits.
BROCHURE: 25 cents

Sources of Cross-Stitch Samplers, Crewel, and Other Embroidery Kits

American Handicrafts. *See listing under* Sources of Kits for Knitted Sweaters and Knitted and Crocheted Afghans

The American Needlewoman
3806 Alta Mesa Boulevard
Fort Worth, Texas 76133
(817) 294-1981
A very nice selection of cross-stitch kits. Many other needlework kits, including needlepoint, some crewel, plus latch hook.
CATALOGUE: Free

Better Homes and Gardens Crafts Kits. *See listing under* Sources of Kits for Knitted Sweaters and Knitted and Crocheted Afghans

Boycan's Craft Supplies
Mail Order Division
P.O. Box 897
Sharon, Pennsylvania 16146
(412) 346-5534
Cross-stitch samplers.
CATALOGUE: $1.00

The Counting House
P.O. Box 155
Pawleys Island, South Carolina 29585
(803) 237-2733
An entire catalogue of cross-stitch designs.
CATALOGUE: Free

Mary Maxim. *See listing under* Sources of Kits for Knitted Sweaters and Knitted and Crocheted Afghans

Old Sturbridge Village Museum Gift Shop
Sturbridge, Massachusetts 01566
(617) 347-9843
Museum reproduction cross-stitch sampler kits.
BROCHURE: Free

Eva Rosenstand Corporation. *See listing under* Sources of Needlepoint Kits

Saddle Valley Stitchery. *See listing under* Sources of Kits for Patchwork and Appliqué

Jane Snead Samplers
P.O. Box 4909
Philadelphia, Pennsylvania 19119
(215) 848-1577
The largest selection of samplers available from one source.
CATALOGUE: 25 cents

The Stitchery. *See listing under* Sources of Needlepoint Kits

Stichin' Time. *See listing under* Sources of Needlepoint Kits

Jane Whitmire. *See listing under* Sources of Needlepoint Kits.

The World in Stitches
The Needlework Shop
Royal Ridge Mall
Nashua, New Hampshire 03060
(603) 888-5589
Hardanger embroider kits.
CATALOGUE: $1.00

Other Sources of Kits for Cross-Stitch Samplers

Country Stitching
P.O. Box 119
Willow Grove, Pennsylvania 19090
(215) 576-7835
As well as marvelous cross-stitch dollhouse rug kits (mentioned in chapter 6), Country Stitching is now beginning to carry a line of stamped cross-stitch samplers.
Write for additional information.

Xstitch
P.O. Box 4235
Parkersburg, West Virginia 26101
No phone listed.
A cross-stitch catalogue featuring the work of more than twenty American designers.
CATALOGUE: $1.00

CHAPTER 8—TRANSPORTATION

Sources of Kits for Boats

Mr. Anders Ansar
Upplandsgatan 19B
113 60 Stockholm
Sweden
Ice-wing air-foil sailboat kit.
LEAFLET: Free

Clark Craft Boat Company
16 Aqua Lane
Tonawanda, New York 14150
(716) 873-2640
Kits for kayaks, canoes, powerboats, sailboats.
CATALOGUE: $2.00

Country Ways, Inc.
3500 Highway 101 South
Minnetonka, Minnesota 55343
(612) 473-4334
Excellent canoe and kayak kits; some small sailboats. 15 percent discount to schools and other nonprofit organizations.
BROCHURE: $1.00

Folbot Corporation
Stark Industrial Park
Charleston, South Carolina 29405
(803) 744-3483
Very stable modified kayak-type boat kits. Can be used with sails.
BROCHURE: Free

Glen-L Marine Designs
9152 Rosecrans
Bellflower, California 90706
(213) 630-6258
Mostly frame kits; all kinds of boats, from sail to dories, to high-speed powerboats.
CATALOGUE: $2.00

Houlton Boat Company
R.D. #1
Berkshire Valley Road
Oak Ridge, New Jersey 07438
(201) 697-5851
Catamaran boat kits.
FLYER: Free

Jamar Industries of Racine, Inc.
1501 Clark Street
Racine, Wisconsin 53403
(414) 632-7561
Boat ramp kits.
FLYER: Free

Luger Industries, Inc.
3800 West Highway 13
Burnsville, Minnesota 55337
(612) 890-3000
Exceptionally complete kits for sailboats and powerboats.
CATALOGUE: Free

Rickborn Industries, Inc.
Rickborn Flying Bridges
175 Atlantic City Boulevard
Bayville, New Jersey 08721
(201) 349-4545
Flying bridge kits. Available through many boat builders, marine dealers, or marina operators. For more information or to find a supplier near you, write directly to Rickborn.
FLYER: Free

Riverside Fiberglass Canoe Company
P.O. Box 5595
Riverside, California 92507
(714) 686-8232
Fiberglass canoe kits.
FLYER: Free

Rotocast Flotation Products
S. F. Austin and Lincoln Roads
P.O. Box 1059
Brownwood, Texas 76801
(915) 643-2517
Pontoon-boat kit.
FLYER: Free

Tri-Star Trimarans
P.O. Box 286
Venice, California 90291
(213) 396-6154
Trimarans, with frame kits available for each.
CATALOGUE: $5.00

Yacht Constructors, Inc.
7030 North East Forty-second Avenue
Portland, Oregon 97218
(503) 287-5794
Fiberglass sailing yacht kits.
BROCHURE: Free

Other Sources of Boat Kits, Plus a Steam-Engine Kit for Houseboats

Semple Engine Company, Inc.
P.O. Box 6805
Saint Louis, Missouri 63144
No phone listed.
Steam-engine kits for use with launches and houseboats.
FLYER: Free

Trailcraft, Inc.
P.O. Box 392
Concordia, Kansas 66901
(913) 243-4235
Trailcraft will special order a Trailfinder premolded fiberglass canoe kit for you if you're interested. They no longer produce their fine wood and canvas canoe kits.
FLYER: Free

Sources of Classic Automobile Reproduction Kits, Plus Kits for Supermodern Sports Cars

Antique and Classic Automotive, Inc.
100 Sonwil Industrial Park
Buffalo, New York 14225
(716) 684-9540
Kits for replicas of fine antique automobiles.
CATALOGUE: $3.00

Classic Motor Carriages, Inc.
200 South Federal Highway
Hallandale, Florida 33009
(305) 456-1500
Fabulous classic replica motorcar kits. You'll probably flip (I did . . .) when you see their reproduction "Porsche" Speedster and their vintage delivery van (both available preassembled only). But their 1929 Mercedes SSK and their 1924 Bugatti replicas (for you to assemble) aren't bad either.
CATALOGUE: $3.00

Daytona Automotive Fiberglass, Inc.
819 Carswell Avenue
Holly Hill, Florida   32017
(904) 253-2573
Daytona MIGI® kits.
BROCHURE: $2.00
MANUAL: $8.00

Fiberfab, Inc.
1000 Turners Cross Road
Minneapolis, Minnesota   55416
(612) 544-2781
(800) 328-5671
Kits for a reproduction of the 1952 MG-TD and for a super-modern sportscar, the Aztec 7.
CATALOGUE: Free

Kelmark Engineering, Inc.
P.O. Box K
Okemos, Michigan   48864
(517) 882-2880
Their Kelmark GT kit is for a beautiful, super-modern sportscar based on the 246 Dino Ferrari.
CATALOGUE: $2.00

Lindberg Engineering
35111 Lodge
Tollhouse, California   93667
(209) 855-8221
Kits for a wonderful "old-time" truck, a car based on the 1936 Auburn Boat Tail Speedster, and one based on the 1932 Mercedes 500.
CATALOGUE: $2.00

Total Performance, Inc.
406 South Orchard Street
Route 5
Wallingford, Connecticut   06492
(203) 265-5667
Replica kit cars. As far as I can tell, the big difference between Total Performance and other kits is that Total Performance uses its own design chassis and suspension.
CATALOGUE: $3.00

Some Additional Sources of Classic Automobile Reproduction Kits, Plus Kits for Supermodern Sports Cars

Bradley Automotive, Inc.
495 Shelard Plaza
400 Country Road 18 South
Minneapolis, Minnesota   55426
(612) 475-2990
(800) 328-7141
These car kits look like ultramodern contemporary classics. They offer at least a couple—the Bradley GT and the GT-II. Each is a fiberglass gull-wing kit with entry gained via nonframed Plexiglas gull-wing doors.
CATALOGUE: Free

Nova Cars, Ltd.
Nova House
6861690 Huddersfield Road
Ravensthorpe
Nr. Dewsbury WF 13 3HU
England
A super-modern sportscar kit based on the Lamborghini Miura and the Corvette Mako Shark prototype. The complete kit runs about $4,000, plus import tax. It's still inexpensive.
Write to them for price of their current catalogue.

RMB Motors
Mill Street
Barwell
Leicester
England
Their car kit is called the Gentry, based on the MG-TF. Front engine, rear-drive. Built on a Triumph chassis.
Write to them for price of their current catalogue.

Sources of Kits for Tractors, R-Vs, a Steam-Powered Bicycle, and More

Dahl Tractor Company
D.V. Dahlco Corporation
P.O. Box 231
Cedarburg, Wisconsin 53012
(414) 377-5707
Rubber-tread crawler tractor kit.
CATALOGUE: 50 cents
FABRICATION PLANS: $7.00

Glen-L Marine Designs. *See listing under* Sources of Kits for Boats. Their "Build-it-yourself" camper kit catalogue costs $1.00.

Carl Heald, Inc.
P.O. Box 1148
Benton Harbor, Michigan 49022
(616) 849-3400
Bike or tricycle kits.
CATALOGUE: Free

Sarlin Steam Works
1237 Glen
Berkeley, California 94708
(415) 843-2523
Kits for converting your bicycle to steam power.
FLYER: Free

Struck Corporation
W51 N545 Struck Lane
P.O. Box 307
Cedarburg, Wisconsin 53012
(414) 377-3300
Mini-Dozer and Magnatrac tractor kits.
CATALOGUE: 75 cents

A Source of Go-Karts

Schmieder Motor Company
R.D. #1
Doylestown, Pennsylvania 18901
(215) 348-8588
Go-Kart kits.
CATALOGUE: $1.00

Sources of Kits for Airplanes, Helicopters, and Gliders

Bensen Aircraft Corporation
P.O. Box 31047
Raleigh, North Carolina 27622
(919) 787-4224
Gyrocopter kits.
BROCHURE: $5.00

Bryan Aircraft, Inc.
Williams County Airport
Bryan, Ohio 43506
(419) 636-1340
15-meter class sailplane kit.
BROCHURE: Free

BW Rotor Company, Inc.
P.O. Box 391
Towanda, Kansas 67144
No phone listed.
Inexpensive Giro Kopter kits.
LEAFLET: Free

Eipper-Formance, Inc.
1070 Linda Vista Drive
San Marcos, California 92069
(714) 744-1514
Motorized glider kits.
LEAFLET: Free

GLA, Inc.
841 Winslow Court
Muskegon, Michigan 49441
(616) 780-4680
Sailplane kit.
BROCHURE: $5.00

Mitchell Aircraft Corporation
1900 South Newcomb
Porterville, California 93257
(209) 781-0778
(800) 344-7280 (for technical help and information)
Sailplane kits.
BROCHURE: $7.00

Mooney Mite Aircraft Corporation
P.O. Box 3999
Charlottesville, Virginia   22903
(703) 296-7711
Airplane kit built along the lines of Britain's "Mosquito" bomber.
INFORMATION KIT: $8.95 (credited against purchase price of the airplane kit)

Barney Oldfield Aircraft Company
P.O. Box 5974
Cleveland, Ohio   44101
(216) 423-3816
Single-place open cockpit biplane kit.
BROCHURE: $5.00

C. Y. Parker
P.O. Box 625
Coolidge, Arizona   85228
(602) 723-5202
Kits for an all-aluminum airplane.
BROCHURE: Send #10 self-addressed stamped envelope.

Pazmany Aircraft Corporation
P.O. Box 80051
San Diego, California   92138
(714) 224-7330
Kits for two sophisticated airplanes, the Pazmany PL-2 and the PL-4A.
INFORMATION PACKAGE: $5.00
PLANS: $140.

Pterodactyl Ltd.
847 Airport Road
Monterey, California   93940
(408) 375-0328
Motor glider kit.
LEAFLET: Free

Rand Robinson Engineering, Inc.
5842 "K" McFadden Avenue
Huntington Beach, California   92646
(714) 898-3811
Two-place side-by-side low-wing monoplane kits.
INFORMATION PACKAGE: $1.00

Schweitzer Aircraft Corporation
P.O. Box 147
Elmira, New York   14902
(607) 739-3821
Sailplane kits.
BROCHURE: Free

Stolp Starduster Corporation
4301 Twining
Flabob Airport
Riverside, California   92509
(714) 686-7943
Wonderful duster-type aircraft kits.
Acroduster I Brochure: $5.00
Starduster II Brochure: $5.00

Additional Sources of Kits for Airplanes, Helicopters, and Gliders

Ken Brock Manufacturing
11852 Western Avenue
Stanton, California   90680
(714) 898-4366
Rotary-wing aircraft kits.
CATALOGUE: $2.00

Bushby Aircraft, Inc.
Route 1
P.O. Box 13B
Minooka, Illinois   60447
No phone listed.
They specialize in plans for home-built aircraft, but kits are available.
CATALOGUE: $3.00

EMG Engineering Company
18518 South Broadway
Gardena, California   90247
(213) 321-8699
Propane-fueled jet engine kits.
LEAFLET: Free
G8-2 TECHNICAL HANDBOOK: $7.50

Sky Rider
2432 Pleasant Ridge
Columbia, South Carolina 29209
(803) 776-4108
Inexpensive motorized hang-glider kits.
INFORMATION SHEET: Free
BROCHURE: $5.00

Spencer Amphibian Air Car
12780 Pierce Street
Pacoima, California 91331
(213) 899-1010

Component kits plus plans for wood-hull-construction amphibious planes.
CATALOGUE: $5.00

Taylor Mini-Imp
P.O. Box 1171
Longview, Washington 98632
(206) 423-8260 (days)
(206) 425-9874 (evenings)
Component parts available for a two-place, towable, folding-wing amphibious light airplane.
INFORMATION PACKAGE: $5.00

CHAPTER 9—OTHER USEFUL KITS

Sources of Down and Synthetic-fill Comforters and Pillows

Altra, Inc.
5541 Central Avenue
Boulder, Colorado 80301
(303) 449-2401
All down or down/feather comforters, plus luggage kits
BROCHURE: Free

Country Ways, Inc.
3500 Highway 101 South
Minnetonka, Minnesota 55343
(612) 473-4334
PolarGuard comforters, luggage kits, plus many others.
CATALOGUE: $1.00

Frostline Kits
Frostline Circle
Denver, Colorado 80241
(303) 457-4484
Down comforters, feather blends; pillow kits; luggage kits, and *much* more.
CATALOGUE: Free

SunDown Kits
14850 Northeast Thirty-first Circle
Redmond, Washington 98052
(206) 883-3997

Down comforter and pillow kits, down coat kits, plus others.
CATALOGUE: $1.00

Sources of Food-related Kits

Bacchanalia
P.O. Box 51
Central Village, Massachusetts 02790
(617) 636-5154
Beer- and wine-making kits.
CATALOGUE: Free

Country Ways. *See listing under* Sources of Down and Synthetic-fill Comforters and Pillows.

Excalibur Products
6083 Power Inn Road
Sacramento, California 95824
(916) 381-4254
Home grain mill kit.
LEAFLET: Free

Foothills Distributors, Inc.
P.O. Box 1758
Cave Creek, Arizona 85331
No phone listed.
Kits for stone-mill kits.
LEAFLET: Free

Garden Way
Charlotte, Vermont   05445
(802) 425-2121
(800) 228-5000
(800) 642-8777 (in Nebraska)
Kits for cider press, grain mill, sausage-making and wine-making.
COUNTRY KITCHEN CATALOGUE: Free

Harvest Home Products, Inc.
3020 Vine Street
P.O. Box 5595
Riverside, California   92517
(714) 787-9080
Food-dehydrator kits.
BROCHURE: Free

Kittredge Bow Hut
P.O. Box 598
Mammoth Lakes, California   93546
(714) 934-7566
Sausage-making kits.
ARCHER'S BIBLE: $1.00

The Woodworkers' Store
21801 Industrial Boulevard
Rogers, Minnesota   55374
(612) 428-4101
Coffee-mill kit.
CATALOGUE: $1.00

Additional Sources of Food-related Kits

Park Seed Company
Greenwood, South Carolina   29647
(803) 374-3341
Mushroom-growing kit.
CATALOGUE: Free

Specialty Products International Ltd.
P.O. Box 784
Chapel Hill, North Carolina   27514
(919) 929-4277
Beer-making kits for light, amber, or dark malt beer.
LEAFLET: Free

Vynox Industries, Inc.
400 Avis Street
Rochester, New York   14615
(716) 254-4771
Beer- and wine-making kits.
ENCYCLOPEDIA OF WINE- AND BEER-MAKING EQUIPMENT AND INGREDIENTS: $2.00

Wine-Brew & Stove Shop
43 North Ninth Street
Allentown, Pennsylvania   18105
(215) 432-6616
Beer-making kits.
LEAFLET: Free

Sources of Kits for Birdhouses, a Doghouse, a Dog Run, and Beekeeping

Audubon Workshop
1501 Paddock Drive
Northbrook, Illinois   60062
No phone listed.
Birdhouse kits and other bird-feeding supplies.
CATALOGUE: Free

Constantine
2050 Eastchester Road
Bronx, New York   10461
(212) 792-1600
Birdhouse and bird-feeder kits.
CATALOGUE: Free

Glen-Bel Enterprises
Route 5
Crossville, Tennessee   38555
(615) 788-5568
Birdhouse and beekeeping kits. Other old-fashioned country-store-type merchandise.
300-PAGE CATALOGUE: $5.00

Nasco
901 Janesville Avenue
Fort Atkinson, Wisconsin   53538
(414) 563-2446
(800) 558-9559
(800) 242-9587 (in Wisconsin)
Birdhouse and bird-feeder kits.
CATALOGUE: Free

Shettel-Way Innovations
P.O. Box 12
Twin Falls, Idaho   83301
(208) 733-6034
Doghouse kit.
LEAFLET: Free

Sporty's Tool Shop
Cleremont County Airport
Batavia, Ohio   45103
(513) 732-2411
Dog run kit.
CATALOGUE: Free

Wild Bird Supplies
4815 Oak Street
Crystal Lake, Illinois   60014
(815) 455-4020
Many fine birdhouse and bird-feeder kits.
CATALOGUE: Free

Additional Sources of Birdhouse Kits

Larson Wood Manufacturing
Industrial Park
P.O. Box 672
Park Rapids, Minnesota   56470
(218) 732-9121
Larson offers the same fancy birdhouse and bird-feeder kits as the ones described as offered by Constantine. Larson's cost 50 cents to 75 cents less.
CATALOGUE: Free

Sources of Kits for Luggage

Altra, Inc. *See listing under* Sources of Down and Synthetic-fill Comforters and Pillows.

Frostline Kits. *See listing under* Sources of Down and Synthetic-fill Comforters and Pillows.

Haan Crafts Corporation
185 South Main
Otterbein, Indiana   47970
(317) 583-4496

Kits for gym bags, tennis totes, diaper bag, plus terrific stuffed animals.
BROCHURE: $1.00

SunDown Kits. *See listing under* Sources of Down and Synthetic-fill Comforters and Pillows.

Sources of Clothing and Accessory Kits for Men, Women, and Children, including Down Coats and Bathrobes, and a Sheepskin Jacket

Charing Cross Kits
Main Street
P.O. Box 798
Meredith, New Hampshire   03253
(603) 279-8449
Extraordinary clothing kits for women and children.
CATALOGUE: $2.00

Family Circle Kits—STB, Inc.
P.O. Box 450
Teaneck, New Jersey   07666
(201) 569-5505
"Victorian" lace blouse kits.
No catalogue, but you can order Family Circle kits you've seen advertised in the magazine for several years after the ad has run.

Frostline Kits. *See listing under* Sources of Down and Synthetic-fill Comforters and Pillows.

Plain Brown Wrapper, Inc.
2200 West Alameda #35
Denver, Colorado   80223
(303) 936-2377
Down coat for women, plus other warm down clothing.
CATALOGUE: Free

SunDown Kits. *See listing under* Sources of Down and Synthetic-fill Comforters and Pillows.

Tandy Leather Company
2617 West Seventh Street
P.O. Box 791
Fort Worth, Texas 76101
(817) 335-4161
Kits for belts, bags, business-card cases
CATALOGUE: $1.50

Allen J. Valero
R.D. #1, P.O. Box 199
Monroetown, Pennsylvania 18832
(717) 364-5160
Shearling vests, jackets, hats.
BROCHURE: $3.00

Sources of Some Useful Kits for Your Home

Black Magic Chimney Sweeps
P.O. Box 977
Stowe, Vermont 95672
(802) 253-4867
Chimney-sweeping kit.
BROCHURE: Free

Dick Blick
P.O. Box 1267
Galesburg, Illinois 61401
(800) 447-8192
(800) 322-8183 (in Illinois)
Rubber-stamp kit.
CREATIVE MATERIALS CATALOGUE: Free

Conran's
145 Huguenot Street
New Rochelle, New York 10801
(914) 633-8200
Window-shade kit.
CATALOGUE: $2.00

Country Ways, Inc. *See listing under* Sources of Down and Synthetic-fill Comforters and Pillows.

Garden Way Research. *See listing under* Sources of Food-Related Kits

Gilliom Manufacturing, Inc.
1109 North Second Street
Saint Charles, Missouri 63301
(314) 724-1812
Power-tool kits.
BROCHURE: 50 cents

Golden Enterprises, Inc.
P.O. Box 1282
Glendale, Arizona 85311
No phone listed.
Air-ionizer kits.
BROCHURE: Free

J-D Hydrolic Sales
P.O. Box 681
Warsaw, Indiana 46580
(219) 566-2957
Log-splitter kit.
LEAFLET: Free

Mother's Plans
Mother Earth News
P.O. Box A
East Flat Rock, North Carolina 28726
Alcohol fuel kit.
For fuller details, see *Mother Earth News* (November/December 1979, page 134). Current issues may include details as well.

Neff's Nifty Chimney Center
P.O. Box 308
McGraw, New York 13101
(607) 836-6062
Chimney-cleaning kit.
Write to them for additional information.

An Additional Source of Chimney-cleaning Kits

Homestead Chimney Sweep
P.O. Box 398
Hampton, New Jersey 08827
(201) 735-7708
Chimney-sweep kits.
BROCHURE: 50 cents

Sources of Kits for Craftspeople

A-1 Kiln Kits
369 Main Street
Ramona, California 92065
(714) 789-3310
Gas and electric kiln kits.
BROCHURE: Free

Armour Products
Hill Street
Midland Park, New Jersey 07432
(201) 652-8895
Do-it-yourself glass-etching kit.
BROCHURE: Free

Basic Crafts Company
1201 Broadway
New York, New York 10001
(212) 679-3516
Bookbinding, book-repair, and paper-making kits.
CATALOGUE: $1.00

Country Ways, Inc. *See listing under* Sources of Down and Synthetic-fill Comforters and Pillows

Mould-N-Mount, Inc.
P.O. Box 130
Priddy, Texas 76870
(915) 966-3776
Taxidermy kits.
LEAFLET: Free

Oak Hill Industries, Inc.
1335 North Utah Avenue
Davenport, Iowa 52804
No phone listed.
Potter's wheel kits.
LEAFLET: Free

Pacifica Crafts
P.O. Box 1407
Ferndale, Washington 98248
(206) 384-1504
Kits for electric potter's wheels.
LEAFLET: Free

Pottery Equipment, Inc.
P.O. Box 428
Silt, Colorado 81652
(303) 876-2935
Electric potter's wheel kit.
LEAFLET: Free

School Products Company, Inc.
1201 Broadway
New York, New York 10001
(212) 679-3516
Loom and spinning-wheel kits, plus many other items for the weaver.
HAND-WEAVING CATALOGUE: $1.00

Sievers Looms
Green Bay Road
Washington Island, Wisconsin 54246
(414) 847-2264
Loom kits.
CATALOGUE: $1.00 (refundable upon purchase)

Van Dyke Supply Company
Woonsocket, South Dakota 57385
(605) 796-4425
(800) 843-3320 (not within South Dakota)
Huge selection of taxidermy supplies and kits.
CATALOGUE: Free

Wallis Designs
P.O. Box 95
East Hartford, Connecticut 06108
No phone listed.
Inexpensive kickwheel kits.
LEAFLET: Free

Other Kits for Craftspeople

Pacific Leather Company
P.O. Box 641
McMinnville, Oregon 97128
No phone listed.
Professional home tanning kit, quite inexpensive.
LEAFLET: Free

Western Products Company
Mason City, Iowa 50401
(515) 423-4584
Home tanning kit that uses no dangerous acids. The
$9.95 kit contains enough to tan two or three deer
hides. Postpaid.
LEAFLET: Free

Where to Buy the Ukrainian Easter Egg Kit

Surma
11 East Seventh Street
New York, New York 10003
(212) 477-0729
Easter egg-decorating kit.
LEAFLET: Free

Where to Buy the Passover Kit

The Jewish Museum Shop
1109 Fifth Avenue
New York, New York 10028
(212) 860-1888
Matzoh-cover crewel kit.
CATALOGUE: 50 cents

Where to Buy the Chanukah Dreidel Kit

Studio 35
P.O. Box 1177
Brooklyn, New York 11201
No phone listed.
Christmas ornament kits, a Chanukah dreidel kit,
and several unusual small needlepoint kits.
LEAFLET: Free

An Additional Source of Chanukah Kits

Stitchery by Henye
5710 West Mariposa Street #1
Phoenix, Arizona 85031
No phone listed.
Kits with Jewish holiday themes.
CATALOGUE: $2.00

Sources of Kits for Christmas Ornaments and Decorations

Aldebaran Educational
84-33 Ninetieth Street
P.O. Box 21132
Woodhaven, New York 11421
(212) 441-8030 (evenings)
Macramé snowflake kits.
LEAFLET: Free

Arts Array
P.O. Box 219
Calabasas, California 91302
(213) 880-5662
Needlepoint tree ornaments.
CHRISTMAS CATALOGUE: 75 cents

Bahlsen of North America, Inc.
34-39 Fifty-sixth Street
Woodside, New York 11377
(212) 898-1692
Terrific gingerbread-house kits.
These kits usually appear before Christmas in stores
like Bloomingdale's and Macy's and in many mail-
order catalogues. If you can't find a distributor near
you, write to them and inquire.

Judy Bean Crafts
P.O. Box 281
Kirbyville, Tennessee 75956
(713) 384-9477
Patchwork Christmas pillows, placemats, and tree
ornaments.
BROCHURE: $1.00

Cher's Kit and Kaboodle
P.O. Box 71
Vernon Hills, Illinois 60061
(312) 438-4242
Wonderful patchwork and appliqué Christmas
stockings, angels, wise men, and tree.
CATALOGUE: $1.00

Creative Needler
P.O. Box 158
Orient, Ohio 43146
No phone listed.
Lovely needlepoint tree ornaments.
CATALOGUE: $1.00

Cross Patch Quilting Center
Route 9
Garrison, New York 10524
(914) 424-3443
Patchwork wreaths, gingerbread house, tree ornaments.
CATALOGUE: $1.00

Ginger Snap Station
P.O. Box 81086
Atlanta, Georgia 30366
(404) 455-4104
Calico wreaths, trees, stockings, tree ornaments.
CATALOGUE: 50 cents

Gloria's Cone Tree
42664 Upper Calapooia
Sweet Home, Oregon 97386
(503) 367-6642
Kits for pinecone centerpieces and wreaths.
CATALOGUE: 50 cents

Harbour Gifts, Inc.
1070 Harbour Drive
Palmyra Harbour, New Jersey 08065
No phone listed.
Exquisite needlepoint stocking and ornament kits.
BROCHURE: Free

The Krick Kit Company
31 N. Brentwood Boulevard
Saint Louis, Missouri 63105
(314) 862-3188
Needlepoint wreath pillow kit.
BROCHURE: $2.00

Elaine Magnin Needlepoint Designs
3063 Fillmore Street
San Francisco, California 94123
(415) 931-3063
Fabulous needlepoint ornaments.
CATALOGUE: $2.50

North Shore Farmhouse
Greenhurst, New York 14742
(716) 484-1430
A few unusual Christmas kits.
CATALOGUE: Free

Papillon
458 Plasamour Drive
Atlanta, Georgia 30376
(404) 872-0440
(800) 228-1244
Unusual needlepoint Christmas decorations.
CATALOGUE: $1.00

Peacock Alley
650 Croswell Street, S.E.
Grand Rapids, Michigan 49506
(616) 454-9898
Needlepoint Christmas stockings and tree ornaments.
CATALOGUE: $2.00

Quill Art, Inc.
11762 Westline Drive
Saint Louis, Missouri 63141
(314) 872-3181
Quilled wreath kits, plus marvelous quill snowflake kits for use as tree ornaments.
LEAFLET: Free

Stitchin' Time
P.O. Box 18063
Rochester, New York 14618
(716) 271-6884
Some of the best needlepoint Christmas stocking kits.
CATALOGUE: $5.00

Studio 35. *See listing under* Where to Buy the Chanukah Dreidel Kit.

Lee Wards Creative Crafts Center
1200 Saint Charles Road
Elgin, Illinois 60120
(800) 972-5858 (in Illinois)
(800) 621-5809
Christmas kits of all types. Ask for their Christmas catalogue.
CATALOGUE: Free

Additional Sources of Kits for Christmas Ornaments and Decorations

Alma's Original Alaska Patterns
Alma Henry
Route 1—227 D3
Salmon, Idaho 83467
(208) 756-4369.
Alma has a very charming set of tree ornaments for you to appliqué. Called "Dorothy and Friends," the kit contains figures of Dorothy, the Tin Man, the Scarecrow, and the Cowardly Lion. About $6.00.
BROCHURE: $1.00

Better Homes and Gardens Crafts Kits
P.O. Box 374
Des Moines, Iowa 50336
(800) 228-3300
Tatted tree ornaments, calico candy canes, embroidered poinsettia table linens, hooked tree skirts, and much more. Do send for their current catalogue.
CATALOGUE: Free

Carousel Crafts Company
7452 Harwin
Houston, Texas 77036
(713) 784-3551
Crewel and stuffable tree ornament kits. They are a wholesaler, and you'll see some of their kits in catalogues like Better Homes and Gardens. They do publish information sheets, however, and you can order directly from them.
LEAFLET: Free

The Cracker Box
River Road (at Pleasant Pike)
Point Pleasant, Pennsylvania 18950
(215) 297-5700
Very elaborate ball or bell-shaped ornaments, mostly studded with plastic and metal doodads. The only one I really like is their calico-trimmed sunbonnet girl design.
CATALOGUE: $2.25

Hill-Looney, Inc.
P.O. Box 1533
Wewoka, Oklahoma 74884
(405) 257-2639
Needlepoint Christmas stockings depicting Santa Claus and a little girl holding a Teddy bear. The latter can be personalized. Nice needlepoint tree ornaments too.
Ask for free Rosene Needlepoint ornaments kits leaflet.

Martin's Gingerbread Houses, Inc.
36 East Twenty-second Street
New York, New York 10010
No phone listed.
Obviously, gingerbread-house kits. Very nice.
LEAFLET: Free

Mary Maxim, Inc.
2001 Holland Avenue
Port Huron, Michigan 48060
(313) 987-2000
Their Christmas catalogue always has a few interesting kits, especially their knitted, personalized stockings, and cross-stitch table linens.
CATALOGUE: 50 cents

The Nest Egg
717 Oakwood Avenue
Hurst, Texas 76053
No phone listed.
Some very nice and very inexpensive calico bow or candy cane wreath kits. Under $7 each.
LEAFLET: Free

Pourette Manufacturing Company
6818 Roosevelt Way, N.E.
Seattle, Washington 98115
(206) 525-4480
Kits for making interesting Christmas candles. Under $7. Their basic kit sells for under $3.
CATALOGUE: $1.00

The Stitchery
Wellesley, Massachusetts 02181
(617) 237-7554
(800) 225-4127
Always some interesting needlepoint and patchwork Christmas kits. Nice holiday table linens, too.
CATALOGUE SUBSCRIPTION: $1.00

INDEX